P9-BAV-444

So Long, Insecurity

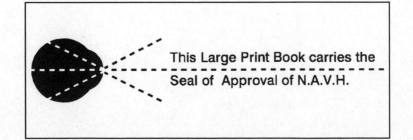

So Long, Insecurity

YOU'VE BEEN A BAD FRIEND TO US

Beth Moore

THORNDIKE PRESS

A part of Gale, Cengage Learning

GALE
CENGAGE Learning·

Detroit • New York • San Francisco • New Haven, Conn • Waterville, Maine • London

GALE
CENGAGE Learning

Copyright © 2010 be Beth Moore.
Thorndike Press, a part of Gale, Cengage Learning.

ALL RIGHTS RESERVED
Thorndike Press® Large Print Inspirational.
The text of this Large Print edition is unabridged.
Other aspects of the book may vary from the original edition.
Set in 16 pt. Plantin.

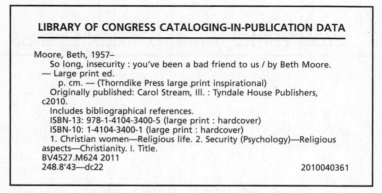

LIBRARY OF CONGRESS CATALOGING-IN-PUBLICATION DATA

Moore, Beth, 1957–
    So long, insecurity : you've been a bad friend to us / by Beth Moore.
    — Large print ed.
        p. cm. — (Thorndike Press large print inspirational)
    Originally published: Carol Stream, Ill. : Tyndale House Publishers,
c2010.
    Includes bibliographical references.
    ISBN-13: 978-1-4104-3400-5 (large print : hardcover)
    ISBN-10: 1-4104-3400-1 (large print : hardcover)
    1. Christian women—Religious life. 2. Security (Psychology)—Religious
aspects—Christianity. I. Title.
BV4527.M624 2011
248.8'43—dc22   2010040361

Published in 2011 by arrangement with Tyndale House Publishers, Inc.

Printed in the United States of America
1 2 3 4 5 6 7 15 14 13 12 11

PERMISSIONS

For Annabeth

CONTENTS

ACKNOWLEDGMENTS

I have never had so many people to thank at the end of a writing project. Over a thousand men and women contributed to this message, and if you're one of them, my words of gratitude will fail to convey my heart and how humbled I am by your willing investment. I pray God will wildly bless your efforts through a harvest of women who stumble on the book providentially and find the freedom they yearn for.

To my beloved online community I affectionately call the "Siestas" — Girls, this book exists because of your input and the courage you gave me to write it. You will recognize yourselves all over it. Wait till you see chapter 7. It is you from beginning to end. I love you like crazy. You are a huge part of my journey and my picture window to a big world. May Jesus continue to be your prize.

To the more than 150 men who invested in the guys' survey — Your perspective turned out to be one of the most important junctures in the journey. Pure gold. Thank you so much for letting me quote you and for even letting me pick on you a bit. You were fabulous. By the way, so many of you asked what you could do to make insecurity a smaller issue for your wives and daughters. I smiled every time and thought to myself, *If you had the insight to ask the question, you were not part of the problem.* I respect you so much. Thank you again.

To my Monday night TMA girls — I had such a blast with you. Thank you for bringing insight from your young generation to an issue that will undoubtedly only escalate. Keep gathering the courage to be the women of God we talked about!

To my friends — Poor things. This was a dangerous time to be my running buddies. Thank you for telling me things you had to wonder later if I'd share in print. Rest assured, I did, but don't worry. Either I didn't use your name or I changed it. I'm throwing back my head and laughing. You might as well too. It helps calm the nerves.

To my second family, my staff at Living Proof Ministries — You are the dearest people on earth to me outside my immediate family. I absolutely adore you. Thank you for all the deep conversations over lunch about this

12

topic and for acting once again like you could hardly wait to get the new book in your hands. I am not worthy of you. I love you and cannot imagine my life without you.

To Sealy and Curtis and the entire staff of Yates and Yates — Thank you for being people I can trust. Thank you for being the very first to catch the vision and for doing everything you could to give it wings. The best part is that you didn't do it because you believed in me but because you believe in Jesus. Thank God He can use anybody, or you and I would never have crossed paths. You are gifts of His mercy to me.

To the Tyndale team — Mark Taylor, I have so much respect for you and your heritage. I am honored to partner with you, sir. Thank you for taking this chance on me. Ron Beers, you are honestly one of the most gracious men I've ever encountered. I bet the women in your life don't struggle with a ton of insecurity. Jan Stob, you were one of the first women to read the manuscript, and I was relieved almost to tears because I could tell you got it. Sometimes I'm such a needy, fragmented person that I wonder if I've written a whole book to myself. You made me know that this one was at least written to two of us. Jackie Nuñez and Stephen Vosloo, I loved working with you guys!

13

Thank you so much for coming to Houston and for making me smile till my cheeks were honestly sore. I had more wrinkles when you left than when you came. Maria Erikson, I am so grateful for your attentiveness to every detail and for not letting up on the questions until you understood the audience. Your professional intensity never left me wondering whether or not you were doing your job. Stephanie Voiland, thank you so much for your hard work on copyediting. How many times did you wonder why I couldn't say it simpler?

To Lisa Jackson —You are an integral part of the Tyndale team but worthy of singling out in this project. As this message began to take shape on paper, I knew the editor would have to be a woman. God knew the editor would have to be you. I loved every minute of working with you. You have an uncanny way of always being available but never intrusive. No small feat. I will long remember the day we spent together knocking out every single edit and without a single awkward moment. How about that? You treated the manuscript with dignity. You won my heart as an editor, as a fellow mom, and as a sister trying to navigate the shark-infested waters of this culture. Thank you from the bottom of my heart.

14

I've written all the other acknowledgments with teeming joy, but as I come to the remaining few, I do so with tears stinging my eyes.

To my wonderful daughters, Amanda and Melissa — Nothing on this earth fulfills me like learning and processing and serving alongside the two of you. I respect no one's opinion more than yours. I have no greater proof of God's grace in my life than the two of you. No one makes me think or laugh or pray or *spend* like you do. You are used of God to continually keep me connected with a generation of women, not coincidentally, young enough to be my daughters. Words don't exist to tell you how much you mean to me.

To my sons-in-law, Curtis and Colin — I am so glad you did not know what you were getting yourselves into. You never could have imagined the implications of having wives thrown this deeply into women's ministry. You are both great sports . . . and the sons I never had.

To Jackson and Annabeth —Thank you for providing countless delightful distractions. Your Bibby is nuts over you.

To my man, Keith — How can I ever thank you enough for sticking it out with me through so many ups and downs and twists

15

and turns? Others come and go, but you have not left my side for thirty-one crazy years. You are my life companion. My very best friend. I place no offering on the altar of God that did not cost you dearly in one way or another. You often say how you could never write a book, but darling, much of your life has been an open book with your wife's name jotted on the cover. I'm somewhere between so sorry about that and so very thankful. Bless you for caring about people so much that you let me tell about you constantly and *on you* occasionally. You are a humble man with a bone-deep desire to see hurting people come to wholeness. I am so in love with you . . . again.

Above and beyond all else I find dear, "now to the King eternal, immortal, invisible, the only God, be honor and glory for ever and ever. Amen" (1 Timothy 1:17).

INTRODUCTION

Well, I suppose what you hold in your hands is the closest I'll ever come to an autobiography. My entire life story grows like a wild shoot from the thorny soil of insecurity. Every fear I've faced, every addiction I've nursed, every disastrous relationship and idiotic decision I've made has wormed its way out of that sorrowfully fertile ground. Through the power and grace of God, I've dealt with so many side effects of it, but oddly, until now, I've somehow overlooked its primary source.

Our family has some acreage in the uglier, flatter, and rougher side of what's generously called the Texas Hill Country. Let's put it this way: if there's a sudden rush on cactus, mesquite, and non-descript white rocks, Keith and I are sitting pretty. While I was there recently, I got a dichotomous glimpse of myself while trudging down a rocky path, dodging thorns. I had my headphones on and my iPod blaring. My left hand, complete with wedding ring and fresh manicure, was up in the air, praising God, and my right hand was down by my side, gripping a shotgun. I know how to load it. I know how to use it. I grinned, shook my head, and thought to myself, *How on earth did this happen?*

Rattlesnakes — and not a few. They're the reason Keith ended up setting empty soda cans on a stump, putting a shotgun in my hands, and saying, "Aim carefully, 'Lizabeth. Now lean in, steady the thing with your shoulder, and when you're ready, shoot like you mean it." I missed the first time, but I haven't missed since. The way I see it, either I can get out in the fresh air and enjoy myself well equipped or I can sit in the stale house like a wimp and sulk about a path full of hazards. Throw me a shotgun. I'm not missing life over snakes.

These are perilous days to be a woman, but to be sure, they're the only days we have and they're passing quickly. We can sit around like victims, talk about how unfair all the gender pressure is, and grow less secure by the second, or we can choose to become well equipped and get out there and do some real living. This book is for any woman who courageously chooses the latter

18

over her own strong compulsion of insecurity in a culture that makes it almost irresistible.

Through all the hype of our society, we've developed an erroneous belief system that is about as subtle as a rattlesnake. It's time we aimed hard and shot some holes in it.

Maybe you've never read a book like this before. Maybe you don't share my belief system, but you've been drawn to open this cover because you share my battle. Glance around you. Do you see another woman? She probably shares that battle too. Regardless of our professions, credentials, or possessions, the vast majority of us are swimming in a sea of insecurity and trying our best to hide behind our goggles. In case we're thinking we'll one day outgrow the challenge, I've learned through the research for this book that chances are, we won't. Left to itself, the chronic part of the struggle may curve downward in our sixties, but insecurity could just as easily haunt us till we die. Honestly, who wants either option? In the best-case scenario, what are we supposed to do with those first fifty-nine years until we feel better?

Insecurity among women is epidemic, but it is not incurable. Don't expect it to go away quietly, however. We're going to have to let truth scream louder to our souls than the lies that have infected us. That's what this book is all about. It invites us to focus solidly on one issue that causes countless others. I hope so much you'll come along with me on this journey to authentic security. I give you my word that I'll shoot you a straight shot and won't try to manipulate you. If I have something to say, I'll just say it instead of trying to get you to swallow something you didn't realize you had on your plate. Risk it from the first page to the last, and if you honestly get to the end without an ounce of insight or encouragement, I'll pack up my books and go home. My hope is that you'll come out with something infinitely greater, however. I want nothing less than for you to close this book *secure*.

This writing process has been unlike any other I've experienced. I'm a research freak and relish the study that goes into a book as much as the writing. Months are spent in other resources before the first word pecks its way onto the computer screen. Not this time. My search for books devoted specifically to insecurity turned up a paltry offering. More resources may have been hiding in the bushes out there, but methods of finding them that have served me well for years failed to produce. In the lack, I discovered resources that were infinitely more valuable. I turned to people as my books. Over 1,200 of them, as a matter of fact, and you might be intrigued to know that I didn't just study women. You'll have to hang with the message to see the parts men play. I think you'll find their contributions very enlightening.

Every woman's story I'll share in these pages is somehow, in some way, a piece of my own. I may not have gone to her lengths. She may not have gone to mine. But we understand each other well. We wish each other well. Perhaps now it's time to walk with each other well.

CHAPTER 1
MAD ENOUGH TO CHANGE

I'm seriously ticked. And I need to do something about it. Some people eat when they're about to rupture with emotion. Others throw up. Or jog. Or go to bed. Some have a holy fit. Others stuff it and try to forget it. I can do all those things in sequential order, but I still don't find relief.

When my soul is inflating until my skin feels like a balloon about to pop, I write. Never longhand, if I can help it. The more emotion I feel, the more I appreciate banging on the keys of a computer. I type by faith and not by sight. My keyboard can attest to the fact that I am a passionate person with an obsession for words: most of the vowels are worn off. The word *ticked* really should have more vowels. Maybe what I am is peeved. That's a good one. How about irrationally irritated to oblivion? Let that one wear the vowels off a keyboard.

The thing is, I'm not even sure exactly

who I'm ticked at. I'm hoping to find that out as I hack away at these chapters. One thing is for certain. Once I figure it out, I probably won't keep it to myself. After all, you know how the saying goes: hell hath no fury like a woman scorned. And I'm feeling scorned.

But not just for myself. I'm feeling ticked for the whole mess of us born with a pair of X chromosomes. My whole ministry life is lived out in the blessed chaos of a female cornucopia. I've been looking at our gender through the lens of Scripture for twenty-five solid years, and I have pondered over us, taken up for us, laid into us, deliberated over us, prayed about us, lost sleep because of us, cried for us, laughed my head off at us, and gotten offended for us — and by us — more times than I can count. And after a quarter of a century surrounded by girls ranging all the way from kindergarteners to those resting on pale pink liners inside caskets, I've come to this loving conclusion: we need help. *I need help.* Something more than what we're getting.

The woman I passed a few days ago on the freeway who was bawling her eyes out at the steering wheel of her Nissan needs help. The girl lying about her age in order to get a job in a topless bar needs help. The divorcée who has loathed herself into fifty extra pounds needs help. For crying out loud, that female rock star I've disdained for years needs help. When I read something demeaning her ex said about her recently — something I know would cut any female to the quick — I jumped to her defense like a jackal on a field mouse and seriously wondered how I could contact her agent and offer to mentor her in Bible study.

Several days ago I sat in a tearoom across the table from a gorgeous woman I love dearly. She has been married for three months, and they did all the right things leading up to that sacred ceremony, heightening the anticipation considerably. After an hour or so of musing over marriage, she said to me, "Last weekend he seemed disinterested in me. I'll be honest with you. It kind of shook me up. I wanted to ask him, 'So, are you over me now? That quick? That's it?' "

I'm pretty certain her husband will perk back up, but what a tragedy that she feels like she possesses the shelf life of a video game.

I flashed back to another recent communication with a magazine-cover-beautiful thirty-year-old woman who mentioned — almost in passing — that she has to dress up in costumes in order for her husband to want to make love to her. I'm not knocking her pink-feathered heels, but I wonder if she is paying too much for them. I'm just sad that she can't feel desirable as herself.

Then yesterday I learned that a darling fifteen-year-old I keep in touch with slept with her boyfriend in a last-ditch effort to hold on to him. He broke up with her anyway. Then he told. It's all over her high school now.

I've got a loved one going through her third divorce. She wants to find a good man in the worst way, and goodness knows they're out there. The problem is, she keeps marrying the same kind of man.

I'm so ticked.

If these examples were exceptions to the rule, I wouldn't bother writing, but you and I both know better than that. I hear echoes of fear and desperation from women day in and day out — even if they're doing their best to muffle the sound with their Coach bags. Oh, who am I kidding? I hear reverberations from my own heart more times than I want to admit. I keep trying to stifle it, but it won't shut up. Something's wrong with us for us to value ourselves so little. Our culture has thrown us under the bus. We have a fissure down the spine of our souls, and boy, does it need fixing.

This morning while I was getting ready for church, my cell phone nearly vibrated off the bathroom counter with six incoming texts from a single friend who was having a crisis of heart. I answered her with what little I had to give, even as I grappled with my own issues. I decided that what I needed was a good sermon to keep me from crying off my eyeliner, so I flipped on the television to a terrific local preacher. Lo and behold, the sermon was about what a woman needs from a man.

Deep sigh.

Actually, it was a great message if anyone had a mind to do what he was recommending, but knowing human nature and feeling uncharacteristically cynical, I could feel my frustration mounting. The preacher had done his homework. He offered half a dozen Scripture-based PowerPoint slides with state-of-the-art graphics describing what men should do for women. "Women want to be told that they are captivating. That they're beautiful. Desirable."

I won't deny that. What woman wouldn't thrive under that kind of steady affirmation?

But here's my question: What if no one tells us that? Can we still find a way to be okay? Or what if he says it because he's *supposed* to, but to be honest, he's not feeling it? Are we hopeless? What if a man is *not* captivated by us? What if he doesn't think we're particularly beautiful? Or, understandably, maybe just not every day? Are we only secure on his "on" days? What if he loves us but is not quite as captivated by us as he used to be? What if his computer is full of images of what he finds attractive, and we're light-years from it? What if we're seventy-five, and every ounce of desirability is long behind us? Can we still feel adequate in our media-driven society? Or is it only possible if our man has gone blind?

A guy told me the other day that normal men never get too old to eye women. Wow. Are those of us who are married to these "normal" men supposed to keep trying to compete with what's out there? Or should we simply tell ourselves that the roving eye of a mate is harmless? I'm not being defensive. I want very much to believe that it is. But if it is, harmless to *who?*

Or what if you're single and there's not a man on the horizon you want to take home to Daddy? Honestly, is there no validation for our womanhood apart from a man?

I find it ironic that many of the women who defensively deny needing one single thing from a man have done one of three things: they've tried to make themselves into men, they've turned to a codependent relationship with a masculine woman, or they've done the *Sex and the City* thing by trying to beat men at their own game.

Don't tell me we don't have man-issues. After all this time in women's ministry, I won't believe you. Maybe you are the rare exception, but this I know: if you are a real, live, honest-to-goodness secure woman who is neither obsessed with a man's affirmation nor nursing a grudge against one, you did not arrive at that place by accident. None of us will.

I want to get a couple of things out on the table as fast as I can:

1) Men are certainly not the only source of insecurity for women. We'll wrestle with other sources on the pages that follow. But we're starting here because a woman with an unhealthy heart toward men will invariably be unhealthy in all sorts of areas, some of which extend far beyond her sexuality.

2) I am not a man-basher. Nothing could be further from my intent

than to blame men for our problems or infer that we should divorce ourselves from them emotionally in order to survive. God would flatten me like a horsefly if I did that. I don't think any male in my life would claim that I harbor repressed anger at his gender. (And if he did, I have a mind to hit him square in the middle of his forehead with a slingshot and a bottle of Midol.)

I'm a big fan of men. I've loved some fine ones and married my favorite one. Thirty years in, I'm still nuts about my husband and can't imagine life without him. Nobody makes me laugh like he does. Nobody makes me think like he does. Nobody has access to my heart like he does. He is worthy of my respect and gets a steady dose of it. So do my terrific sons-in-law, and if anybody on this earth is an object of my unbridled affection, it is my grandson, Jackson. I dearly love my guys and highly esteem so many others.

Men are not our problem; it's what we are trying to get from them that messes us up. Nothing is more baffling than our attempt to derive our womanhood from our men. We use guys like mirrors to see if we're valuable. Beautiful. Desirable. Worthy of notice. Viable. We try to read their expressions and moods in order to determine whether it's time to act smart and hard to get or play dumb and needy. Worse yet, we try to tap into their inner equestrian by acting like the damsel in distress. When XX meets XY and tries to pry that X away from him so she can have an extra one, she is attempting to mutate both of them.

I say this with respect and great compassion: we're attempting to get our security from a gender that doesn't really have much to spare. Our culture is just as merciless on men as it is on women. Their insecurities take different shapes, but make no mistake: they've got them. You know it. I know it.

Let's face it. Men want us to get a grip anyway. They don't like the pressure of being in charge of our sense of value. It's too much for them. The candid ones will gladly admit it, and for those who don't, you'll know it by the flapping of their shirts in the wind as they run for their lives.

A man is infinitely more attracted to a secure woman than to an emotional wreck who insists he could complete her. As my friend Christy Nockels says, "Men are not drawn to hysterical, needy women." I'm embarrassed to say that I know this fact from personal experience. No, it's not my normal approach, but sometimes life offers me such a monumentally irresistible opportunity to act like an idiot that I cave.

I have had the blessing and curse of being married to a very honest man. Keith is the kind who has prayed for forgiveness for impure thoughts even when I was sitting right there next to him with my head bowed. Needless to say, it didn't stay bowed. There I was, thinking nothing on earth was safer or more secure than praying with my husband . . . then *bam!* Honestly, the man would not purposely injure me for the world. And goodness knows, after my first big reaction, he never did this type of prayer-confession again. He is a very loving guy. But he had no idea that one innocent comment (even about guilt, ironically enough) had the capacity to sting my self-esteem, let alone send me into all manner of vain imaginations, depending on my present frame of mind. The worst part of it is, I could still be thinking about what he said a solid week later while he remained oblivious.

Now that's a key word that raises an important point. Are we honestly going to insist on drawing our security from people — men *or* women — who are oblivious to the inordinate amount of weight we give to their estimation of us? Seriously? Maybe others in our lives are not so clueless. Maybe they revel in the power they hold over us. Either way, are we just going to live our lives hurt and offended? The thought is exhausting. The reality is ultimately debilitating.

In countless ways, Keith has been the best medicine in the world for my terminal case of idealism, as bitter as a dose may taste. I will never forget a brief dialogue we had about ten years ago after I'd suffered a permanent fracture in a friendship. Suddenly his fairly self-sufficient woman (whom he'd married specifically because of that trait) started trying to suck the life out of him and, oddly, thought he'd be glad about it. After considerable deliberation and the careful planning of one committing herself for life, I made a brave and tearful declaration to Keith that went something like this: "I'm going to focus my attention on you. You are my best friend. In many ways, my only friend. I've decided that you are the only person on the earth I can really trust." He looked at me like a scared rabbit and said, "Baby, you can't trust *me!*" It was vintage Keith. Though he had never been unfaithful to me nor did he plan to be, it was his spit-it-out-and-prepare-for-carnage way of saying, "You can't put all your trust in me! I can't take the pressure! I'll fail you too!" I was utterly bewildered. Back to square one.

A beautiful place to be, actually. A place I'm trying to find. Again. Maybe the person I'm ticked at is me. Maybe I'm furious at myself for needing any part of this journey for my own sake. How could I need anything else in this world beyond what I already have? Lord, have mercy. What more could a woman want? As a matter of fact, I'd like to tell you exactly what more this woman could want — and not just for herself. I want some soul-deep security drawn from a source that never runs dry and never disparages us for requiring it. We need a place we can go when, as much as we loathe it, we *are* needy and hysterical. I don't know about you, but I need someone who will love me when I hate myself. And yes, someone who will love me again and again until I kiss this terrestrial sod good-bye.

Life is too hard and the world too mean for many of us to grasp a lofty sense of acceptance, approval, and affirmation early on and keep hold of it the rest of our lives . . . come what may. Circumstances abruptly change, and setbacks happen. Relationships unexpectedly end. Or, just as cataclysmically, *begin.* Schools change. Friends change. Jobs change. Offenses happen. Betrayals happen. Tragedies happen. Engagements end. Marriages begin. Kids come. Kids go. Health wanes. Seasons change. An old situation creeping up in a new season of our life can be more complicated than ever. We can think we've murdered that monster once and for all, and then it rises from the dead and it has grown another head.

As if the battle isn't hard enough, we sabotage ourselves, submerging ourselves with self-condemnation like a submarine filling with water. How often do we think to ourselves, *I should be handling this better?* So is it okay to ask why we're not? Like, what's at the root of an ugly knee-jerk reaction?

God did not create static beings when He breathed a soul into Adam. Dynamic creatures that we are, we are ever changing and ever spiraling up — or down. Please don't misunderstand. God forbid that we live life in a vicious cycle of gaining ground and losing it. I've learned some lessons that have lasted decades, and I hope to heaven I don't ever have to relearn them. However, I've never arrived at a place where injury or

35

uncertainty no longer issues an invitation to some pretty serious self-doubt even when I make the tough decision not to bite the bait. I still get thrown for a loop more easily than I would like and find myself in a temporary but painful setback of insecurity — one that affects me too chronically to deny that something is broken somewhere. Often when a situation warrants a minor case of injured feelings, I tend to respond with a classic case of devastation. "I know better than this," I chide. "I can't believe I've fallen for this again. My head knows good and well that this doesn't define me. Why can't I get that message to my heart?"

Listen carefully: the enemy of our souls has more to gain by our setbacks than by our succumbing to an initial assault. The former is infinitely more demoralizing. Far more liable to make us feel hopeless and tempt us to quit. We can rationalize — even truthfully — that an initial assault caught us by surprise. Setbacks, on the other hand, just make us feel weak and stupid: *I should have conquered this by now.* I happened on a question not long ago that perfectly expresses this mentality: How many times must I prove myself an idiot?

I hate that I can still be so easily shaken, and somehow I convince myself that if I could just develop a healthy enough psyche, life couldn't touch me. I'd be completely immovable. Steady Eddie. A rock. One thing keeps nagging at me, though. A man with an incomparable heart for God once confessed, "When I felt secure, I said, 'I will never be shaken.' O Lord, when you favored me, you made my mountain stand firm; but when you hid your face, I was dismayed" (Psalm 30:6–7).

Just when I'm feeling all secure, like I'm God's best friend, an earthquake splits that lofty mountain right down the middle. And boy, am I dismayed. I have a feeling we can never get so secure in ourselves that we cannot be moved. Can a rock ever move forward?

Is the goal of the believing life to get to a place where we simply hold steady till we die? Maybe that's part of my problem. Maybe I just get bored easily. I'm forever wanting to go someplace with God. I forget that in order to really want to go, something has to happen to make me want to leave where I am. Maybe we're all just sick to death of taking three steps forward and two steps back. Call me a math wizard, but isn't that still one step forward? Isn't that still some pretty big progress as we run against the hurricane winds of a godless culture?

And if we don't lose that ground, aren't we on our way somewhere new? Willing to take three more steps — even if we lose two?

Maybe this process is just for me. I've never written a single book out of expertise. I usually write to discover something I myself am yearning for. Even desperate for. I have given myself over to a lot of things along the way, but God help me, somebody tell me to retire when I start writing books just to talk about myself. That kind of self-importance makes me want to hang my head over a toilet. God has sustained this women's ministry with its one simple approach: I'm a common woman sharing common problems seeking common solutions on a journey with an uncommon Savior. If something hurts me, I conclude it probably hurts somebody else too. If something confuses me, I figure it probably confuses somebody else. If something helps me, I hope against hope that it might help somebody else. After all, "no trial has overtaken [us] that is not faced by others. And God is faithful" (1 Corinthians 10:13, NET).

To be honest, I don't know whether you and I are at a common place right now. I just have a hunch. See if this sounds like something that could erupt from your own pen: I'm sick to death of insecurity. It's been a terrible companion. *A very bad friend.* It promised to always think of me first and meticulously look out for my best interests. It vowed to stay focused on me and help me not get hurt or forgotten. Instead, insecurity invaded every part of my life, betrayed me, and sold me out more times than I can count. It's time I got healthy enough emotionally to choose my lifelong companions better. This one needs to get dumped.

By the grace and power of God, I've had the exhilarating joy of winning many battles, some of them against no small foes. I've experienced dramatic victory over sexual sin, addiction, unhealthy relationships, and other equally fierce opponents. But I have not won this particular battle against the stronghold of insecurity. *Yet.* God help me, I'm going to. This one's too sinister and deeply woven into the fabric of my female soul to deal with amid a bagful of other strongholds. Thank God, a time comes in a willing life when you're ready to face a Goliath-sized foe all by itself and fight it to the stinking death.

You hold in your hands one woman's quest for real, lasting, soul-changing security. I'd be honored if you care to join me.

Chapter 2
Insecure Enough to Matter

We all have insecurities. They piggyback on the vulnerability inherent in our humanity. The question is whether or not our insecurities are substantial enough to hurt, limit, or even distract us from profound effectiveness or fulfillment of purpose. Are they cheating us of the powerful and abundant life Jesus flagrantly promised? Do they nip at our heels all the way from the driveway to the workplace? Scripture claims that believers in Christ are enormously gifted people. Are our insecurities snuffing the Spirit until our gifts, for all practical purposes, are largely unproductive or, at the very least, tentative? Maybe you can answer each of those questions with an honest no. The only reason I'm bothering to write a book instead of leading a small group, however, is because I believe if you can, you'd be in the vast minority.

I'm convinced that many women — if not

most — have enough insecurity to hinder them. I recently surveyed more than nine hundred women and found that 78 percent admitted to having feelings of insecurity at or above a level that bothers them.[1] That qualifies as a major cry for healing. Of the total number of respondents, 43 percent described their issues with insecurity as anywhere from "pretty big" to "huge." If those nine hundred women are remotely reflective of the rest of us, we need to own up to a serious problem and seek serious solutions from a Creator who wonderfully crafted us.

Before we inch any further, let's start shaping some working definitions of insecurity so we can figure out if ours warrants attention and healing. Later in our journey, we'll also discuss various experiences that can feed those insecurities. Rest assured until then that there are often plausible explanations for why one person's insecurities exceed another's.

I am well enough acquainted with the issue to know that as we start defining and describing this malady, those of you with fairly chronic cases are going to begin to feel insecure even about your insecurities. (It takes one to know one.) Try not to go there. There was a time when I would have been tempted to put away a book that magnified my vulnerabilities, but these days I'd rather press through the discomfort of staring at my weaknesses than live in denial and bondage. The enemy of your soul has a tremendous amount to gain if you don't deal with your insecurities. Don't let him have that kind of victory. Let's just stay honest and courageous, and trust that help is on the way.

Okay, let's start by looking at one specialist's definition of insecurity:

Insecurity refers to a profound sense of self-doubt — a deep feeling of uncertainty about our basic worth and our place in the world. Insecurity is associated with chronic self-consciousness, along with a chronic lack of confidence in ourselves and anxiety about our relationships. The insecure man or woman lives in constant fear of rejection and a deep uncertainty about whether his or her own feelings and desires are legitimate.[2]

I hope that definition conveys to some extent the idea that insecurity is not the same thing as sensitivity. The latter can be a charming trait that is often evidenced in

42

thriving individuals and relationships. Not everyone who is sensitive is insecure, but make no mistake: everyone who is insecure is usually sensitive to a fault. Confusingly, these are often people who can dish out all sorts of things they can't take. As you glance over this first definition, keep in mind that you don't have to possess every description or element to qualify as insecure and in need of healing.

For instance, I don't have anxiety about all my relationships, but I have enough to bother me in a few. Likewise, I don't live with a constant fear of rejection in all my associations, but a handful of experiences have left some sizable wounds. I also don't grapple with feeling like I have no place in this world. In fact, like so many other women who are in over their heads in responsibility — moms, teachers, caretakers, doctors, and corporate executives, to name a few — some of my insecurity stems from being uncomfortable with the place that I *do* have. Whether we feel insignificant or overrated or drunk on some loony cocktail of the two, insecurity lands with both feet on two words: self-doubt. I step in it. Then I swim in it. Then I nearly drown in it.

This morning I went on a walk to listen

to praise music on my iPod and hold the themes of this book out before God in hopes that He would speak to my heart. He spoke, all right. I realized that maybe I don't just doubt myself. Maybe I subconsciously doubt God for using me. Let me be frank: if I were God, I wouldn't have given me a second look. I constantly feel unqualified, inadequate, and out of my league. I realized this morning that I not only lack security, I also lack faith. I don't just doubt myself, I also doubt God *about* myself. It was a revelation to me. Almost a horror. I wonder if you can relate.

If you know Jesus Christ personally, He has chosen you, too, and has appointed you to accomplish something good. Something that matters. Something prepared for you before time began (Ephesians 2:10). Something meant to have a serious impact within your sphere of influence.

Perhaps, like me, somewhere deep inside you entertain the lie that you know yourself better than God knows you and that you've somehow successfully hidden something from His omniscient eye. This could be the only explanation for why He bothers with you. For those of us who try to live in the light of Scripture, this thought process is far more subtle than outright. Roots always extend underground. Sometimes the only way we know one of these roots exists is when we see what's growing from it. If we have false assumptions like, "If God really knew me, He wouldn't like me" hidden somewhere in our core, it will feed our insecurities like a zookeeper shoveling hay to an elephant. We only know that assumption is there because something big, alive, and destructive is growing from it.

Some of us never seek healing from God for our insecurities because we feel like we don't fit the profile. We think insecurity only looks one way — mousy, maybe even inept — and that's not exactly who we see in the mirror. At least not once the mascara's on. And it certainly is not the woman we present to the public. Insecurity's best cover is perfectionism. That's where it becomes an art form.

Keep an open mind to what an insecure woman looks like, and don't be too hasty to let yourself off the hook just because one dimension of the portrait doesn't look like you. The fact that she can be a complicated mix of confidence and self-consciousness is the very reason it took me so long to identify it in myself and admit it.

As I was preparing to write this book, I took an insecurity inventory and found that many of the statements did not apply to me at all.

Do I cry easily? No.

Do I avoid the spotlight in social situations? Uh, no. There's a reason some of my best buddies call me "Beth La Ham."

Other suggestions on the inventory, however, were so descriptive that I felt my face flush like someone had caught me cheating.

Do I have a strong desire to make amends whenever I think I've done something wrong? Are you kidding me? I have a strong desire to make amends even when I *haven't* done something wrong! And not solely because I want to do the godly thing. I battle an inordinate desire to make peace that can't always be others- or God-centered. I dread the backlash of people far more than the backlash of God at times. He's infinitely more merciful. Depending on how insecure I feel at the moment, having someone upset at me is very unsettling even if I was on the right side of the conflict. I cannot count the times God has had to tell me to cease trying to fix something that insists on staying broken. Loss of favor and approval and harmony is excruciating to people with insecurity.

Here are a few other survey questions that hit the bull's-eye:

46

If someone gets angry at me, do I have a hard time not thinking about it? I try to limit myself to obsessing.

Do I sometimes feel anxious for no apparent reason? God knows I do.

Does it hurt my feelings when I learn that someone doesn't like me? Breaks my heart.

Do I fear that my husband might leave me for someone else? Not all the time. Not most of the time. But more often than I think is healthy.

Did you catch the part of the definition that describes insecurity as "a deep uncertainty about whether his or her own feelings and desires are legitimate"? How often do you have to ask yourself if what you're feeling is even real? Or if your desires should be quashed or pursued? If you're discerning or just suspicious? If you were supposed to do "this" or not? If you're like me, it's more often than you want to admit.

You might protest with something like this: "But Beth, I feel all those same things, and I don't consider myself insecure." My question in response would be, How intensely do you feel those things? If you feel as intensely as I do, that woman you see in the mirror probably has a bigger insecurity problem than you're giving her credit for. Or, more important, seeking healing for.

Intensity is a key factor in insecurity. A fissure in a relationship might sting one person but devastate the other. Obviously, the latter party is most likely the least secure. Insecurity is not just about how many of the qualifications you possess. It's about how much the ones you own really get to you.

The length of time you've been plagued by insecurity is another key factor to consider. Maybe you caught the repetition of the word *chronic* in the specialist's definition of insecurity. This was a medical term used by Hippocrates from the Greek word *chronos*, meaning "time." It referred to maladies that persisted for many days. In modern medicine, the term is still used to describe conditions that have lasted three or more months. Humor me here for a moment. Have your insecurities bothered you for more than ninety days? Mine have. Then they've been chronic. Enough said. Let's press forward.

Let's lock in for a few moments on the element of self-consciousness from our earlier definition. At the mention of the term, our minds once again start sketching

48

an image of what a self-conscious person looks or acts like, and we know we don't want to be her. After all, we have too much pride to be her. But the truth is, she's not nearly as easily pegged as that seventh grader in the locker room who perfected the art of changing into her gym clothes without first taking off her dress. I hate to state the obvious, but all it takes to be chronically self-conscious is to be chronically conscious of self. Self-consciousness is acute self-awareness and a preoccupation with self, no matter how it's externalized in life. Suddenly the broader scope changes everything we picture about her.

The self-conscious person may protect herself with plainness and try to blend into the paint, but she also may dress herself to perfection and stand squarely in the spotlight. In either portrayal — or anything in between — she is ordinarily more aware of herself than she tends to be of any other person in the room. Whether she feels inferior or superior, she takes a frequent inventory of her place in the space. She may like it or hate it, but she's rarely oblivious to it. Never think for a moment that pride and self-centeredness have no role in insecurity. Since she keeps confusing her insecurity with humility, however, she never recognizes

49

the self-centeredness so she can turn from it.

Now for the part of the specialist's description of insecurity that had me at hello:

> The insecure person also harbors unrealistic expectations about love and relationships. These expectations, for themselves and for others, are often unconscious. The insecure person creates a situation in which being disappointed and hurt in relationships is almost inevitable. Ironically, although insecure people are easily and frequently hurt, they are usually unaware of how they are unwitting accomplices in creating their own misery.[3]

That's me! Or at least it *was* me. It's becoming less and less descriptive, only because I decided to declare war on it and let God get to it if it killed me. Here's the confusing catch: I've rarely been called out on this issue. As the definition suggests, I was not consciously aware of putting undue pressure on the relationship, nor was I accused of it, but in retrospect it is embarrassingly obvious. Let's face it. Many of us appear far more together on matters of the heart than we are.

Like you, I've been confident and secure in many relationships while others were nearly the death of me. No matter how healthy some of my associations were, the ones where I harbored unreasonable expectations caused me considerable pain and innumerable disappointments.

Can you say the same thing? How honest would you be if it were just the two of us and God talking? Let's try to relate like that through these pages. What does your own relational track record look like? Do you tend to put a fair amount of pressure on some key relationships? Do you have a few unrealistic expectations?

I once heard a comedian on television say that he'd finally come to the conclusion that what a woman wants in a man is another woman. Isn't that the truth? Don't we frequently wish our men were more sensitive and nurturing? Don't we wish they liked to eat at Souper Salad, see a good chick flick, and talk afterward about how it made them feel? Don't we wish that just one stinking time they'd offer a massage instead of asking for one?

And then there are other times when we think if we have to hear another woman whine (no, not all women are whiners), we're going to put our heads in the washing machine and hold our breath. You know you're on the verge of unrealistic expectations when you want to tell your girlfriend to get some hair on her chest and take her situation like a man.

Understandably, we develop relationships in large part based on what we derive psychologically from them. Maybe you have a very sanguine friend who buoys you or brings an element of excitement to your life. But what if she doesn't happen to be in a terrific mood when you meet up after work that day? Is that okay with you, or do you tend to be disappointed even if you don't show it? Is there a part of you that feels like she let you down? You might have a mentor you look to for spiritual guidance, but she doesn't seem as focused on you as she used to be. How easily do you roll with that kind of transition?

We can be so blessed in certain relationships that our unrealistic expectations often seem met and, therefore, reasonable. We can get away with thinking we're secure people because, for a time, we have the important things just like we want them. But then change happens, and suddenly we are thrown for a severe emotional loop. We realize we weren't secure. We were spoiled. One way we can detect insecurity is by our

52

knee-jerk reaction to any level of change in a relationship, particularly if we perceive that the focus has shifted away from us. The more easily threatened we are, the more insecure we are. You can take that one to the bank.

I know what it's like to inadvertently create an atmosphere where some measure of hurt is inevitable. In my vastly unhealthy days, I tended to handpick relationships in which I'd get mistreated in some ways. There have been other times when I've put so much stock in certain relationships that a crash was unavoidable. Thankfully, only a few of those collisions have been fatal. The rest of them, however, either stayed wrecked or took a good while to repair. If we let too much ride on a relationship, a blowout is inevitable. The very nature of pressure is to blow. The ramifications of this kind of insecurity reach all the way from a pattern of disappointment to unabated abuse.

Oddly, both the victim and the victimizer in toxic associations suffer from a similar malady. They're both chronically insecure. Both have false belief systems shoveling hay into the mouth of that destructive elephant. The great news is that when we let God bring some wholeness to unhealthy propensities within us, we will not only make healthier relationships, we will also enjoy them immeasurably more. For crying out loud, we might even start *liking* some of those people we love but can hardly stand.

I'm going to take the risk of saying something pretty bold at this point so you'll have a heads-up. In your pursuit of God-vested security, the only relationships in your life that will suffer rather than improve are the significantly unhealthy ones. I'll go one step further. Those that are the unhealthiest might not even survive at all — and maybe they shouldn't. But more on that later.

Right now we're picking on ourselves, but later in our journey, we're going to pick on the people in our lives who prefer us to be insecure and have a sick need to keep us that way. They are what the same specialist I quoted earlier calls "emotional predators." No, you are not the only one to blame, but girlfriend, you are the only one you can change. God is willing. God is able. Let Him get to that terrified part of you that devalues the rest of you.

As we draw this chapter to a close, let's not allow our focus on personal relationships to fool us into thinking that this is the only area of our lives at risk over insecurity. It's just the most painful. The same self-doubt, self-consciousness, and fear that dog us at home will dog us all the way to work and bark like a miniature schnauzer at our desks. Not only will insecurity cheat us of reaching and then *operating consistently* at maximum potential, it also will turn our coworkers into threats and trap us into becoming posers. It will also chase us to church, where we'll be so distracted by who we know or don't know, where we sit or don't sit, what brand we are or aren't wearing, that we probably won't hear three words of the message.

This is the perfect spot to try my own hand at a succinct definition of insecurity: self-sabotage.

Insecurity is miserable. That's the bottom line. We don't need it. We don't want it. And we really can live without it. So what would happen if we quit being accomplices in our own misery?

CHAPTER 3
SHE DOESN'T LOOK A
CERTAIN WAY

Sometimes wide, sweeping explanations are a big help. That's what I hope we got in the last chapter. Other times we just need a concept boiled down to its most basic form. That's where we'll start this one. According to *The American Heritage Dictionary of the English Language,* the first definition of the word *insecure* is this: "Not secure."

There you have it. Sometimes it's just that simple. If you frequently don't feel secure, you're insecure. It's just a matter of finding out why and what to do about it. Sometimes you know in your own gut that you struggle with insecurity even if you can't get many people to believe you. I've had conversations that go like this:

"What on earth do you have to be insecure about? You have everything."
Nope. Actually, nobody has everything. Beware of appearances.

56

"Your husband loves you." Yes, he does. And I love him. But we are flawed people with flawed hearts. We don't always say the right thing or choose to do the thing that would build the other up. We love each other deeply and know each other like no one else. We are well versed in each other's weaknesses and starkly aware of the other's vulnerabilities. Most of the time we avoid those areas. Some of the time we aim at them. Our hearts are fully exposed to each other: big, round, thumping red targets. That kind of susceptibility makes the joys ecstatic and the offenses horrific. Anyway, no person on earth can love you perfectly enough to mend a tear in the crimson fabric of your soul. Furthermore, if a person ever gave unwavering, undivided attention to loving every part of us and made us the solitary object of his undying, unhindered, unhidden affection, we'd probably start feeling smothered. Maybe that's a little of what Ovid meant when he wrote, "Love fed fat soon turns to boredom." I don't know about you, but I like people who have a life. I just want a healthy piece of it.

"A lot of people like you." Those are

beautiful words to a sanguine like me. But for every person who likes me, there's another person who doesn't.

Making assumptions about who struggles with insecurity and who doesn't based on what they appear to have going for them suggests how little we understand the nature of insecurity and what feeds it. Convinced that security is wholly circumstantial, we make false assumptions that add all sorts of trash to the heap we're in. I'm hoping that somewhere along the way our quest will make us rethink our typecasting and develop some real insight concerning what makes people tick. If in high school you were eaten alive with resentment toward that perky cheerleader type with the blonde hair, blue eyes, and dark tan, you probably still hate the grown-up version of her in your present social or work circle *unless* you got to the root of why you felt that way in the first place.

You're not alone. Every female at one time or another has been jealous of the resident "it-girl," and no one is a darker shade of green than the girl most recently dethroned. Here's what a lot of people don't get about that type: she may be bloodier in the battle with insecurity than the sum total of all those who hate her.

If you knew what her heart was going through much of the time, you might even feel a tad sorry for her. You'd definitely save yourself the energy of wishing you were her for very long.

If having it all is a myth, then keeping it all is science fiction at its furthest fetch. The pressure is impossible, and the appetite of that beast is insatiable. She wouldn't know the concept of carefree if it jumped on her flat iron and hit her upside her head. You see, no one is more thoroughly seduced by the lie that security is circumstantial than somebody who has *almost* everything. The more believable the myth, the less likely she'll be to buck it and break free. She feels so close to the goal, she can almost grab it. It dangles right there at the edge of her solar tips (not knocking them — typing with them), but she can't quite get her fingers wrapped around it. She is often the last person to come around to the truth, sometimes believing to her dying breath that if she could just do this or control that, she could quell that ache inside of her. She is driven to the ridiculous by her chronic need for affirmation. And, Lord knows, nobody is unhappier with aging than she is. Maybe she was genuinely enviable her freshman year in college, but boy, would you ever want to avoid being in her heels from forty to the grave. Especially when the doctor tells her she needs to switch to flats.

The wounded in this war are not always the ones we would expect. In my twenty-five years of conferences and retreats, no group has ever fostered more anguish in my heart than professional athletes' wives. Most of those I spoke to personally had souls that were in shreds. Those who didn't poured their lives compassionately into those who did. They knew the pain of insecurity. The trap of it. Some of them knew how to escape from the game of it — and I'm not talking about the comparative child's play on the field. Each time I've had the opportunity to serve a group of professional athletes' wives, they were the most gorgeous women I'd ever encountered. The kind who make you gawk. I might have envied how some of them looked, but I never once envied what they faced.

Don't miss one of the chief purposes of this chapter: Be careful who you covet. Be careful how you judge. Be slow to size somebody up and think you know all about her type. She's not so different from you. Nobody's unbreakable here on this planet. Only the dead don't bleed when they're cut.

We all fear that we aren't who we are pretending to be. The more careful we are about what we're projecting, the more driven we tend to be by fear.

Maybe you're onto the fact that many of the women I've pinpointed with chronic insecurity are physically attractive. I won't keep hammering the point, but I want to establish early on that if you're thinking really attractive women don't have this issue, you are out of your darling little mind. If you happen to be thinking that average looks are the problem, they're not. An injured soul is the problem. Improving her appearance can make a woman feel better about herself and arguably improve some quality of life, but it still won't heal her insecurity. The more she thinks it will, the more she's setting herself up for another blow. Each woman has within her capabilities various ways of looking her best. Not somebody else's best, mind you, but her own. If our pursuit has moved from reasonable attention to a veritable obsession, however, we'd better search our souls for what's driving us.

Do you ever stop in your tracks and ask yourself out loud, "What am I doing?" Boy, I do. It's a terrifically important question, but it needs a few others to follow it up, like, "Why am I doing what I am doing? What am I hoping to achieve?"

Thankfully, we don't always get a scathing result when we perform a soul search. Sometimes we might actually discover that our motives are not that off base. The more afraid we are to ask ourselves hard questions, however, the more we probably need to. Sometimes we may have a pretty acceptable motive, but the outcome is something altogether different from what we expected, and we can't handle it. Case in point: a woman I know got liposuction last year and decided recently that she looked good enough to get a better man, so she dumped her husband. They have children, for crying out loud. Something's whacked somewhere. Needless to say, not everybody who gets liposuction leaves her spouse. Something much deeper than the desire for smooth thighs drives an outcome like that.

There's a woman in my neighborhood who has been the envy of other women around here for years. Her face is nearly flawless. Worse yet, so is her body. Amazingly, she has kept it up for what seems like forever. *Lord have mercy, does this woman ever have an off day?* I've stayed physically active, but trust me when I tell you this: we are not running bases in the same ball-park.

I can remember many times power walking through the neighborhood when she'd nearly blow me off the sidewalk, sprinting like a twenty-year-old in her black and red spandex. I always thought how terrific she looked and marveled that she was only a few years younger than I am. Recently I was on my millionth walk through this subdivision where we've lived for twenty-five years when she whizzed past me again. This time on a bike. And in spandex. And looking fantastic. But suddenly I felt sorry for her. I thought, *Shoot fire, that must be exhausting to keep up.* And I felt a little sorry for myself, too. Sure, I want to keep my own stuff up as long as I can, but what about when I can't? Is that okay?

I hear that voice deep within me saying, *Don't ask if that's okay with them. Here's the real question: is that okay with you?* You and I are going to have to come to a place where we stop handing people the kind of power only God should wield over us. Change will not come easy. Old habits die hard. But we *can* make the radical decision to rewire our security systems.

Before we do so, we'll need to widen the scope on those false assumptions. Not only do we misunderstand attractive women to have fewer insecurities than others do, we also misunderstand married women to have fewer insecurities than single women do. I won't argue that a good man and a good marriage can't vastly enhance a woman's sense of well-being, but you can mark my word on something: if a woman is married to a man who somehow feeds her sense of inadequacy, she has double the issues of her single friend. A bad marriage can make you feel worlds more insecure than singleness. The answer for the married woman is not to dump her husband, nor is it for a single woman to marry someone just for emotional coverage. The answer is to deal with the insecurity, believing that everything God says about us is true.

You see, the trap is not only in placing our security in something that gives a false positive. It's also in fighting like a mad dog to keep it there. Whether our false positive is appearance, marriage, moneymaking, position, education, or notoriety, it only works enough to keep us seduced and distracted, and we never get to the real issues. Even if we could make everybody believe we were "every woman," we ourselves would know better. Self-doubt would devour us. In one way or another and sooner or later, we'll give ourselves away. Security in any earthly thing simply cannot be sustained.

Right now I'm completely eaten up with this subject. Every woman I encounter for any amount of time inevitably becomes a book in my library of research for this message. If she'll open up, that is. A few days ago I met a really good friend at our neighborhood mall. She's years younger than I am, but we have similar tastes in coffee and in clothes, so we have a blast together. She said, "Hey, somebody at your office told me you were writing a book on insecurity." This friend is refreshingly honest about her weaknesses and could have well gotten away with hiding them behind an exquisitely put-together exterior, but she plowed right ahead: "Girl, you know good and well that's my big issue! I want the first copy!" See what I mean? Refreshingly bull-free. She continued on. "You know, Beth, people who don't know you really well would never be able to imagine that you struggle with insecurity." Then she made a comment that really got my mind rolling. "After all, you're so tiny."

That's when it hit me. Most of us have what I'll call a prominent false positive: *one thing* that we think would make us more secure in *all things.* You want to know how you can pinpoint your own prominent false positive? The thing you tend to associate most with security? Think of a person you believe to be secure and determine what earthly thing he or she has that you don't feel like you possess, at least in matching measure. That's liable to be your prominent false positive: the *one thing* that would make you more secure in *all things.* Needless to say, we would all like any number of things to give us the security we're after, but we each have a tendency to prioritize one above the rest. Our attachment to it is not a cerebral thing. Few of us would reason that the weight we're giving to the object or circumstance makes sense intellectually. It's an emotional thing. Often we're not even aware of it, but we demonstrate it by the inordinate power we assign to it.

My friend conveyed (openly, because that's her style) that much of her insecurity is tied up with her weight. That's why she would be inclined to think that I would be more secure. Her prominent false positive might be thinness. Her exact struggle is not so much mine. And trust me when I tell you, mine is not so much hers. Lord have mercy, does she ever have some things I don't have! Mind you, my friend has a fabulous shape most women would envy, but she says she has some pounds that drive

66

her crazy. Two other women could have taken the conversation a totally different direction. Picture a different writer and a different friend:

"You know, _____, people who don't know you really well would never be able to imagine that you struggle with insecurity. After all . . .

. . . you're married to the most fabulous man in the world." *Prominent false positive: A great man would make me secure.*

. . . look at this house! Girl, you never have to worry about money." *Prominent false positive: Financial success would make me secure.*

. . . you've got the best personality of anybody I know. Everybody likes you." *Prominent false positive: Popularity would make me secure.*

. . . you're young and in the prime of your life!" *Prominent false positive: Recapturing youthfulness would make me secure.*

. . . you're gorgeous! I'd give anything to see that in the mirror!" *Prominent false positive: Beauty would make me secure.*

. . . you run this whole corporation.

Look how people jump through hoops for you!" *Prominent false positive: Power would make me secure.*

. . . everybody looks up to you!" *Prominent false positive: Prestige would make me secure.*

. . . look at all those degrees on your wall. Are you kidding me? You're the smartest person I know!" *Prominent false positive: Credentials would make me secure.*

. . . you've got tenure! What are you worried about?" *Prominent false positive: Job certainty would make me secure.*

I'm not naive enough to think that any one of those things couldn't add a layer of security to a sliver of our lives. At least temporarily. I'm saying none of them, nor all of them in sum total, would fix our core issue. We'd still slosh around in self-doubt or worry over whether or not we'll have tomorrow what we have today. Most of us would wrestle with how much we don't deserve what we have, and that alone can make us feel insecure. Acquiring your prominent false positive is like putting a finger in the crack of a bulging dam. You can try to stop up a leak in one place, but the pressure's going to build up in another, and one day that levee's going to burst. Having a dab of security here and there is a long way from being a secure person, and that's what you and I are after.

I know some folks who think publishing a book would totally cut it for them. No, it won't. Neither will a nose job. (Obviously, I can't tell you that from experience.) Neither will money. Neither will breast implants. Neither will a big house. Or a man who calls you six times a day. Or great hair, although I'm often happily seduced by the hope that it will. Neither will a big office in a financially solid corporation . . . if you can still find such a thing. Not even losing that proverbial ten pounds will fix what insecurity has broken. Any of those things might soothe the savage beast for a while, but it will inevitably wake back up, and the hope deferred will make it angrier than ever. No one solitary thing on this entire planet has the power to secure everything else. Not even a long-awaited child, as dear as he or she would be. I write those words with compassion and tenderness. There are countless amazing things children bring into a life. Just don't put security in that Pack 'n Play. Children will bring out every insecurity you've got. Count on it.

I guess you know I'm not casting stones.

You're safe with me even if your false positive is the furthest thing from mine. After all, at least you don't have such a chronic case of insecurity that you are willing to become a public poster child. Frankly, I don't care who knows I struggle. What kind of nut would think I don't? I'm on my way to freedom and bound and determined, God willing, to take some women with me. The journeys that brought the two of us to this juncture may be as different as day and night, but the one that will take us to the security that sticks around longer than a circumstance is very much the same.

Not long ago I was having one of those days all women have — at least occasionally — feeling down and probably hormonal. You know the kind: those days when we look in the refrigerator and wonder when somebody's going to go to the grocery store, and in the closet and wonder why in heaven's name we bought all that hideous stuff. Those days when we look in the mirror and mumble, "Sick." Or if we're more spiritual, "Bless your heart." Those days we are too down on ourselves to lift ourselves up, so we usually go looking for someone else to do it. It should have been God, but for me that day it was Keith.

If I don't feel like I look good, somehow I

rationalize that since God looks on the heart, He's not the threat, so I don't need to go to Him. When on this earth will I learn to go to Him about every single thing? Instead, I rationalize that Keith could be the threat. He may not love me as much if he doesn't think I look good. You know the pathetic drill. I wouldn't have been caught dead asking him the real question: "Am I still beautiful to you?" It would be too humiliating. Leave me too wide open. As I tell on myself, humor me if I choose not to imply that I'm more pathetic than I am. I'll save that for better opportunities. I'm being as honest as I know how when I tell you that, while I hope other women think I'm cute — and if not in looks, at least in personality — I don't have a deep emotional need for them to think beyond that. My primary "looks" issue is tangled up with my husband. He's the person whose attraction I crave *and* to whose occasional bouts of disinterest I cave. He's the one holding the arrow that can hit this particular Achilles' heel.

So instead of asking Keith the question on my mind, I simply tried to see if I could get him to volunteer the information. Otherwise it doesn't count. Please somebody fess up to doing this too. Don't leave me hanging here. I put on something I thought he would really like: the jeans and sweater kind of thing, because Keith doesn't like a skanky look on his woman. I then proceeded to walk between him and that interminable fishing show no less than twenty times. Nothing. Not a word. Well, maybe a "Hey there, sweetie," but I wasn't fishing for "Hey there, sweetie." I was fishing for a mere "Man, I must be the luckiest guy on earth." Nothing. Two hours later, still nothing. Keith *can* be affirming, so it wasn't a far-fetched idea. It just didn't work this time.

I eventually plopped down at the table on my back porch and heard a voice from my own handicapped soul mimicking Keith's: *No, the simple fact is, you're not still beautiful to me.* Not surprising coming from the voice of my soul; self-condemnation is the strong suit of people with my kind of background. But that's when the freaky part happened. A moment later I heard a deeper voice — not out loud, of course, but from the innermost place within me — say, *Yes. Yes, indeed you are.* The thought came out of left field. In fact, it shocked me. Listen, I'm not given to those kinds of thoughts when I'm in that kind of emotional funk. I knew that voice was not mine. It was Christ's. I also knew that it had absolutely nothing to do with my looks and everything to do with the kind of beauty that really is sustainable — even improvable — no matter what happens to us, who rejects us, how handicapped we are, or how old we get.

The thought had occurred to me before but never in this context: sitting at that porch table, I realized with fresh astonishment that, although we may have something unhealthy deep inside of us, those in whom Christ dwells also have something deeper. Something whole. Something so infinitely healthy that, if it would but invade the rest of us, we would be healed.

I don't know. Maybe this isn't a big revelation to you, but I am so thankful that at no time since I received Christ as Savior have I ever been a total wreck. Partial? Lord, have mercy, yes. Humiliatingly so. But total? Not on your ever-loving life. And if He resides in you, neither have you (Romans 8:9). Jesus is not unhealthy. Not codependent with us. His strength is made perfect in our weakness. This thought never grows old to me: He has no dark side. In Him is *no darkness at all.*

That, beloved, is our challenge. To let the healthy, utterly whole, and completely secure part of us increasingly overtake our earthen vessels until it drives our every emotion, reaction, and relationship. When we allow God's truth to eclipse every false positive and let our eyes spring open to the treasure we *have,* there in His glorious reflection we'll also see the treasure we *are.* And the beauty of the Lord our God will be upon us (Psalm 90:17, NKJV).

CHAPTER 4
GOOD COMPANY

If you're coming to the same conclusion I did — realizing you have a sizable issue with insecurity — take heart! We are in fine company. I started flipping through Scripture looking for tell-tale signs of insecurity, and I had a veritable field day. In fact, with your indulgence, I'd like to select winners in both the male and female categories for the most insecure people in Scripture. I'll never make it past the Old Testament without doling awards. There are too many winners to resist.

I would start with Eve as our first runner-up, because I feel sure that all our female troubles began with her. But since the only real hint of insecurity I can find is her affinity for fig leaves, I'll leave her alone. Insecurity often displays itself in a woman's wardrobe, but who can blame Eve for grabbing the closest thing on a hanger? There wasn't a darn thing in her closet. Not many women are secure enough to walk around for long without some kind of leaf. I have a wraparound monogrammed towel that I wear when I blow-dry my big hair. Keith calls it a red potato sack because it doesn't have any real shape, but actually it's just a huge wraparound, terry cloth leaf, and I, for one, am thankful for it. Enough about Eve. Or was it me? Let's move on to better candidates like Sarai and Hagar.

Their conflict goes to show that monu- mentally foolish decisions can catapult you into insecurities you might have lived the rest of your life without. You can be sure we'll hear more on that subject later. After years of trying to conceive a child with Abram, Sarai came up with the bright idea to hand over her young maidservant, Hagar, to him in hopes of producing an heir. Can you spell I-D-I-O-T? I know, I know. It was a different culture, but no matter what the local mores are, there's something inside every woman that says it's wrong to share her man. Then again, desperation opens the door of insecurity with the gentility of a wrecking ball. Genesis 16:4–6 tells us what happened next.

He slept with Hagar, and she conceived. When she knew she was pregnant, she began to despise her mistress. Then Sarai said to Abram, "You are responsible for the wrong I am suffering. I put my servant in your arms, and now that she knows she is pregnant, she despises me. May the Lord judge between you and me."

"Your servant is in your hands," Abram said. "Do with her whatever you think best." Then Sarai mistreated Hagar; so she fled from her.

Nothing makes a woman battle insecurity more than feeling like she can't give her guy what he wants. Nothing except handing him another woman, that is. I need you to chase a rabbit with me for a moment. Do you know that recently someone tried to convince me of the marital benefits of swinging? (I don't mean the kind of swinging first graders do on the playground.) Rumors of swingers have circulated for years around the cul-de-sacs in our family-friendly suburb. I have no idea if they're true, and Lord knows I don't want to know. Nevertheless, here's the argument I heard: "You can stay married to one partner, yet [hesitation while searching for the right word] *sleep* with others in a mutually agreed-upon situation." Blood pressure rising. Trying to stay in control of my volume. *Are you out of your ever-loving mind?* Sorry, buddy, but that's not what most people call staying married.

It simply cannot work. No couple on earth can maintain emotional intimacy with one another while they have sexual intimacy with other partners. Our bodies, souls, and spirits are far too intricately woven. Eventually hearts follow bodies, and bodies follow hearts. Thank God, most couples aren't crazy enough to think swinging would help, although plenty of marriages *are* crushed by unfaithfulness. I am absolutely convinced that couples can be restored by God after betrayal and infidelity if both the husband and the wife are willing to do the hard and long work — but not until relations *of every sort* have been completely cut off from the third party. (And even then it's a miracle. But thank God He does indeed perform miracles. I've seen the evidence in more marriages than I can count.)

These examples may seem worlds apart from Sarai and Hagar, but in reality, the only difference is the goal. The carnage is all too similar. Any time a third party enters the intimacy of marriage, someone is eventually going to get thrown out. And even though it wasn't Sarai, the experience nearly skinned her alive. Glance back at that

Scripture segment for a moment and notice that Hagar despised Sarai and Sarai mistreated Hagar. We naturally despise people whose company we are forced to share if we feel largely threatened by them.

Threat. That single word captures one of the most powerful drivers of insecurity. More often than not, if we're willing to make the connection, we can trace feelings of insecurity to a perceived threat, especially when it comes in a sudden rush.

What are we afraid of?

Who are we afraid of?

What are we afraid of losing?

Why are we afraid of being displaced?

Studies have long since proven that much of what we fear is fueled by our imaginations, and in fact, most of what we fear never even happens. However, as we seek healing for our insecurity, it does us absolutely no good to work from the premise that we have nothing to be insecure about. Sometimes our fears *are* founded. Sometimes a valid threat really does arise. What happens then? Not long ago a woman wrote me a letter describing how her best friend systematically seduced her husband. That, girlfriend, is a threat. My suggestion is this: even when fears are founded and threats are real and we are about to be swept away

79

in a tidal wave of well-earned insecurity, there is divine power, wisdom, and clarity of thought to be found. The person who responds with strength instead of hysteria at a time like that may be a stranger to you right now, but finding that person is precisely what we are doing here.

If you can't find resolution when faced with a persistent threat, bad feelings can quickly turn into bad behavior, and somebody's going to get mistreated. Take Sarai or Hagar, for instance. Neither one of them had what they wanted. The mistress would never hold the esteem of the wife, and the wife would never be the surrogate heir's real mother. Hence, Hagar despised Sarai, and Sarai mistreated Hagar. No emotion is uglier than jealousy, and you can jot this one down in bold print: jealousy is always the result of a perceived threat. And a threat always places a 911 call to insecurity.

Oh, but I can one-up Sarai and Hagar. In the entire canon of Scripture, no competition among women compares to the one recorded in Genesis 29 and 30, in which a man with more than one woman has inadvertently signed himself up for more than double his share of turmoil. Jacob had two wives. Worse yet, they were sisters, and Jacob didn't love Leah. He loved Rachel, but her sister, Leah, was a baby-making machine in a culture that placed a high premium on baby making. Each of Leah's sons and her maidservant's sons bore the mark of her insecurities by receiving names that reflected her emotional state at their births. Here are just a few:

- Reuben: "The Lord has seen my misery. Surely my husband will love me now."
- Simeon: "Because the Lord has heard that I am not loved, he gave me this one too."
- Levi: "Now at last my husband will become attached to me." (She'd given up on love. Now she'd just settle for an attachment. Pathetic. Let's avoid that, sister.)

And those were only the first few sons. In the ancient world, names were often given to the infant on the seventh day. Imagine what our children might have been named if we had chosen something that reflected our postpartum frame of mind.

A name meaning "I guess I'll never sleep again"?

Or "Fetch that man so I can flail him"?

Or "I've never been in so much pain in all

my life"?

Or "Where in the world is my mother when I need her"?

Or "She's not as cute as her big brother was"?

Or just something short and sweet like "Hemorrhoid"?

It would be awful, just as it had to have been for those two sisters. Leah needed counseling. Rachel needed to go with her.

When Rachel saw that she was not bearing Jacob any children, she became jealous of her sister. So she said to Jacob, "Give me children, or I'll die!" Jacob became angry with her and said, "Am I in the place of God, who has kept you from having children?"

GENESIS 30:1–2

Nothing like thinking God doesn't like you as well as He likes someone else to make you a smidge insecure. This was only the beginning of Rachel's madness. Before all was said and done, she'd dragged her maidservant into the middle of it, and all her sons' names were emotionally regurgitated too. That's why I'm co-awarding Leah and Rachel with the Most Insecure Women in the Word Award. They earned it. And they might as well share it. After all, they shared Jacob.

I'm ready to turn the spotlight on some men, lest we think insecurity is only a woman's battle. So let's pick on Moses. After encountering the fiery, self-existent God of heaven and earth — the great I Am — then being used by Him to turn a staff into a snake and a diseased hand into healthy flesh, and then being commissioned by Him to proclaim deliverance, Moses offered this retort: "O Lord, I have never been eloquent, neither in the past nor since you have spoken to your servant." (Translation? Nothing has even changed since You showed up. Same old, same old.) "I am slow of speech and tongue."

So the Lord said, "I will help you speak and will teach you what to say."

But Moses said, "O Lord, please send someone else to do it."

Yep. That's some insecurity. Heaven knows how many people never fulfill their destinies simply because of their own insecurities. God finally gave in to Moses' request to have someone else talk for him, but lo and behold, Aaron was the very person who offered to fire up a golden calf from the wanderers' jewelry ("I threw it into the fire, and out came this calf!") so the Israelites would have something to worship while Moses was delayed. The kind of insecurity that makes us reluctant to believe and obey God not only leads us into sin, it also ends up dragging a few other people into it with us.

But now, for my selection for the Most Insecure Man in the Word Award. No one was the king of insecurity like the first crown of Israel. You can't fully appreciate his earnings without knowing that Scripture introduces Saul as "an impressive young man without equal among the Israelites — a head taller than any of the others" (1 Samuel 9:2). He's exhibit A for dispelling the theory that impressive people must be inwardly secure. When the people of Israel tried to coronate Big Boy, they couldn't find him anywhere. I love this part:

> When they looked for him, he was not to be found. So they inquired further of the LORD, "Has the man come here yet?"
> And the LORD said, "Yes, he has hidden himself among the baggage."
> 1 SAMUEL 10:21–22

Insecurity's expertise is hiding its victim in some baggage. I know that from personal experience. Believe me when I say that God has had more than a few occasions to say of me, "Yes, she has hidden herself among the baggage." Some months ago I flipped on the television and took in an *Oprah* show on record setters. One woman held the world record for the shortest length of time it has ever taken anybody to zip herself up in a suitcase. Nine seconds. What I wanted to know was this: whatever made her say to herself the very first time, *I believe I'll zip myself up in a suitcase?* If I were a betting woman, I'd put my money on family. But back to Saul.

> They ran and brought him out, and as he
> stood among the people he was a head
> taller than any of the others.
> 1 SAMUEL 10:23

Scripture had already acclaimed Saul's stature, so why bother telling us again? I think God wanted to make sure we knew He had ancient Israel's Baby Huey on His hands. If you want to see an insecure person make an idiot of himself, put him in a leadership position, stick a very talented and together up-and-comer right next to him, and then stand back and watch. Talk about threatening! Here's what threw a teetering Saul right over the edge:

Whatever Saul sent him to do, David did it so successfully that Saul gave him a high rank in the army. This pleased all the people, and Saul's officers as well. When the men were returning home after David had killed the Philistine, the women came out from all the towns of Israel to meet King Saul with singing and dancing, with joyful songs and with tambourines and lutes. As they danced, they sang: "Saul has slain his thousands, and David his tens of thousands." Saul was very angry; this refrain galled him. "They have credited David with tens of thousands," he thought, "but me with only thousands. What more can he get but the kingdom?" And from that time on Saul kept a jealous eye on David.

1 SAMUEL 18:5–9

Insecurity lives in constant terror of loss. Insecure people are always afraid that something or somebody is going to be taken from them. Saul feared the loss of power and admiration, and he quickly ascertained that David would be the one to try to take them from him. He didn't quite get that God alone was in charge of his destiny and the only one who could jar that crown off his head. Saul sloshed fuel on the fire of his

86

jealousy until he developed such an obsession with David that he lost his gourd.

One thing that might have driven Saul to such distraction was that his feelings were so conflicted. Did you notice in the segment above that Saul was the very one who promoted David? I'd like to suggest the probability that he liked David and despised him at the same time. That's not an uncommon response toward people we admire but who also make us feel threatened and insecure. We're not jealous of people in whom we see nothing admirable. In fact, it is the fear that they have something we don't that makes us most insecure.

We've all felt insecure over somebody else's success. But that's not why I am giving Saul the Most Insecure Man in the Word Award. He won because he let his emotions get so out of control that his insecurity morphed into complete instability. It happens. Interestingly, Saul had moments of emotional sobriety when he knew how far left he'd gone and even wept with regret over his actions toward David. Nevertheless, he refused to call out to God for deliverance from his own unhealthy emotions, and before the dust of regret settled, Saul wanted the source of his threat dead. That's the kind of thing that can land you in prison.

I just want to whisper something to you in the safety of this environment while no one else is listening: by the time you wish something bad would happen to the person who makes you feel insecure, you need urgent care. Sometimes we need an outside voice to say, "You're spinning out of control here. Let somebody help you reel that thing in."

These examples are just a touch of that familiar insecurity from the fingerprints on the pages of the Old Testament. The New Testament would offer us no fewer picks, but with the point made, I'll just hit a few highlights. How about when the disciples picked the inopportune time of the Last Supper to get into a fight over which one of them was considered to be the greatest? The need to be considered the greatest is always rooted in the gnawing fear that we're not. Unrelenting self-promotion always carries the lingering scent of insecurity.

Or how about the woman at the well in the fourth chapter of John's Gospel? If marrying five losers and living with number six isn't a waving red flag with the letters I-N-S-E-C-U-R-I-T-Y appliquéd on it, one doesn't exist.

And then there's Paul. I love the apostle

Paul. Honestly, he's one of my favorite people in the entire stretch of Scripture, but maybe one reason he appeals to me so much is because he was enormously used of God *in spite of himself.* Don't think for a moment he didn't fight his own flesh just like the rest of us. Take, for instance, the way he felt the need to affirm his credentials to the people he served in Corinth by using this little twist:

> I do not think I am in the least inferior to those "super-apostles." I may not be a trained speaker, but I do have knowledge.
>
> 2 CORINTHIANS 11:5–6

Tell me that's not insecurity. If you're not convinced, take a look at what blurted from his pen only a chapter later:

> I have made a fool of myself, but you drove me to it. I ought to have been commended by you, for I am not in the least inferior to the "super-apostles," even though I am nothing.
>
> 2 CORINTHIANS 12:11

Do you think just maybe he protests too much? In all probability, he fought the awful feeling that he wasn't as good as the others who hadn't done nearly so much wrong. I totally grasp that. At the same time, Paul also battled a big, fat ego. He was a complex mound of clay just like the rest of us, belittling and boasting in himself in a dizzying psychological zigzag. The beauty of Paul wasn't his superhumanity but his unwillingness to let his weaknesses, feelings, and fears override his faith. Like us, the fiercest enemy he had to fight in the fulfillment of his destiny was himself.

To Paul, the essence of the crucified life was daily dying to the part of himself that would deny, destroy, or distract from the great work of God in him. The great work of God *through* him. After untold wars with his own inner man, Paul watched as his wounded ego was wrestled to the ground by the Spirit of Christ, and up stood a person he had no inkling he could be. A stranger, you might say, to the man he'd mirrored for so long. "By the grace of God I am what I am" (1 Corinthians 15:10). And his mission was accomplished.

The fact that the inspiration of the Holy Spirit on the pages of Scripture is not dampened by the insecurities of those God chose to pen it is perhaps the greatest testimony to its incomparable potency. After the likes of Adam, Eve, Abraham, Sarah,

Hagar, Leah, Rachel, Saul, the woman at the well, the super-apostles, and Paul, surely we can breathe a sigh of relief that we are not alone in our struggles. Human flesh and blood have no weakness so strong that God's strength is made weak.

He's got what we need. It's up to us whether or not we're going to let the worst of us get the best of us.

> May the LORD answer you when you are in trouble; may the God of Jacob make you secure!
>
> PSALM 20:1, NET

CHAPTER 5
ROOTING IT OUT

That was then. This is now. Where on earth is all our insecurity coming from? And what makes some people struggle with it so much more than others? We're going to sit down in the dirt for a little while and dig down deep until we discover some roots. If you've dealt with insecurity much of your life like I have, you've surely wondered where you picked it up or if you managed to come out of the womb with it like a giant invisible birthmark.

You've probably also marveled at a few people along the way who don't seem to give insecurity the slightest shrug. Of course, you and I don't tend to befriend them. After all, they'd make us feel even more insecure, but we can admit that we're baffled by them. What makes some people decidedly less susceptible than others? And how could so many of us with a hundred things going for us be so pitifully rattled by this one persistent thing?

Let's go ahead and unload ourselves of considerable culpability: the only thing it takes to develop insecurity is to be born human and raised on planet Earth. We live in the information age. We wake up to a dozen news-breaking reasons to feel the ground quaking beneath our feet. Practically every morning while I'm leaned over the sink toward the bathroom mirror, putting on my mascara, Keith sits on the edge of the tub and reads me excerpts out of the *Houston Chronicle.* It's far more interesting than reading it for myself because Keith provides his own very colorful editorials, for which he often gets chided to watch his mouth. Still, I keep listening. At times he'll read silently and then blurt out some kind of slang that tells me he's totally disgusted. It piques my curiosity every time.

"What, Baby?"

"I'm not telling you."

I'm not a very naive person about most things. I purposely stay plugged into world events, so I know that if he's refusing to read me something it must be a prime exhibit of humanity's total depravity. A few days ago, he pitched the whole paper on the floor and said, "I'm not reading it anymore. I'm sick of it. Nothing but bad news." He didn't mean it, though. We're both news freaks. He was on the edge of the tub with the very next edition. But he was dead right about one thing: there's no apparent end to bad news. Much of the world is racked with enormous debt and economic instability, threats of terrorism, wars, fallen heroes, rabid perversity, and violence for the pure pleasure of it.

About the time we stop hearing about one natural disaster, another erupts with a death toll so high we go numb. Add to that a demoralizing list of acquaintances or loved ones diagnosed with life-threatening diseases, and you've got yourself enough fear to dig a hole of insecurity six feet deep. Hop on the Web with your own symptoms, and you'll find enough criteria to diagnose yourself with three months to live, and about that time, your six-foot ditch starts looking like it might come in frighteningly handy.

If we didn't have a single earth-shattering reason to feel insecure, simply growing up would do the trick. As parents, we do our best to build our children up in those preschool years, and then we send them off to elementary school only to have them come home with something like, "The kids at school say I look like a turtle." A *what?*

"I'm never going back!" Tears gush and we start trying to figure out what kinds of professions require only a kindergarten education.

Life is rough. It's also beautiful, but if we can't get some respite from its cruelty, we will never have the healthy vision to savor its tender beauty.

Growing up, we are all surrounded by people with such generous portions of insecurity, they'll gladly share them. In fact, one terrific way to develop a chronic case is to have somebody project their own onto you. I'm not casting stones. I've done it.

My oldest daughter turned sixteen before most of her friends, and since they couldn't wait to be freed from the tyranny of the parental car pool, the attainment of her license was a much-celebrated affair.

To my daughter's unbridled delight, Keith's parents gave her the coolest gift ever for her birthday: a maroon convertible Mustang with a huge bow on it.

Perhaps you can imagine how thrilled I was over the prospect of our brand-spanking-new driver having a cloth-top sports car. I think I recall muttering the words *death trap* under my coffee breath even before the cake and ice cream were served. After a few days of driving to school,

Amanda quipped to me almost as a side note that she needed to work on her parking. She kept getting it in the spot crooked, and a couple of her friends made fun of her. Leave it to me, the worst driver in the free world, to put on my sunglasses and make a trip to the high school parking lot for the next couple of days in order to repark her car so they'd stop teasing her. What an idiot. I projected my own insecurities right on top of hers like a hard top on a convertible. I didn't tell her for years, and she nearly flipped when she found out. Do you want to hear something pathetic? If I had it to do all over again, I would probably do the same thing. Why? Because growing up can be brutal. And if not for you, for your mother.

But for some, it's more brutal than others. Take, for instance, any two people who happened to have lived similar lives and suffered the same kinds of traumas. While they can probably find loads of ways they can relate to one another, if they are given enough time and enough depth, they'll probably also discover how different they really are. We are each completely and complexly original, whether or not it happens to be convenient. It's the way our Maker made us. Our DNA weaves in and out of every experience and emotion like a needle and a long blue thread. The writer of Proverbs puts it this way: "Each heart knows its own bitterness" (14:10). The more intense the pain, the more it feels like nobody fully understands. Try as I might, I can't fully comprehend how a particular event affected your life, even if we both shared the same experience. Your personality and history shapes your response, just as my own unique background affects mine. We'd go only so far in one another's shoes before the laces came loose.

A host of troubles are common to humankind, but when it comes right down to it — and all things being equal — almost nothing is equal. For me, this is one profound reason that God, omniscient and omnipresent, has been the vital element in my healing. During particularly lonely or frustrating times, perhaps you, like me, have felt that nobody else gets it. But He gets it better than we do. So many times He has shown me where I was coming from instead of the other way around.

That said, there really are a number of common contributors to chronic insecurity. Even bad fruit has a vine, and where there's a vine, there's a root. As we dig up a few of these roots, stay mindful to the fact that the impact of each can differ dramatically from

97

person to person. I won't pretend to have the expertise to present a complete and comprehensive list, but I do believe the origins we'll discuss could offer us a couple of helpful "aha!" moments. Few of these roots will surprise you, but I believe that the reminder alone will stir up the sensation of insecurity so we can make the personal connection. Don't fight it. Recognition is the first step toward letting God get to an issue and healing it. Get some things up there on the surface, and let God validate your challenges. Somewhere along the way, we've been made to believe that these things aren't that big of a deal, but actually they are.

Instability in the home

This is a no-brainer. Perhaps your parents fought like wildcats, and maybe one continually threatened to leave. Or maybe they got along reasonably well, but your home was rocked by layoffs and financial woes. The disintegration of a family can jerk the rug of security out from under a couple of generations. If you're a mom who has suffered through a divorce, please don't crawl under a rock of condemnation. Just realize the potential fallout and seek to counteract it with the power of a redeeming God and a community of support.

An alcoholic parent or a mentally ill parent also stirs up an environment of chaos and uncertainty. Like many of your families, my family of origin has been touched by mental illness. Thankfully, it wasn't a constant presence in ours, but it erupted often enough that flashbacks of certain moments of madness can still send shivers down my spine. I feel the terror of them again just like I felt at fourteen.

A parent's physical illness can also create significant fear and insecurity for a child — even if that parent would give anything on earth to be the best possible caretaker. If you happen to be that infirm parent, I pray you will not give way to despair over these words. I also pray that God will show you wonders unceasing. We who are in Christ are never hopeless, never without recourse or divine help, even when our bodies are weak. If we find ourselves facing the frightening prospect of serious illness, we must exercise the courage to cry out for help, seek the support that we and our children need, and learn to create open and honest dialogue. Inviting even the worst and most unfair circumstances out into the spotlight sets the stage for a miracle. In the meantime, never forget that God still reserves the right to favor the suffering.

Many invitations to insecurity within a home are unintentional and largely unavoidable, no matter how a loving parent might be trying. But make no mistake. Some parents are *not* loving. Their children, so worthy of affection, may live their entire lives without ever discovering exactly why their parents couldn't show it. In cases like this, let's first offer parents the benefit of the doubt. It *is* possible to genuinely love without ever becoming genuinely loving. An unfortunate disconnect exists somewhere. But other times a parent is not only unloving, he or she — to quote my grandmother — is meaner than a snake.

At the root of chronic insecurity is often the primal fear that no one will take care of us. Every single thing that underscores that fear is like fertilizer in the soil. And there's nothing that makes a home less stable than abuse. Any kind of abuse — emotional, mental, physical, verbal, or sexual — not only causes immediate effects, it also goes straight to the core of our belief system and parrots our worst nightmares: *I'm on my own. No one will take care of me.* And not only does it teach us that no one is there to take care of us, it also affirms that those who are *supposed to* care will instead harm us.

Even if you have loving people in your life, if they cannot or will not stop your abuse (even if they are oblivious), your fear is still confirmed. We can't underestimate the repercussions of that kind of perception, and the earlier it is affirmed, the louder it speaks.

The residual ongoing sense of being unprotected can obliterate personal boundaries until our emotions are black and blue. We end up putting ourselves into one messed-up relationship after another trying to find someone who will take care of us. *Someone who will not disappoint us.* And it never works. For one thing, that kind of motivation draws us to the wrong kind of people. For another, it's too much pressure to put on any human relationship. I speak to you as one who knows. Not surprisingly, the gender of an abuser also has a strong connection to the direction the insecurity grows. The human mind and emotions are far too complex for many hard, fast rules, but if a female was a sizable source of our insecurity early on, we will tend to struggle more with security around or with women. If it was a male, as in my case, we will tend to struggle more with security around or with men. The gender of the person who originally made us feel defenseless will often continue to make us feel either defenseless or *inordinately* defensive until we are restored.

Because I suffered victimization, I also realize how painful reminders like this book can be. No one wants to reflect on times we were abused or misused, but as we take this journey together, look at it this way: those of us who share this background can rest assured that we didn't conjure up our insecurities out of thin air.

Recently I read a few lines to a song that touch the frayed nerve of anyone whose perpetrator of abuse or misuse was supposed to be a protector. These lyrics were written by a woman with a life and belief system very different from my own, but somewhere along the way our conclusions were the same.

I don't say much, I just talk a lot,
I don't know what love is,
But I will tell you what it is not.[4]

Actually, by the time you realize that what you're experiencing is *not* love, some significant healing is already beginning to take place. It hasn't reached into the deepest canyons of the soul, however, until you come to a place where you can echo across that great expanse, "Now, *that's* love." The ability to know the difference is, in itself, a glimmer of health in a war-torn soul.

Before we start digging up the next root of insecurity, I want you to know something. I believe with all my heart that every adult still has a need to be loved like a child. I didn't say every adult has a need to be *treated* like a child. We'll leave that to the narcissists. I said we have a need to be *loved* like a child. That's why losing both parents is often a profound life transition — no matter how old you are when it happens. Just wait and see. I get that orphaned feeling every time I kneel at my parents' graves. But here's the good news: you can indeed look for that kind of love from God, and He will always love you and take care of you like the perfect father does his child.

> Even when you are old, I will be the same. Even when your hair has turned gray, I will take care of you. I made you and will take care of you. I will carry you and save you.
>
> ISAIAH 46:4, NCV

If you've lived your life looking for someone

to take care of you but always end up taking care of everyone else, your search is over. God has what you need, and you'll never wear Him out.

A Significant Loss

Losses that contribute to chronic insecurity come in a variety of forms. It could be the loss of anything that you genuinely prize or derive stability and self-worth from. It might be the loss of a home, a peer group, a relationship, a best friend, a long-term babysitter, or the permanent loss of a loved one due to death. In this section, we will primarily focus our attention on losses that occurred earlier in life because of their impact on developing belief systems, though loss at any age can be traumatic and can stir up terrible insecurity even in a person who has hardly struggled with it before.

A few days ago my husband, his parents, our oldest daughter, and I attended the Catholic graveside service of Keith's elderly aunt. While he and his mom circulated through the crowd of relatives, my beloved father-in-law stood to the side with Amanda and me and talked. Almost out of the blue he said, "Duke is buried right under here." He pointed with his cane to the artificial green turf the funeral home had spread around the burial site. "Probably close to where we are standing." I nearly jumped like I'd been hit by lightning. I'm sure, as sensitive as Amanda is, she probably did too.

Duke was my in-laws' adored firstborn. When he was a lively and darling three-year-old cotton-top, he and my husband, Keith, who was two years old at the time, slipped unnoticed into the garage. In minutes they turned over a gas can, spilling gasoline under the water heater and creating an inferno. Duke lived only a few excruciating days. Keith survived but with emotional scars that have taken as much painful grafting as if his body had been cloaked with third-degree burns. After research for this book revealed the powerful connection between loss and insecurity, I realize that he is a marvel, scars and all. I have mourned the loss of Keith's older brother many times even though I came on the Moore scene eighteen years later. I have never been more tender to it, however, than I have been recently. My grandson, Jackson, is now exactly the same age as Duke was when he died, and the thought of losing him is utterly unbearable. I can't even pause here to think about it.

"Pawpaw, is Nalda buried here, too?"

Amanda asked. He obviously wanted to talk, so the question was appropriate coming from his oldest grandchild. "No, honey. She's buried over there." Are you ready for this? Nalda was Keith's younger sister. She died of an aneurysm at twenty-three. Too much. *Way too much.* And since Duke's grave was mercifully covered that day, the three of us made our trek to the markers in the adjacent area to pay our respects to their beloved daughter. Soon Keith saw us across the way and joined us.

Moments later, while we were still standing at Nalda's grave, I glanced over at the awning and tried unsuccessfully to spot my mother-in-law amid the few remaining relatives. Then I saw her. She'd gotten into the car. We could stand at her children's graves all we wanted, but she'd wait in the car. And I didn't blame her. Those two deaths profoundly affected every member of that large family — but did they all respond in the same way? Not on your life. "Each heart knows its own bitterness" (Proverbs 14:10).

A primary loss in childhood is a surefire setup for insecurity. If you lost a parent to cancer when you were a child, girlfriend, your search for the root of your chronic insecurity is over. You earned it. No, you can't have your loved one back in this lifetime, but you can indeed have your security back. That loss does not have to be permanent.

Insecurity can result from a broken attachment of any kind, even one that seems relatively minor to others. If it translated as something huge to your heart, it is huge to God on your behalf. Before we move on, remember to always think broadly when you're trying to analyze losses and their links to your insecurity. Even the loss of face or respect through some kind of public shame can have an immense impact. Wondering if everybody hates you takes no small toll on your soul.

The loss of innocence is also a powder keg of insecurity. Although my husband was not touched inappropriately like I was, a few of his father's employees had the audacity to show him pornography in his boyhood. Both of those examples, as different as they may seem, constitute a loss of innocence. Simply put, if you didn't get to be a child when you were young, you suffered a loss of innocence. As the apostle Paul inferred, children are supposed to talk like children, think like children, and reason like children (1 Corinthians 13:11). When they are forced to grow up too quickly, they lose something that no one can give back.

Rejection

After years of working with women and hearing their stories, I've observed that few forces can catapult a female into a season of insecurity with the swiftness of rejection. We've danced a few steps on the topic already and will do so again before we close the book, but to overlook it as a thick, gnarled root of insecurity would be a mistake. Nothing shouts a more convincing lie about our personal value than rejection, and it can reverberate with deafening pitch from any direction.

Anywhere there is relationship, there is potential for rejection. Mind you, we were created by God precisely for relationship, so disconnection is not the answer. Restoration is. First, however, we need to take a good look at our insecurities and see if they are tied to our perception of a rejection that sent us reeling.

I used the word *perception* because it is entirely possible to perceive that we've been rejected when we haven't. If our hearts are tender or unhealthy enough, we can turn a reasonable boundary into a full-fledged rejection. In other words, we might have wanted *all* the attention of someone who was only willing to give us a significant portion. We may, for instance, want to be treated as the favorite child of a parent of two or a stepparent of four. Or we may want to be the only friend of *our* only friend. Or we may want to be the absolute apex of our man's attention, and when we don't get what we crave in the relationship we've exalted, we feel rejected. We can confuse 80 percent reciprocation with 100 percent rejection.

We could be laid off from work, but instead of seeing it as a bad break, we feel totally rejected. Someone we want to be attentive to us might suddenly have a preoccupation like a family crisis or a health problem. The shift may feel like rejection when it's not.

But let there be no confusion. Real rejection does indeed occur, and when it does, it's a mind bender. Unfortunately, it is possible to suffer the crushing rejection of a parent, a friend, an associate, a stepchild or child, a boyfriend, or a spouse even if it's never admitted or addressed. No matter the source, the shout translates into the language of the soul as one jolting message: *I do not want you!* Here's the even trickier part: nothing elicits quicker concurrence on our part than feeling rejected. Our equally deceptive agreement with the original lie doubles the strength of the bond, and through that betraying handshake, we find ourselves nodding. *You are so right . . .*

I'm not worth wanting.
I'm not worth loving.
I'm not even worth liking.
I'm not worth pursuing.
I'm not worth fighting for.
I'm not worth keeping.
I'm not worth hiring.
I'm not even worth noticing.

Henceforth and until healing comes, we plot our course out of a smoldering sense of worthlessness. It's that powerful. Rejection doesn't have to happen in childhood for it to pitch someone into profound insecurity. Even grown women with comparatively successful track records personally and professionally can sustain a rejection that nearly sends them over the edge. In fact, if we're not careful, we could dangle right there on that fragile cliff for the rest of our lives and appear to everyone who comes in close contact with us as a person on the brink of breaking. Be careful not to give too much credence to the old adage that time heals. Mark my word. It's God that heals. Time only tells. The passage of days, weeks, and years can as easily amplify an old voice as weaken it. Given enough time, rejection will set up history to repeat itself over and over until the rejected person forms relationships based on the likelihood that she'll be rejected.

I know no other way to say it. Taken badly enough, rejection can muster up some temporary insanity. Reflect on your own history, and I imagine you'd come up with the same summation that I would: the craziest, most uncharacteristic things I've ever done have occurred in the wake of major rejection. It's insecurity with a serious fever. Yesterday my daughter Melissa was talking about a friend who was devastated over being dropped by a guy who had hardly raised her brow prior to his abrupt exit. The fact is, she was basically using the dude to have a dating life until somebody she liked better came along. Melissa said, "You know, Mom. It's that rejection thing. There's nothing like it to make you obsessed with someone you didn't even want." How true is that?

I'll tell you something else I've noticed about women and rejection. We tend to wear it like a sign. You can't always tell right away when someone has come from an unstable home or endured a significant loss, but in thirty minutes flat a discerning eye might make out a woman who has been rejected.

No matter how we try to disguise it, there it hangs in neon red. We try to act self-assured, but the light still flashes: "Vacant." "Lonely." "Desperately available."

Rejection has a nasty way of making the healthy people we're hoping to attract high-tail it like a scared rabbit the opposite direction. Last night our family and some friends went to an Italian restaurant in a swanky part of Houston to celebrate a special occasion. My grandson, Jackson, was sitting right beside me and downing a sizable Sprite through a straw, so about halfway through the meal I did what any good grandmother would do. I asked him if he thought we'd better head to the potty. Of course, any chance of getting up from the table was fine by him, so his feet hit the floor before I could finish the question. As we were making our way to the restroom, we passed the bar, where two women wearing very short skirts and extremely low tops were perched on stools. I don't mean the sexy kind; I mean the pathetic kind. This wasn't just cleavage. It was like bulls busting from the pen. I'm talking about the kind of exposure that leaves no hint of mystery. The why-bother-getting-to-know-me kind. The kind that screams, "I'm desperate! I'll do anything! I'll take anyone!"

The thing about it is that I love all kinds of women — I guess because I've been so many of them. The jagged death trap of thinking that we're only as valuable as we are sensual and that if no one loves us, at least they could want us is all too familiar to me. My heart wrenched over those two women, and they might have even caught me staring for a few seconds, but not for the reasons they probably supposed. I could've been them back in the day. I've been that desperate. I thought how I'd give just about anything to know their stories and tell them mine. They weren't looking for me to shimmy up on the next stool, however. They were trying to get the attention of the men at the other end of the bar who were trying equally hard to get the attention of that cute twenty-year-old hostess at check-in. There's no telling what those women had been through, but you could probably take this one to the bank: somewhere along the way, they had been dumped on their uncovered behinds. They were both wearing rejection and begging for more. It broke my heart.

Sleazy is certainly not the only way rejection dresses. It has a much larger wardrobe than that. You'll just as often see it dressed down and defeated or cold, acrid, and cynical. One thing is for certain: when we bear it, we wear it.

And let's not get the idea that women are the only gender reeling from rejection. Nobody takes this one well. We're not going to jerk up a single root of insecurity that would not also grow into a choking vine in a man. The point is, generally speaking, the way men and women behave in the aftermath can differ substantially. Take romantic rejection, for instance. Where a man might turn to a string of superficial relationships in which he never gives his heart away, a woman might give her heart away before she even has a relationship. Of course, the reverse can also happen. We're only talking in gender tendencies here.

We'll run into the topic of rejection a few more times before the end of our journey and learn how to break out of insecure mind-sets like the reject mentality. For now, rest assured that it's a major root of insecurity. If you've suffered a serious case of rejection, you need to make sure that you're letting God tend to it. Each root we've mentioned so far is painful, but this one is poisonous. Putting up a front doesn't work. That neon light has a way of burning through every cover we throw on it. God knows exactly what happened and what a toll it took. He knows the number it played on your mind. Let Him bring you peace. Let Him tell you you're worth *wanting, loving, even liking, pursuing, fighting for,* and, yes, beloved, *keeping.* Whatever you do, don't reject the only One wholly incapable of rejecting you.

> I have chosen you and have not rejected you. So do not fear, for I am with you; do not be dismayed, for I am your God.
>
> ISAIAH 41:9–10

Dramatic Change

Some people really do have reasonably stable homes and haven't suffered a major loss. I don't happen to know many of them, but surely they exist out there somewhere. Goodness knows, I probably don't interact with many personally because I tend to attract recovering wrecks like myself. Of course, I prefer the term *redeemed* over *recovering wrecks,* but I'd answer to either one as long as you'll let me tell you about my Redeemer and Recoverer. You might be one of those rarities who has enjoyed a fair amount of stability and a minimal amount of loss, but none of us can avoid change. In fact, you can't get past the delivery room without experiencing sudden and dramatic

115

change. We take our first breath of terrestrial air in total shock. Christ alone is "the same yesterday and today and forever" (Hebrews 13:8). We, on the other hand, are in constant, hair-raising, stomach-turning flux. As the old saying goes, nothing stays the same but change.

Most women find a tremendous amount of security in sameness. Sometimes we'll stay in a destructive situation because we reason that what we know is better than what we don't know. We'll stay in a job we hate because we'd have to change insurance companies. We'll keep going to a church God has long since prompted us to leave, because it's what we know. We'll stay best friends with somebody we haven't liked in ten years because it's too much trouble to make a new one. And anyway, the new friend might want us to change. And we hate change. If we're big enough control freaks, we might manage to keep a handful of things the same, but to be sure, we don't just hold on to them; we strangle them half to death.

But then, some of us experience bigger changes than these. Dramatic changes. Changes that change everything. A skiing accident, a bankruptcy, or a stock market crisis. Hearing from your nine-year-old that your ex-husband is getting remarried. Finding out from the obstetrician that three babies are showing up on that sonogram. You see, dramatic change isn't always bad, but it's always big. Our security is easily threatened by anything unknown yet suddenly unavoidable.

Many of us have learned the hard way that one phone call from a relative or an employer can be the end of life as we know it. Even when we know that God is in the picture and every end leads to a new beginning, right at that moment of discovery, we tend to feel that everything wonderful is over. Does it suddenly sound like we're talking about loss again instead of change? As we keep digging around for roots of insecurity, we're going to find that most of them are intertwined underground. Case in point: our hearts often translate sudden and dramatic change as either instability or a form of loss. Sometimes it hits us as both.

When I was fifteen years old, my dad moved our family from a small Arkansas town where we'd lived for thirteen years to Houston, Texas, the biggest city in the South. I went from a high school of 900 to one splitting at the seams with 4,700 kids. That dramatic life change not only brought a heightened sense of instability to an already unstable home, it also brought the loss of lifelong peers — many of whom I needed to lose, incidentally. Though change ended up working in my favor, the process of working through that loss was still difficult.

I chose to make dramatic change a category of its own because even though it's such a fact of life in the human experience, we tend to dismiss its potential impact on our souls. But a history of unwelcomed changes can be a breeding ground for insecurity, because it invites you to become addicted to dread. You learn to live life with the constant expectation that something bad is about to happen. And because life is life, eventually something bad *will* happen, deepening your commitment to forecasting doom. You develop into your own false prophet, and if you don't stop yourself, you won't rest until you're proved true. It's a miserable trap of self-inflicted insecurity. You can cheat yourself of ever enjoying the terrific season you're experiencing because you're waiting any moment for it to change — and always for the worse. When we become psychologically dependent upon crisis, it actually becomes our life motivator, and if we don't have a present crisis, we'll learn to create one.

The truth is, God uses change to change *us*. He doesn't use it to destroy us or to distract us but to coax us to the next level of character, experience, compassion, and destiny. I hate to display such a firm grasp of the obvious, but how will we ever change if everything around us stays the same? Or what will ever cause us to move on to the next place He has for us if something doesn't happen to change the way we feel about where we are? God is thoroughly committed to finishing the masterpiece He started in us (Philippians 1:6), and that process means one major thing: change.

> Don't be misled, my dear brothers and sisters. Whatever is good and perfect comes down to us from God our Father, who created all the lights in the heavens. He never changes or casts a shifting shadow. He chose to give birth to us by giving us his true word. And we, out of all creation, became his prized possession.
>
> JAMES 1:16–18, NLT

Personal Limitations
A learning disability can sow a harvest of insecurity. So can a physical handicap, abnormality, or anything that makes us feel

particularly different or inferior. Sometimes limitations are matters of perception. Something one person finds almost debilitating might seem trivial to an observer. Acne is a prime example. A girl struggling with a bad complexion at a hard age might feel humiliated and inhibited by it, while her parents can't figure out why she's making such a big deal out of it. After all, they reason, it will pass soon enough. On the other hand, maybe the parents do everything they can to help the situation, but the invitation to inferiority persists. What happens then?

Attitude is everything when it comes to limitations, and the way you view yourself will acutely shape how others view you. Nothing is more impressive than a person who is secure in the unique way God made her. A very good friend of mine taught me to look at limitations as providential redirections. Years ago I received a phone call that ended up totally changing the course of my life. Lee Sizemore worked for the largest Christian curriculum publisher in the world. He explained that he had a vision for video-driven Bible courses and he wondered if I would consider being one of the teachers. Though I would be teaching in front of a small studio audience, our target would be women watching the video in their living rooms, churches, and classrooms.

The concept had almost zero appeal to me; I couldn't imagine teaching a group of women I couldn't see. The interaction is what I enjoy most in any class setting. I was also very satisfied doing what I was doing. Lee said he and a small team would like to come to Houston to meet with me, and if the idea still didn't strike a chord, they would know God was leading them elsewhere. You cannot imagine my surprise when a man with slightly disfigured hands and feet came rolling up to me in a wheelchair. He had not been on his feet in years and would not be on his feet again until he stood before his very wise Maker in heaven. What I didn't realize then was that the very format I initially resisted would eventually become the engine that drove everything else God would call me to do. Those video series took us all over the world, and don't think for a second that Lee let us go on location without him. We wheeled him up the Mount of Olives and down the streets of old Jerusalem and across a boat ramp to Greece, Turkey, and the islands of the Mediterranean.

Before all was said and done, that "handicapped" man produced over one hundred video series with numerous authors and was used of God to change the entire face of Bible study in America. And all from a wheelchair. I am absolutely convinced that Lee's mind and vision went as far and wide as they did because his body was trapped in that chair. His disability was actually his freedom. His limitations in one area redirected his full release to another like a pressure cooker that had finally found a spout. His wheelchair took him somewhere the strongest legs never could have carried him.

Lee is one of countless examples we have of people who display security in spite of limitations The great writer Anne Rice had a learning disability that made reading extremely difficult even through young adulthood. Ironically, from that very travail with words, numerous best-selling novels were born.

I'm not trying to lead a pep rally here. I'm simply telling you what I believe is gospel truth: God can bring freedom and vision to your life because of those limitations that you would never have discovered without them. You can let your limitations make you either insecure or unstoppable.

Personal Disposition

It is possible that you know people who have experienced the kinds of situations I've just described — instability, loss, unwanted change, or limitations — but are as genuinely secure as anyone you've ever met. On the other hand, you might know someone who has experienced the best life has to offer, yet is so insecure you can hardly stand to be around her. What is the difference? Sometimes it boils down to our most basic personal components: disposition and temperament. Although insecurity and sensitivity are not synonymous, people who are especially tenderhearted are significantly more predisposed to insecurity.[5] In other words, the more tenderhearted we are, the more vulnerable to insecurity we'll likely be. Some people take things harder and deeper to heart than others. It's not a matter of weakness. It's a matter of personal sensitivity.

I don't know how it hits you, but identifying disposition as a possible contributor brought me significant relief and understanding. Even though my childhood abuse and unstable home offered ample ammunition for insecurity, I have come to the conclusion that, with my hypersensitive disposition, I probably would have battled it to some extent anyway. I feel everything. My joys are huge, and so are my sorrows. If I'm mad, I'm really mad, and if I'm despondent, I wonder how on earth I'll go on. Then I get up, pour some coffee, and move on to the next emotion and forget how depressed I was an hour ago. Ever done that? Most of the time my emotional nerve endings are exposed like live wires. I can't even see a smashed toad on the pavement without feeling sorry for it. I boycott movies where animals die and could still use a counseling session over *My Dog Skip.*

Perhaps you'll be relieved to know that my sensitivity does reach further than animals. When I see people saying an emotional good-bye to one another at the airport, it is everything I can do not to embrace them in a group hug. For the next half hour, I'll think about them so much that I'll write their whole story in my head. I feel such pity for elderly people who live alone that I have to force myself not to go straight to the pound and fetch them a stray dog. Imagine their faces when they opened the front door. Yep. That's what has kept me from doing it. I'm afraid I'll get bitten. (And I don't mean by the dog.) God gave me this tender heart, and though I want to give up my chronic insecurity, I really do want to hang on to my heart. I like to feel. When I don't feel something, it's like being dead.

You may not be nearly as sensitive as I

am, but perhaps you've suffered losses or struggled through limitations that help explain where on earth your insecurity originated. Remember, you're not looking for all of the above to qualify. Then again, if every single root we've discussed so far is under your family tree, girlfriend, you are already a living, breathing miracle.

I've saved two roots of insecurity for the next chapter because, as you'll see, they come from a different part of the soil than those we've discussed here. With the exception of personal disposition, those in this chapter — instability in the home, significant loss, rejection, dramatic change, and personal limitations — are, in many ways, scars on the soul left by hardship. Insecurity that results from the way we've coped rather than healed.

Life really is hard. No one can escape it. No one is unscathed by it. But we are not just flailing aimlessly in a universal black hole. There is purpose. There is order — because there is God. Several months ago my younger daughter, Melissa, insisted upon going with me to a follow-up appointment for a suspicious mammogram. No, I've never been diagnosed with breast cancer, but because my mother died with it, I have to be more cautious. We were sitting in the waiting room, each of us crossing one leg then the other, sipping our Starbucks and making an attempt at small talk. We're both big readers, but instead of a *People* magazine to pass the time, the only reading material the office offered was a rack of brochures about every imaginable cancer.

Melissa took one after another and glanced over them, shaking her head. She looked up at me with that classic expression of hers and said, "Life is brutal, man." I nodded. We both sat silently for just a moment. Then she said one of the most profound things I've ever heard.

"He knows it's scary to be us."

Yes, beloved, He does. He does not take lightly that some of us were raised in a veritable madhouse. He does not take lightly that some of us have been mentally berated or physically beaten or sexually abused or simply abandoned. He does not take lightly that some of us are still trying to recover from that midnight phone call. He does not take lightly that some of us were born with legs that don't work. Or eyes that can't see. Or ears that can't hear. He does not take lightly that some of us have endured the cancer treatment of our very own children. He does not take lightly that some of us, Lord help us, have buried our own children.

He knows it's scary to be us.

Son of David, have mercy on us! It's almost too much to bear here at times, Lord. No wonder we're insecure!

The thunder crashes in the heavens, and the earth grows dark in the middle of the afternoon, and a man, beaten to a bloody pulp, cries from a cross between two thieves, "It is finished!" Because He did, one day God will wipe away every tear from the eyes of those who trusted Him, and there will be no more death or mourning or crying or pain, for the old order of things will pass away and all our hardship will be *finished.*

CHAPTER 6
A COCKTAIL OF
EGO AND CULTURE

Let's dig in a couple of other places for roots of chronic insecurity before we move on. The roots we talked about in the previous chapter — instability in the home, significant loss, rejection, dramatic change, personal limitations, and personal dispositions — are timeless. Any one of those factors could have challenged the inhabitants of planet Earth five thousand years ago just as readily as they challenge us today. They are part of life in any era, at any time, but in this chapter we are about to draw a deep line in the sand. After all the talk from our grand-parents about how much worse life was for them and what lightweights we are in comparison, we've finally found a genuine area in which we trump them.

Our Culture
As God would have it, I'm writing this chapter from a tiny, century-old German

farmhouse that sits on some acreage Keith and I own out in the middle of nowhere. Keith had talked incessantly about owning some ranch land ever since we were married three decades ago. In fact, he insisted that it was the dream of almost every little boy reared in the Lone Star State and that the dream unrealized would put a Texan in the grave dissatisfied even if they buried him with his boots on. We didn't have two dimes to rub together when we were first married, and practically before I learned to sign my new name, our first child was on her way.

Keith's dream was a long while coming, but two years ago, after a few good fights and a few bent knees, we signed the papers on some desperately neglected land begging for love. A friend of ours had snatched it up in foreclosure so he could flip it. Trust me when I tell you the land wasn't the only thing that flipped. Learning to love this rough country was no small education. For a woman raised amid the hills, lakes, and piney woods of Arkansas, it was a reach. Very little about our land of mesquite, cactus, rocks, and rattlers is beautiful to the untrained eye, but it is ours, and we honestly adore it. What it lacks in aesthetics it makes up for in sunrises and sunsets so beautiful they could make you bawl. That's what I've come to love about the flatlands.

While we were on our first drive through the acreage, our friend said, "There's an old dilapidated farmhouse there that you could tear down and then build something in its place. It's in a good location for a view of the old red barn and the western horizon." A few minutes later, Keith and I walked gingerly on creaky wooden floors that contained holes so big you could crawl through them and under the house if you had a mind to meet a rattler. The house was so far past condemned that you couldn't have found a place to nail a warning sign that wouldn't collapse. And Keith and I loved it. Everybody thought we had lost our minds, but to two history buffs, there was something so charming about the house that we couldn't bear to tear it down. Real, live people with real, live stories had lived within those walls one hundred solid years ago. They deserved respect.

Keith began a mammoth six-month project with one goal: to restore that tiny German farmhouse as close to original as he could — without bankrupting us. Today, almost everything in this house is one hundred years old: every door inside and out, every single window, as much of the floor as we could salvage, many of the pictures, and much of the furniture, which belonged to somebody a century ago. Only the heavy white and black Magic Chef stove is new by the house's standards. We had to settle for a 1924 model, and yes, every burner still works. It's true. They just don't make them like they used to.

Every time I'm here, I wonder what life was like for the family who most certainly bulged from these tight walls years ago when another man fulfilled his dream. His body has long since turned to ashes, yet we walk through the very same doorposts he did. What was his wife like? What kinds of things occupied her thoughts? How alike are we, if at all? When did she flip through her first Sears and Roebuck catalog? If they went to church on Sundays, what did she and her friends chat about? What were her insecurities? Or did she even have enough time on her hands to give insecurities a second thought? I can hardly imagine her world, but in her wildest dreams, could she have ever pictured mine?

Life has changed dramatically for American women since the first nails were hammered into the wood of this old house. So dramatically, in fact, that we were told the property foreclosed on people who lost their priorities — and maybe even their minds —

to cocaine. Ironic, isn't it? I thought that was an urban addiction. No century on record has ever clocked the dramatic changes of the twentieth. We wheeled into it on a horse and buggy and out of it on a rocket. We split the century wide open with our feet on the moon. Years into the twenty-first century, I peer through these wavy windows at a postmodern world and bear its growing pains as much as anyone in it.

Life has changed — and in countless ways, it has changed for the better. But here's that line in the sand I promised you: our fore-mothers did not have to put up with the media madness that we women do today. They did not check out their groceries next to a magazine rack of gorgeous, half-dressed, airbrushed women. They did not rinse the leftover Hamburger Helper off the supper dishes while their husbands watched Victoria's Secret models traipsing around in high definition. They did not stumble on pornography or chat rooms tucked in the closets of their computers — nor did they seek it out for themselves. They did not get explicit mail from complete strangers in their in-boxes. They could never have imag-ined the quick trip a woman could take from double-X chromosomes to triple-X movies. They were not immersed in a society where a woman is only as valuable as she is sensual. Simply put, they were not surrounded by our harrowing culture.

I'm not foolish enough to suggest a list of ways we have it harder than the women who graced this earth before us. We have rights, conveniences, occupations, and health care they never dreamed of having. My goal is to pinpoint one way their lives were dramatically easier than ours. But it's a whopper: *media exploitation.* We're so accustomed to it now that we're growing oblivious to the toll it's taking on us. It's our new normal. Let's wake up from our shell shock long enough to reflect on the image onslaught that has overtaken us like a tidal wave in the last seventy-five years.

Consider this for a moment: though television only became commercially available in the 1930s, even well into the next decade, very few American households could boast of having one. It was not until the mid-1950s that the phenomenon exploded and spawned into every imaginable offshoot. Anything with a screen can call television "Daddy."

My generation is the first in all of history to grow up in a media-driven society. What we're dealing with is unprecedented; we cannot look to the generations before us to

133

see how to handle it. We are drowning in uncharted waters, and it's time we learned to swim. Most of our great-great-grandmothers had access to compare themselves to a few hundred women in a lifetime. We can now throw ourselves up against tens of thousands if we're willing — and apparently most of us are. We've got travel, television, the Internet, magazines, books, billboards, movies, storefronts, advertisements (even on the back of the cab in front of us and the bus beside us), camera and video phones, texting, sexting, and Twittering to remind us what's out there. We'd better step it up if we want to compete, and if we don't, we might as well have the word *loser* inked on our foreheads.

In a telling article in *Psychology Today,* studies show that "women who are surrounded by other attractive women, whether in the flesh, in films, or in photographs, rate themselves as less satisfied with their attractiveness — and less desirable as a marriage partner."[6] Since the mark of real security is the ability to be around anyone, regardless of how attractive or intelligent, and still maintain personal confidence and contentment, that study says a lot about our need for a change. The primary point for now, however, is that we no longer feel inferior to ten other women the way our great-grandmothers might have. We feel inferior to thousands, and as a result, we become less and less satisfied with ourselves until much of our lives are lived on the slippery slope of self-loathing. We honestly talk ourselves into believing that media princesses, whether on the page or the stage, are the norm and that we are the pathetic few in the entire universe who can't keep up. We hang these near-perfect images like an enormous collage on the walls of our brains, making common experiences like acne, extra pounds, a flat chest, or a large nose twice the benefactor of insecurity that they once were.

That's not all. The high premium on youthfulness has skyrocketed to the point that a woman in her midtwenties now fears she's getting old. (If you're young, I don't want you to dread what you're about to hear and put the book down. Answers and new attitudes are on their way, and you'll be far more equipped to handle aging than my generation is.) Let me be loud and clear: our culture is just as merciless on men. Those men who have done their best to handle themselves with integrity in a society where sex sells and age smells are true warriors and worthy of a medal. None of us girls can imagine what it's like to have the genetics of a guy and deal with such a wholesale assault on the senses. The same trap that demoralizes women as bait discounts men as animals. No one walks away from the snare without a limp.

There are places in which our challenges take different turns, however. As we address some of those ways, I'll need a little elbow room to speak in gender generalities. Keep in mind as I proceed that not all men or women lean with the cultural sway; some are remarkably unaffected by it. That said, generally speaking, our culture does not hold men to the same standard of youthfulness as women. I'm not telling you something you don't already know. I'm just trying to show you how the double standard intensifies our gender's insecurities. Case in point: a few days ago I was watching one of those murder-mystery documentaries on television. A woman was dead, and her husband was the primary suspect. The couple in question had been married for thirty years and had raised several great kids. From all outward appearances, they seemed happy. The husband was first suspected of murder after authorities discovered his long affair with a younger woman. The evidence mounted from there, and he was eventually convicted of murder.

Here's the part that caught my attention: the dead woman's own sister, believing her brother-in-law was innocent, explained away the affair by saying something like, "Well, his wife had gotten older. . . ." A *woman* said that! She had bought the double standard hook, line, and sinker until it made perfect sense to her. My thought? *If she's right and that was his rationale, somebody wheel that dude in front of the mirror and show him somebody else who has gotten older!* Why, I ask you, had *she* gotten older but not *he?* His hair was mostly gray (come to think of it, his wife colored hers), and his face was appropriately lined by time. Oh, I know. Men are supposed to be more visual, and women are more relational and emotional. Is it really that simple? For the life of me, I don't know a single woman with decent vision who has been married awhile who can't see that her man is aging too. Or gaining weight. Or dressing differently. Women are not blind. As a gender — and I'm speaking in blatant generalities here — we may be a tad gentler. But that's probably because we're emotional.

It's maddening sometimes — and not just for women who have kissed their twenties good-bye. I well remember being a very young woman cognizant of my culture and wondering how quickly I would be dismissed and outdated. I don't think there are many women — of any age — in Western culture who are oblivious to how quickly the clock ticks. We don't get that luxury. The dot on the cultural time line that separates the young from the old is inching closer and closer to the left-hand margin. If we women are to believe our culture's press, our window of relevance is so small we have to squint to see it. Furthermore, by the time we develop some semblance of vision and wholeness, our time has come and gone, culturally speaking. We need to start looking out a new window.

Our culture offers us five minutes — okay, maybe five years — to feel fairly good about ourselves. The least we can do is refuse the offer and instead look for a reasonable ethic to live by. The One who created us in His own image and then bragged about His own handiwork extends such an ethic to us, but we have to be willing to redirect our preoccupations.

This youth-obsessed movement would lose half its steam if we quit puffing our breath into it. Listen, men didn't shape this culture by themselves. Women did just as much to contour the mind-set. We've even

shot our own wounded so we could minimize the competition. God has entrusted
each of us — male and female — with a
brief measure of time on this planet, and
each season is meant to be lived abundantly,
effectively, powerfully, and pricelessly. It's
our right as His prized creation, and we're
living like people scratching to reach our
five-minute peak and then sliding downhill
from there, all the while wondering if we
felt anything.

When I was in my forties, I was hit with
my first memorable wave of jealousy toward
younger women. Though I have lost battles
with numerous other insecurity struggles,
God and I won a fast victory on this one,
and for some reason it stuck. When that
jealousy first reared its unwelcome head in
me (I hate that feeling), it occurred to me
that not one woman out there would be
young a second longer than I was. Generally speaking, we all get the same amount of
time. I'd had my turn. They would have
their turn. And all of us, God willing, will
get the chance to age. I've not experienced
many immediate cures, but in that very moment, I felt God shove aside my jealousy,
flood me with empathy, and impress upon
my heart the need to do my part in making
it easier on those coming behind me. I want

to be part of a coalition of women who feel the same way. Not bitter women. Not angry women. Not women with an ax to grind. Gracious, loving women who have found some relief and release. I don't doubt that it was the beginning of this book.

Oh, that one generation could teach the next how to survive this culture with security intact! We'd better come up with some chutzpah, though, because this I promise you: media exploitation is not going to let up on us. We can scream about the double standards and injustices all day long, but it probably won't make one bit of measurable difference. It must happen in our thinking, in our processing, in our feeling, in our relating.

It's up to us to change the way we react to media influence and to quit emotionally buying into everything we see. Dr. Rick Rigsby says, "Truth is the first casualty in a media-crazed society."[7] How right he is. Absorb this thought for a moment: a medium (the singular form of media) is "a channel or system of communication, information, or entertainment."[8] It is a go-between. An intermediary. You can see the obvious connection when you set the words *media* and *mediate* side by side. Everything that qualifies as media stands between "us"

140

and some form of "them," whether they're politicians, nations, entertainers, teams, or some similar entity. Anything that's not the general "us" qualifies as a "them." While mediators like newspapers and newscasts were originally meant to be unbiased, mediators of entertainment and advertisement are now blatantly selling agendas and subsequent emotions. If we do not have a measurable reaction, they have failed.

Boy, are we having a reaction. We've spent ourselves blind, and worse yet, allowed an imaginary system to mediate our very real personal values. Listen, I'm a media addict just like most of you. I have no intention of throwing out my television, newspaper, or Internet access; nor do I plan to blindfold myself at the supermarket checkout counter or refuse to buy another movie ticket. But I'd better learn to be wise, moderate, and discerning. If we don't learn to separate entertainment from identity and hyped images from real womanhood, our feminine souls are going to pass straight through the shredder. We must stop affirming and reaffirming to ourselves how inferior we are. It's extremely unhealthy, and in reality, it's the furthest thing from God's concept of humility. We'd be wise to take note of how fickle the media is with its own stars and how short lived the friendly spotlight is.

Have you ever seen one of those magazines with photos of unsuspecting celebrities in unflattering swimsuits plastered right across the cover — cellulite and all? Their faces are always blacked out, and the question in the caption is usually something like, "Do you recognize these stars?" Then you're told to read page such and such for their identities. I never do. I'm too horrified for them. I can't help but picture my own thighs on the cover, and I try not to yell from the top of my lungs, "It's me! Lord, help me! It's me! Right here in front of the whole world!" Of course, that might explain why I'm writing this book and not somebody else. A slight psychosis.

We're going to learn some practical tools along our journey to help us live real life as secure people and, yes, even right here in this treacherous culture. This is a terrific time to interject a couple of tools. First, we need to recognize when we're overloading ourselves on media hype and back off when we sense it tripping our insecurity switch. Let's learn how to put something down or turn something off when it's just too much or makes a lie too believable.

We also need to make sure we're deliberately exposing ourselves to materials that edify the human soul rather than erode it. If you deal with a measurable amount of insecurity, poring obsessively over *InStyle* magazine or amusing yourself with online shopping probably isn't doing you any favors. If you don't know if your hype of choice is a problem, try putting it aside for a while, and once you get past the initial withdrawal, see if you feel better about the person God made you to be. If you do, rethink how much you want to reintroduce that particular media outlet. Our culture molds addicts like cavemen molded clay, so moderation can be even more challenging than avoiding it altogether. Moderation is a practice that begs to be recaptured in our society, however.

Second, we need to start looking for ways in which we set ourselves up for failure. For instance, if we know in advance that a movie is going to have a lot of skin in it and will probably make us feel like a zero sitting next to our man, we really can suggest seeing something else. We don't have to ask for trouble. Needless to say, there are significant parts of life we simply need to learn to deal with. On the other hand, there are other areas that are not unreasonable to avoid.

Perhaps you legitimately need to figure out a way to attend your man's work parties without lapsing into old insecurities, but you really could opt out of going to Hooters. It's good to learn to socialize without seeing others as a threat, but if there is a particular person who gets to you over and over and makes you feel small or stupid, perhaps he or she needs a quick shift to the B-list. Or if you find that whenever you and your man spend time with one particular couple you end up fighting, you need some new couples to befriend.

The point? Learn what you can handle and what you can't. As you become more and more secure, you will discover with great satisfaction how much more you can handle and, at the same time, come to recognize what you should not have to handle at all. There's a volume of wisdom in knowing the difference.

Okay, can you handle digging up one more root of chronic insecurity? Allow me to reiterate that we don't have the time or space, nor do I have the expertise to offer you the definitive, all-inclusive list. Hopefully we've covered enough ground with these first seven, however, to recognize a similar setup when we see one. Here's the last one I'll include here:

Pride

Yep, pride. Capital P-R-I-D-E. It's an ugly word, isn't it? At least we got to put it off this long. Every other root of insecurity falls into the category of influences largely beyond our control. Instability in the home, significant loss, rejection, dramatic change, and the surrounding culture each constitute circumstances imposed on us rather than invited by us. Personal disposition and many legitimate limitations are part of our DNA package and therefore also not of our own choosing. Our last selection, however, is one we have to own.

And it's as old as humankind. We would make a severe mistake if we went to great lengths to dig up every other root of chronic insecurity but left this one firmly in the ground. We'd never be free.

This one is not about culture. It's about ego, and we all have one. Let's face it. Sometimes people and situations make us feel insecure because they nick our pride, plain and simple. All the blows of life aside and every other root yanked out of the ground, we wrestle with insecurity because we wrestle with pride. Give some thought to the glaring connections between the two:

We're not the only women in our men's

145

lives, and that hurts our pride.
We're not the most gifted people alive, and that hurts our pride.
We're not the first choice every time, and that hurts our pride.
We're not someone's favorite, and that hurts our pride.
We can't do everything ourselves, and that hurts our pride.
We're not somebody else's top priority, and that hurts our pride. We don't feel special, and that hurts our pride.
We don't get the promotion, and that hurts our pride.
We don't win the fight, and that hurts our pride.
We're not paid what we're worth, and that hurts our pride.
We're not paid at all, and that *really* hurts our pride.

I'm not minimizing the authentic pain of these kinds of realizations. Just because pride fills a heart doesn't keep it from breaking. It just keeps it from healing.

I have come to the conclusion that we have no greater burden in all of life than our own inflated egos. No outside force has the power to betray and mislead us the way our own egos do. Pride talks us out of

146

forgiving and steers us away from risking.

Pride cheats us of intimacy, because intimacy requires transparency. Pride is a slave driver like no other, and if it can't drive us to destruction, it will drive us to distraction. Think about the madness this one little trait can cause:

If we can't be the most attractive, at least
we can be the best at something.
And if we can't be the best at something,
we can at least be the hardest working.
And if we can't be the hardest working,
we can at least be the most congenial.
And if we can't be the most congenial,
we can at least be the most noticeable.
And if we can't be the most noticeable,
we can at least be the most religious.
And if we can't be the most religious,
we can at least be the most exhausted.

And it never ends, because big egos insist on our being a "the." Not just an "a." We're that desperate for significance. We live our lives screaming, "Somebody notice me!" And do you want to hear something interesting? That's exactly how God made us.

That very need is built into our human hard drive to send us on a search for our Creator, who can assign us more significance than we can handle. He not only notices us, He never takes His eyes off us. Every now and then a moment of clarity hits us, and we feel *known* by something — *Someone* — of inestimable greatness. These words fell from a psalmist who experienced such a moment:

O LORD, you have examined my heart and know everything about me. You know when I sit down or stand up. You know my thoughts even when I'm far away. You see me when I travel and when I rest at home. You know everything I do. You know what I am going to say even before I say it, Lord. You go before me and follow me. You place your hand of blessing on my head. Such knowledge is too wonderful for me, too great for me to understand! . . . You made all the delicate, inner parts of my body and knit me together in my mother's womb. Thank you for making me so wonderfully complex! Your workmanship is marvelous — how well I know it. You watched me as I was being formed in utter seclusion, as I was woven together in the dark of the womb. You saw me before I was born. Every day of my life was recorded in your book. Every moment was laid out before a single day had passed. How precious are your thoughts about me, O God. They cannot be numbered!

PSALM 139:1–6, 13–17, NLT

In the radiance of His greatness, we are made great. Our search is over and our egos silenced. We no longer need pride to drive us, because we've found something infinitely more fulfilling: purpose. *He is the reason we are here.* And finally our souls are at rest . . . until once again we forget. Then instead of looking for ourselves in God, we look once more for God in man, and just when we think we've found someone who can hold us high enough and long enough to assuage our fear of forgottenness, we get dropped. Pride is a driver, and it invariably drives us in the opposite direction than it promised.

I chose to discuss these two final roots of insecurity together because the outside influence of culture and the inside influence of pride can get tied up so easily into a big, fat knot. As tempting as it may be, mustering up our pride is not the answer to our culture's vicious assault on women. We really can regain confidence without stirring up arrogance. Pride lives on the defensive against anyone and anything that tries to subtract from its self-sustained worth.

149

Confidence, on the other hand, is driven by the certainty of God-given identity and the conviction that nothing can take that identity away. That's what you and I are after, not an outbreak of bloated ego.

Humility is a crucial component in true security. It's the very thing that calms the savage beast of pride. More important, humility is the heart of the great paradox: we find our lives when we lose them to something much larger. Perhaps the writer of Ecclesiastes had a hint of this in mind when he wrote that God "has also set eternity in the hearts of men" (Ecclesiastes 3:11).

Eternity. In the hearts of mortals. It doesn't get bigger than that. Created in the image of God, we instinctively know that something enormous is within us. Pride is the result of mistaking the eternal for the temporal. We end up looking in to look up instead of looking up to look in. We get fixated on every self-gain and every self-loss until, in our inordinate self-protection, we end up licking our wounds to the point that they can't heal.

Pride. A root of insecurity if there ever was one. We will never feel better about ourselves by becoming more consumed with ourselves. Likewise, we will never feel better about ourselves by feeling worse about others. Superiority can't give birth to security. Neither, by the way, can the relentless pursuit of perfection. Earlier in our journey, I suggested that perfectionism is insecurity in art form. It never looks prettier and never acts deadlier. Perfectionism is perhaps our culture's biggest temptation. In his fascinating book *Perfecting Ourselves to Death,* psychiatrist and theologian Richard Winter offers this intriguing insight:

> Although perfectionists seem very insecure, doubting their decisions and actions, fearing mistakes and rejection, and having low opinions of themselves, at the same time, they have excessively high personal standards and an exaggerated emphasis on precision, order and organization, which suggests an aspiration to be better than others.

> Most psychological explanations see the desire to be superior and in control as compensation for feelings of weakness, inferiority and low self-esteem. But it could also be that the opposite is true; we feel bad about ourselves because we are not able to perform as well, or appear as good, as we really think we can.

We believe we are better than others, but we keep discovering embarrassing flaws. Perfectionists' black-and-white thinking takes them on a roller coaster between feeling horribly inadequate and bad about themselves, and then, when things are going well, feeling proud to be so good. Low self-esteem and pride coexist in the same heart.[9]

Dr. Winter then goes on to quote psychologist Terry Cooper in this vivid snapshot of the coexisting odd couple:

If I search around long enough, I'll find insecurity beneath my grandiosity and arrogant expectations beneath my self-contempt.[10]

We are complex people indeed. Perfect messes. Pridefully insecure. But let me tell you what isn't complex: owning our own pride problem and confessing it to God. That's when He'll move it out of the way so we can deal with the roots of our insecurity we didn't plant. Until we sort the pride out of our insecurity, we can't, in every sense of the saying, see the forest for the trees. Everybody's got a pride problem. Owning it is a relief. Every time I do, I sense the glorious God-given release that follows repentance, and I wonder what took me so long. I don't feel shamed. I feel freed.

Fortunately, pride is not hard to spot. It's not emotionally complicated like the effects of instability in the home, significant loss, or dramatic change. It's ego, and we know it. In that very moment, we can whisper the words, "That's nothing but pride. God, forgive me. Self, get over it." If I'm by myself, I don't whisper. I say it out loud like I mean it. Pride is one of those roots that God can jerk up in a second. We just have to pry our sweet little fingers loose. Our culture has done us no greater injustice than training us to avoid taking responsibility for our own issues. In trying to relieve us of the whole concept of personal sin, our culture's reordered values have cheated us of the right to repentance and sublime restoration. They have hijacked our healing. A clear heart and a clean path are still only one sincere confession away.

CHAPTER 7
DON'T LET IT FOOL YOU

Insecurity. It will make a fool of you. What follows just might be one of the most profound sections of this book. In the pages to come, you will find the stories of women very much like you and me who were willing to answer one simple question I posted on my blog: "Has insecurity ever made a fool of you?"

When I first posted the question, I wasn't sure what kind of response I would receive. But I got enough answers on the blog to fill every page in this book and make us feel pathetic and sorry for ourselves for the next six months. Fortunately, that couldn't be further from my aim. I'll be completely up-front with you about my goal: I want us to see the price we're paying when we don't deal with our insecurity. Unchecked and unhealed, it makes an idiot out of us over and over. Sometimes in small ways. Sometimes in enormous ways. But at the end of the day, even a small idiot feels like a big idiot. Reading stories like the ones that follow can help us see in others the things we desperately need to face in ourselves. Since we don't have the space for all the stories, I chose certain selections because they were either highly representative or particularly poignant. Before we throw ourselves into these testimonies, I need to make a deal with you.

You're probably going to be tempted to skip parts of this chapter because, for starters, it's so much longer than the rest. Further than that, it's purely painful to read at times. Reading these stories not only causes us to feel for the people sharing them, it also sparks the memory of a few difficult circumstances of our own. In one way or another, insecurity has made fools of all of us. Naturally, we'd just as soon not remember how. But dear one, if we're going to get serious about letting God deliver us, we must look in the mirror and realize how disfigured we are — far from God's original intent for us. Until we do that, we'll continue to settle for what we have.

Maybe your story is completely unlike most in this chapter. Others might be so close, you'll wonder if you wrote them in your sleep. I ask you to risk the vulnerability and read every word that follows. When we wrap up this journey, many of you may well have decided to cooperate with divine healing precisely because you didn't want some of these snapshots to find their way into your photo album. Now for the deal: if you'll see it through, I promise to throw in some amusing examples for comic relief, and I promise this will be the last entire chapter I devote to the ugly side of insecurity. We'll get to the beauty of healing after this.

Okay, here goes. I'll loosely categorize these stories by the insights they offer, and with your permission, I'll also let the women speak in their own words. To edit their language would be to edit their emotions. Let's just let them have their own voices.

INSECURITY CAN MAKE YOU ACT LIKE AN IDIOT IN FEMALE FRIENDSHIPS.
Me and a friend of mine recently had a relationship problem. This person is also a family member, so we *have* to make our friendship work no matter what. But we sometimes just have a difficult time because we're so different. She also can be very intimidating. Well, with this most recent relationship tiff, I realized my error, so I wrote an apology (via e-mail —

we live far apart). I didn't hear back from her — thought she must hate me — very insecure about our friendship! So I wrote another e-mail . . . still haven't heard back from her! I read back over my e-mails and realized that I wrote some really stupid stuff because I was so insecure. I wrote yet one more short e-mail telling her to just forget about me and everything I said. I'm so tired of being in such a tizzy! I feel like a fool and have been in such emotional turmoil over all of this! It's still not resolved to my satisfaction. I'm waiting to see if she'll ever talk to me again.

Haven't some of us been there? We gnaw on a relationship like a dog on a bone. We worry a detail half to death out of insecurity, get no response, and then overcommunicate yet again to say, "Forget I communicated all of that." And they rarely do.

Here's another example involving women friendships:

I had a friendship about twelve years ago that consumed me. She was everything I thought I wasn't. So I attached myself to her. We worked at the same place, and we saw each other every day. She was in executive leadership, and she was very concerned about our relationship being unprofessional or something so everything had to be secret. (She was also extremely controlling.) I lied more than I care to remember to "protect" this friendship . . . to my coworkers, family, etc. It was awful. But I couldn't let go because I was so locked in. What made me a fool beyond that is that so many people knew what was going on and just didn't say anything. I was caught in some lies. It was a mess. We moved out of state, and the foolishness followed me as I discovered more people who were onto it the whole time. How embarrassing. I still wince every time I think about it.

Sister, you and I have to learn to be secure enough to question any relationship that involves secrecy. Secure people live in the light. Here's another story about female friendships:

I had two good friends at work, but they weren't really friends with each other. I secretly liked it because I thought if they got to know each other, they would really hit it off and I would be useless to them. Wouldn't you know, they did get to know each other and totally hit it off. They would have lunch together [and] went shopping after work. While I should have reminded myself of the many lunches and shopping outings I had with both of them separately, I let it upset me so much. I would cry to my husband at night that they didn't like me anymore. I should have been praising the fact that they had become friends, and all I could do was feel sorry for myself. I didn't have the confidence to realize that they still enjoyed my friendship. I felt [like I was] twelve all over again.

Jealousy of our friends and the fear that they'll like each other better than they like us is always a product of insecurity, and too often it's the sharp blade to a decent relationship. Permit me to share one more story because this one moves from the emotional arena to the sexual — something that catches many women by surprise:

Because I was not finding my worth in Christ and I had a lot of hatred toward males as a result of things that happened in my childhood, I attempted to find it through my relationships with my female friends. This resulted in three codependent sexual "friendships" with other insecure, hurting ladies. I rationalized with every possible excuse because I needed the feeling of being chosen in order to believe that I was worth something. I cannot believe that I was so deceived. To this day, I often wish that life had an eraser so that I didn't have a testimony that scared away [many in] the church and hurt three people I really cared about in ways that still impact them today. Praise the Lord for His mercy being new every morning!

INSECURITY CAN CAUSE A MOM TO BE OVERCONTROLLING OR JUST GENERALLY OUT OF CONTROL.
I keep making a fool out of myself in front of my daughter. I am so afraid that every little thing she does is some kind of "pre-" to everything I did, I act like a controlling nutcase.

Another:

Wow. As a mom of a sixteen-year-old . . . yes I am still insecure. I am watching when other girls tell her she is fat, but she is not. She believes them and not me. She wants a boy to like her so much that I watch her try to be something different just to be liked. I try to tell her over and over again she just needs the love of Jesus, not some man, to be accepted. Sometimes I feel alone in this. I want her to learn she is enough, just by being who she is right now. I don't want her to go down the road I did, sleeping with a guy just to feel loved and accepted.

And another:

My insecurities increased tenfold when I became a mother. I had such a harsh upbringing that I just knew I would turn out to be my parents. I let Satan sneak into my thoughts daily, and I believed all the "you can't do this" and "go back to work because they would be better off without you." I fell into a depression that I have never experienced before in my life. I started to become what the evil one was telling me. After years of this I got help, and I am now the best mom that I can possibly be with the Lord standing right beside me. I still have flashbacks of those lies, but I am so past believing them. Thank You, Lord,

161

for bringing me out of the pit! I am who You say I am!

If you think insecurity makes run-of-the-mill parenting difficult, it can make the challenges of stepparenting nearly debilitating:

I married a man twenty years older than me, and along with that marriage I became a stepmother to his three kids. Six years ago when we were first married, we attended one of his company dinners. This dinner included roughly forty of his team members, plus their spouses. At that time, I was incredibly (and I can't stress *incredibly* enough) insecure. I was a full-blown mental mess. Anyway, my husband and I got into an argument *at* the table during dinner. He had said something about having three kids with his ex-wife — and I just came unglued. For one, I hated any mention of her name in the first place. I was so irrationally fearful that he still had feelings for her. And for two, I was jealous that they weren't *my* kids. I thought for so long that because they weren't my birth children, he loved them more than me. Keep in mind, he is twenty years older than me, and his kids are closer to my age.

Everyone at the table kept trying to include me in conversation — and I acted like an idiot. I was short and unpleasant and just downright *rude* because I was so ticked off at my husband. God love him, he was so embarrassed. I was so out of my ever-loving, insane mind that when he got up to go to the restroom (because he had just had enough of my whining), I *followed* him. It was a unisex restroom (we were in a private party room), and it had only one stall and the door locked. I charged into the restroom after him and chewed him up one side and down the other (for what? God only knows). And I ended up bawling and acting like a psycho. Oooooh, bad memories. When we left the restroom, the two main gossipers of his work group were standing outside in line waiting for the restroom. Bottom line: I looked like some sort of freaking psycho, and my husband suffered from my foolishness as well.

Another:

I'm a stepmom. When my husband

and I first got married, his former significant other lived a thousand miles away, and my husband was raising his son on his own. His son was four when I first met him and six by the time we were married. My stepson's biological mother only saw him a couple of times a year. The day I married my husband, my stepson asked, "Can I call you Mommy now?" He did, and I was — for about five years — the only mother figure in his life. Then news came that made me want to cry, throw up, scream, and a million other things all at once. *She* was moving back and wanted to start visitation with her son. I felt terrible [that] she was coming and guilty that I felt terrible. It should have been a good thing. But I was totally insecure about my role in this little boy's life. So I spent a few years not only being miserable about the situation, but sometimes miserable to my stepson, always miserable to his mother, and quite often miserable to my husband whenever issues arose involving visitation. Hate grew in my heart. I tried my best to get it all under my control, to be in charge and make things just the way I wanted them to be. Do you know how *tiring* that is? We tried and tried to have children of our own. I thought then I could be a mom again! The one and only mom! Then I could feel secure! But I could not get pregnant. I was just in pieces inside. When it came to the place where I just couldn't handle it anymore, I just had to give it to God. Should have done that first, right? Healing didn't happen overnight, and I think it is still an ongoing process . . . but I now know my place in that little (over six feet tall now) boy's life.

INSECURITY CAN TURN A GIFTED PERSON INTO THE COMPETITION.
God has blessed me with the ability to play an instrument, and I have played at my church off and on for the past twelve years. For some reason, I almost always get insecure when another player of my instrument comes to orchestra. It's like this "queen bee" mentality comes over me, and I turn into a possessive, distant, and mean-spirited person. Thankfully the Lord is faithful and patient with me, gently showing me my faults and helping me to recognize my place in *Him* alone. He is the *only way* that I am able to get through it.

INSECURITY WEIGHS HEAVILY IN WEIGHT ISSUES.

I feel so silly writing this. Putting it down on paper (well, computer screen, anyway) shows me just how embarrassing this is. Sheesh. I'm about fifteen to twenty pounds overweight, and I have a rather large bottom (ahem). There have been several occasions when I have been scheduled to sing in church or to lead the service or to make an announcement up front, and I have ended up coming up with excuses (lies) as to why I can't. The thought of walking up front and then climbing the stairs while everyone can see my backside brings out insecurities galore. I feel so ashamed that I allow *that* to stop me from ministering.

Another:

Can I just say how very glad I am that I am the mother of two *boys?!* Growing up female and knowing how hard it is, I don't know if I could stand having to see a daughter go through it. (And yes, I am sure boys deal with much of the same; it's just that I know what it feels like to be a girl.) My parents separated when I was seven. My father was moving on to wife number four. I always *knew* he loved me, but I never *felt* he loved me. My mom would often tell me that he had left us and didn't love us, and [she] would get very angry at me for wanting to see him. She went from an average-sized lady to [one who weighed] 220 pounds, and throughout my adolescent years she would not pass up an opportunity to say, "You've gained weight. You're going to end up looking just like me." I hated the way I looked. I was five feet six inches tall and weighed between 128 and 135 pounds and had a very curvy body type. I envied my girl-friends who were stick-straight size fours. Can you believe it? Looking back, [I think] they probably envied me! When I see pictures of myself then I am stunned. I was beautiful, absolutely beautiful.

On top of that, nothing I did satisfied [my mother]. I was a straight-A student, never got into trouble, and yet I could do nothing right in her eyes. I was always insecure about guys. In hindsight, I think I tended to sabotage relationships for fear of being rejected.

And another:

My appearance changed after a surgery I had to remove cancer from my body. I was already overweight, but it got worse after the surgery. I had also been divorced for quite a few years, and I wanted to one day be remarried. After the surgery, my insecurity was full-blown out of control. I kept thinking, *Who would want me now?* That played in my head like a recording. After recovery, I went back to work, and a man acted interested in me, and that was all it took. Sexual immorality for months. Sneaking around and trying to hide it from my family and friends. I was a complete fool. My sin looked far worse on me than my appearance after the surgery. I hated myself [and] what I had done and actually could not believe I had done it. I did something I said I would never do; insecurity that is not dealt with is disastrous.

INSECURITY CAN TURN A PRICELESS DAUGHTER OF GOD INTO A BOOT-LICKER.

I have seven brothers (no sisters; I am in the middle), and once when I was about ten years old, we went on a ski trip with oodles of cousins and stayed in a lodge.

The folks all went out for the evening, and us kids were all left to ourselves. (What were they thinking? I won't even tell you the pranks my brothers pulled and the trouble we all got into for it!) I came running into a room where everyone was gathered, and they had said something I couldn't hear, so I asked them to repeat it. Well, they wouldn't, so I just begged and begged. I didn't want to be left out, and I so wanted to be "in." My oldest brother said he'd tell me if I licked the bottom of his boot. So without hesitation, I did! They laughed and laughed at me (still do) for that and wouldn't tell me what they had said. (What was I thinking?) Well, that hasn't helped my insecurity at all, and I still have a bad taste in my mouth!

I bet she does! And I hope we do too. I'd imagine most of us have licked the bottom of some boots over insecurity. I used this fairly benign example to introduce us to one that is so malignant, it could turn deadly in the blink of an eye.

I was violated against my will on a date at sixteen. I worked as a cashier at the time, and when the friend of the violator (we'll call him Vinnie) came into the store three weeks later, I blurted out, "Have Vinnie call me." Just makes me weep. Not only did I not call the police when it happened, I went soliciting for it again. By God's grace, the phone never rang, and I eventually got help for the insecurity.

In order to avoid having to deal with the fact that we've been violated, sometimes we will reframe a situation, making ourselves out to be free agents who wanted it. We sometimes think it's better to prove crass than weak. We think so little of ourselves that we end up not calling a wrong a wrong or a crime a crime. Insecurity and all its attending emotional unhealthiness can cause us to embrace people who abuse us. And if we don't wake up, they could kill us. Let me be blunt: security means we know a jerk when we see one and we know a crime when we experience one. It's not a gender thing. Men also need to recognize a poisonous person when they encounter one and run for their lives before she gets her fangs into them.

INSECURITY CAN VEIL OUR VISION AND BLIND US TO HOW BLESSED WE ARE.

I was adopted and have the best parents ever. But all through school and high school I felt insecure. My parents always told me how much I was loved and wanted. But I let insecurity make me feel like I was not good enough. I mean, how could a mother not want and love her child? Something had to be wrong with me. So I carried that with me for forty-eight years. I let it control me and make me feel like I could not win and did not deserve to win. Even after I was a Christian, it still would pop up. Then one day I was walking and talking to God, and He made it clear to me that He loved me and I was placed where He wanted me. That He had chosen my parents before I was even conceived! Wow, it was an awesome moment. A huge weight was lifted off my shoulders. I can look back now and see so many areas that Satan used with that insecurity. Makes me mad that so much waste came from that.

INSECURITY CAN EVEN REAR ITS HIDEOUS HEAD AT THE DRIVE-THROUGH. I used to be so insecure that I would avoid drive-through windows. I didn't like the way my voice sounded, and I was afraid the person on the other end would think my voice was weird. How silly is that? I mean, whose voice doesn't sound strange when they're in a drive-through, and even if it does, *who cares?* I laugh about it now because it's so silly.

Imagine the tragedy if you're a Starbucks freak like me. Picture the needless lethargy! Get over it and make that order! And while you're at it, I'll have a grande nonfat cappuccino with an extra shot.

INSECURITY CAN CONFINE US.
At work, if there are a lot of people standing in the hallway outside of my office, I won't leave my office. I am so insecure that I feel that if I do walk by, they are judging me or they will talk about me. It gets to be overwhelming, and I end up becoming angry with myself because of my insecurities.

INSECURITY CAN TALK US INTO DOING THINGS WE DON'T EVEN WANT TO DO.
Insecurity has made me do things I knew were dead wrong. Several "sophisticated" friends invited us to Manhattan to have dinner at a place made famous by *Sex and the City.* Never having seen

the show, I didn't know what it was all about. We arrived at this dark, dungeon-like place, and I knew not to go in. Insecurity scooted me in the door, and there were normal-looking people enjoying their filet mignons, while the waiters and waitresses were semi-naked and wearing dog collars. I was so amazed at everyone in my group acting like this was normal. I went right along until they came to the table offering a menu of foot massages while you eat. I got up from the table, went in the restroom, and got on my knees. *God, get me out of this filth, and forgive me for being so flimsy that I ended up here.* With that, I walked to the table [and] said I was going home. And home I went. Never did see my sophisticated friends again.

It's very worth noting from her story that insecurity also causes us to accept things as normal that aren't. That's one of many reasons we need to stay in relationships with lots of transparency. At one time or another, each of us needs somebody to say, "Now, that's just plain weird."

Insecurity can get us into the worst relational nightmares of our lives. Oh, the affairs evolving from insecurity! These are just a few of the many stories:

I married young and never felt that I had my husband's attention in the way I wanted it — I wanted to be his every waking thought, I guess. I attributed what I perceived to be his lack of attention to my lack of desirability. During a very stressful time in our family and after twenty years of marriage, I set out to have an affair — I think to prove to myself that I was attractive. I set out, and I achieved. My affair with a married Christian man lasted several years and almost destroyed my marriage. This situation was the "slimy pit" the Lord lifted me out of (Psalm 40:2). After my husband discovered the affair (discovered in the worst possible way, I might add), I had his attention all right. My betrayal consumed his every thought. As I write this, images of my foolish, disgusting, embarrassing, sinful behavior flood my mind, and my stomach turns. Thank You, Jesus, for rescuing me! And I can also say, with a hallelujah praise, that God restored our marriage — not to where it was before, but to a new marriage with His gloriousness at the center.

And another:

Insecurity has had a devastating effect on my life. Years of severe sexual, emotional, and physical abuse for my entire childhood led me to be a closed-off and distant woman who could not see her value and beauty and worth at all. My innermost desire to be cleansed of my shame over my abuse and to prove that I could be desirable led me to have inappropriate friendships with males, which eventually led to my committing adultery. The affair was with a man who was a sexual predator and addict, and the things I did with him were so demeaning and degrading that I still have a hard time thinking about it. And I did all this because I so desperately wanted someone to love me — anyone to love me.

Not only can insecurity talk us into disastrous relationships, it can talk us out of great ones. This is one of many examples:

Because of deep insecurity and shame, I said no to marrying my very best friend and the most godly man I have ever known. Fifteen years later I am often caught off guard with memories that reveal that I still miss him and his friendship dearly.

I remember breaking up with a really great guy in high school who actually had enough respect for me not to maul me by the third date. (If you had seen how I dressed — what I called *subtly sensual* so I could keep that innocent front going — you'd know it wasn't all their fault.) I was so sure that he would break up with me, I beat him to the punch. I regretted it for years.

Insecurity can make us panic and act like freaks when we can't get in touch with our significant other:

I have driven three hours to go and "check" on a guy I was dating because he wasn't answering his phone. I probably called a hundred times, and no, that's not an exaggeration. Of course there were points leading up to this. I felt I had reason to be suspicious. Another time with that same guy (after I moved closer) — again over him not answering the phone — I parked down the road and snuck up behind his house and stayed there watching for an hour or so. I once even went so far as to go in his house when he wasn't home and go through all his stuff. I used to do the occasional drive-by to "check." I almost got caught and tried to do a turn in an unpaved driveway — ended up getting stuck! Had to go and enlist some of the people who lived nearby to shovel out my car. Talk about embarrassing.

Beloved, let me pause here a moment because she just pegged the goal of this entire book: we need to let God shovel us out of insecurity, because without Him, we're stuck. This one's about to hit a familiar nail right on the embarrassing head:

We are so insecure about our men. We would never tell them this, so we feel like such fools to God. This doesn't happen every day but often enough to bother us. If the men do not accept our calls or don't call us, we immediately start the wheels of disaster, torment, crushing agony, stomachaches, panic, etc. So much so that it stops everything we are doing, and we obsess until we reach them. And we are seriously praying they are okay and they will call, text, something. We feel like foolish freaks! Where does this insecurity come from? Is this the enemy, or do we have underlying stuff to deal with? It feels like total rejection! Then the enemy starts with lies! Such terrible lies. *He must be mad at me! What did I say? Who is he with?* And the best: *What in the world could he be doing that is better than talking to me?* So after listening to the lies, the freak show really starts to take place: *I will call his mobile again; e-mail him — no answer; text him — no answer; call his work desk phone — no answer. Yikes! Panic, anxiety!*

We desperately need to learn a different response when we're tempted to panic and overcommunicate with people. Except in an understandable emergency, leaving ten voice mails and twenty-five texts makes even the people who love us think we're bizarre. Remember, no one is endeared by hysteria. How many of us have tried to figure out how to erase a voice mail we already left or retrieve an e-mail we already sent? As the writer of Proverbs suggests, it's better to stay quiet and be thought a fool than to speak rashly and remove all doubt.

One more:

My high school sweetheart and I were having a fight, and I wanted to talk to him to convince him not to break up with me, but I couldn't find him. I went over to his house and begged and pleaded, and yes, got into that "ugly cry" for his dad to tell me where he was, but he wouldn't. I even ended up going to his grandparents' house.

Don't you just hate the times insecurity has caused you to do the ugly cry in front of somebody who thought you were nuts? And if not before, after? I have a memory of something similar in college, and every time it comes back to me, I sit and shake my head in self-disgust.

INSECURITY CAN MAKE US GIVE AN ENTIRELY WRONG IMPRESSION.
I am a pastor's wife. My insecurity can definitely get the best of me. I'm not real good at small talk and tend to be stand-offish because I don't think people will like me or want to get to know me. Therefore I give off the wrong impression to the other women at church. They see me as being a snob. Oh, if they only knew I'm scared to death of them. I feel so intimidated by them because I don't feel like I have much to contribute to their lives or even the conversation. I am trying to work on this, and it isn't as if it

consumes me night and day. It has been this way for so long, it is just who I am: *Hi, my name is* _____, *and I'm insecure.*

Me, too. But I'm getting over it. You, too?

INSECURITY CAN MAKE US OVERCOMPENSATE.
I grew up with a serious overbite. My mouth was smaller than the set of teeth that grew in. I couldn't close my mouth at all. I was teased constantly. I would sit in my room for hours looking in the mirror with a bent-up paper clip over my teeth, picturing what I would look like with braces. I did everything I could to take the focus off my mouth. My hair always had to be perfect, and so did my eye makeup. The clothes I wore over my petite frame had to make my body look appealing as well. Anything to make people notice something other than those teeth. I joked around a lot, and I was such a pushover. I just wanted to be normal. It didn't help that I was living in California, where the "beautiful people" lived. I did the dumbest things to try to get people to like me. They would say, "Are you getting braces? You

would look so pretty with your teeth fixed." I'll never forget how differently I was treated after I finally had straight teeth. I almost bawled when a waiter in a restaurant told me I had the most beautiful smile. I had never heard those words in my life. I used to say, "If only I could get my teeth fixed, then I wouldn't care about anything else about my appearance." Satan has a field day with me on that when he can. I have to keep reminding myself and other women that God thinks we are beautiful no matter what. He is enthralled with our beauty.

INSECURITY CAN KEEP US FROM ACCEPTING COMPLIMENTS AND, FAR WORSE, FROM ACCEPTING LOVE.
I feel like a fool every time my husband tells me he loves me or that I am beautiful (which happens a lot). I desperately want and need to believe him, but my heart just can't because of his ten-year struggle with pornography and the insecurity it has caused in me. Then I feel like a fool because I am a Christian and can't seem to "break free" and live in freedom. Insecurity has crippled me to where I doubted if God loves me anymore.

181

INSECURITY EXPLODES WITH REJECTION AND CAN TWIST OUR PERCEPTIONS.

Nine years ago my husband left me for another woman. I was beside myself with grief and humiliation and hurt. I begged him to come back. I told him I would change; I would make things better; I would make him happy. Hello? *He* was the main one who needed to change and make things better, not me, and he was responsible for his happiness. He came back, and I tried. I did everything I thought I could do to make him happy. I did wrong things to spice up our marital relations. He left again. And I begged some more. He came back, and I knew things wouldn't work, but I so foolishly thought I could do this. I was afraid to let him go out the door to work because he worked with *her.* He left again for the final time after a couple of months. I was so broken. So humiliated. So angry. So bitter because I had failed. I took him back and forgave him, and he left me again. I compromised who I was and who I was in Christ to please a man who couldn't be happy no matter what because he didn't have a personal relationship with God. Wow! I see now that *he* was the one with the primary problem, not me. The whole divorce was pretty bad, but I wasn't secure enough at the beginning to be able to tell my husband that he had crossed a line. Forgiveness is one thing, but allowing ongoing abuse and deception is quite another.

Another one:

My insecurities have plagued me for the past twenty-five years, yet the majority of that time I did not identify insecurity as the culprit in my "adventures" and "disasters." My husband left me for another woman after fifteen years of marriage, and I was totally unprepared for dealing with the pain and rejection that his decision brought. I had always been my father's pride and joy, and I thought my husband adored me in that way as well. We had married extremely young, so after the divorce I decided to live any way I wanted, and also to prove the great mistake my husband made in leaving me. I became (in my mind) the funniest, sexiest, smartest woman in any room. I managed to do all this in a way that attracted most people and didn't repel them. I am sure God was repelled, and I know that by following my lead and direction, many men (and women) joined me in behaviors that were immoral and damaging. I was involved in affairs with married men, and the relationships I had with single men were invariably doomed by my incessant jealousy of their time and attention. Knowing what a "nice" person like myself was capable of and knowing what my ex-husband and numerous others had done to me led me to distrust any man (and most women) I met.

You would not have guessed I had all these issues if you met me. I appeared the most functional person in the room. My insecurity was this thing that I hid even from myself. I am now married to a wonderful guy, but this insecurity still rears its ugly head after twenty-five years and much repentance on my part. I question my husband too much and feel an icy grip of jealousy on my heart too often. Thank God he and I are talking about this. (It is really annoying to him that Satan has such sway with my mind and I have such unwarranted doubts.) With God's help and immersion in the Word, my insecurity and anxiety are subsiding. I still have much ground to recover, though. And even now, very few people recognize my brokenness.

INSECURITY CAN MAKE A FOOL OUT OF YOU BY MAKING A LIAR OUT OF YOU.

I grew up very insecure because we were poor, my parents were divorced, we lived in the projects, and I wore clothes that were given to me by others. Because of my not fitting in, I lied to make myself and my life better. My lies soon found me out, and I realized I had a habit (lying) that was hard to kick. I took all that lying into adulthood, and it continued to find me out. God truly saved me, and I am now a miracle of His.

Another:

As a child, I remember wanting attention from adults, and when I was a fifth grader, somehow my teacher (who I adored) thought I had been on the receiving end of a brand-new haircut — even though I hadn't. I am unclear how she thought that, but as I was wearing a hat at the time, I just let her think that was the case. I was the center of attention for a few moments, as everyone wanted to see the new do. Never thinking of the consequences, I just went along with it, and then when the big reveal happened, I remember feeling so bad that I had lied the whole time. I was willing to lie for a few minutes of attention.

And another:

Insecurity has caused me to lie more times than I can count. I don't know what it is, but if someone asks me if I've read a book or seen a movie or even know where a certain road is, often I'll lie and say I know exactly what they're talking about. Obviously, if they ask for my opinion I feel like a fool, because I've dug myself into a stupid, ugly pit. I don't know what it is about me that refuses to acknowledge that I don't know something or haven't experienced it myself, but that has often led to me feeling like a fool later on.

Lying has a titanic link to insecurity. Incidentally, research shows that one mark of insecurity is the urge to lie when someone asks us if we know someone we don't, remember something we can't, or have ever heard of something we haven't. We deceive people out of fear that they will think us ignorant or out of the loop.

INSECURITY CAN MAKE YOU WEAR WEIRD STUFF TO SCHOOL.
When I was a freshman in high school, my dad took me shopping for a new pair of shoes and saw a pair of Nike Aqua Socks (you know, the shoes you wear on the beach or out on the boat to keep from slipping or stepping on shells). They were aqua blue and black, but I didn't know they were for water. My dad said they were cool and I would start a new trend (I'm laughing so hard at myself right now I can barely type). So I believed him and I wore those shoes to school every day. In the '80s we did not wear ankle socks but big puffy socks that reached mid-calf, and we tucked our jeans into our socks or rolled them up above our socks. To make it worse, a guy I had a crush on even picked on me for wearing them, but I was sure he was just jealous that he hadn't gotten some first.

If in order to be cool, you are wearing Aqua Socks to school, work, or even to the movies, you have earned the right to be insecure. There is help.

INSECURITY CAN TURN YOU INTO A PUBLIC FOOL.

Most of the time my insecurity comes out as raging anger. In the early years of our marriage, my husband struggled with an addiction to crack cocaine. He is what I call a binger (sober for months, and then he would rent a hotel room and "binge" on it for about a week). During one of his binges, his sister called me and wanted to go looking for him, so I agreed. We got to a hotel, and while we were standing at the registration desk checking to see if he was there, his face popped up on the surveillance monitor in the elevator. We ran down the hall toward the elevator and got there just as it opened. I was so angry and insecure about our relationship that I jumped in the elevator and started just swinging at him — my sister-in-law later described it as the scene from *When Animals Attack* of a deer attacking a hunter. Anyway, he ran out of the elevator and out the back door with me in hot pursuit. He ran (with me chasing him) into the woods behind the hotel, through a car dealership's service bays (it was a weekday, and yes they were busy) and back into the woods, where he finally collapsed from exhaustion. His only defense was a dead tree limb he grabbed to try to ward me off. We laugh about it now. I mean, can you imagine seeing a man come running through a car dealership, into the service bays, and all the while with a woman running about ten feet behind him yelling her head off? We wound up having to call an ambulance to come get him out of the woods.

INSECURITY CAN TURN US INTO POSERS.
As a single girl on the lookout, and one who is highly insecure around boys, I find myself in these "fake" situations all the time. Normally when I know I am going to be meeting a guy or even if I am around a bunch of single guys, I automatically think that one of them could potentially be my husband. Big fat mistake. The thing is, I can't look at them like that, because then I feel the need to act perfect or act how I think would make them attracted to me, instead of just being me. It's awful, because I always, without fail, get all caught up in what I say and how I say it,

what words I am using, how I carry myself, and blah, blah, blah. I walk away kicking myself every time, because I wasn't secure in who I really am. Bottom line, I need to act like me so they'll like *me,* not some made-up girl. But those boys bring out the biggest insecurities in me. I need to stop looking at them as potential mates and start looking at them as just friends. Then it's not such a big deal.

INSECURITY CAN MAKE A GIRL ACT LIKE A GUY.
When I was in elementary school, my mother sent me in with a haircut that was a wee bit shorter than I was used to. Apparently my classmates agreed, because all day I heard, "You look like a boy!" and it's the only comment I remember. After a few hours, I believed it. So when we got to our physical education class at the end of the day and the coach told the girls to skip to the back wall and sit down, I wavered. I knew he would instruct the boys to gallop to the back wall next. Yup, you guessed it. I galloped. And you should have seen the look on Coach's face.

I'm using a silly example to take a little heat off a serious situation so we can stand to discuss it. Countless women are so insecure about their womanhood that they act like men. Sometimes, because a male failed to protect them, they wrap themselves in a masculine exterior to protect their own femininity. I'm not talking about tomboys. I'm not talking about women athletes. I'm talking about women who hide themselves behind a masculine exterior so no one can get to their vulnerable female interior. I pray with all my heart that when this journey ends, we can each find the security to be the women God created us to be.

Speaking of acting like a guy, guys can make fools of themselves out of insecurity too. Oh, to have that list! Another time, another book. Here are a couple I have to pitch into the mix now, however, so that we'll feel better knowing we're not the only gender with insecurity issues:

Okay, this one is about my husband, and we still laugh about it. When we were in college (not married at that point), my husband, Andrew, made an appointment to get a haircut. When he got there, the guy cutting his hair kept accidentally calling him "Ian." Well, Andrew was too shy/embarrassed/insecure to correct the guy, but he really liked how he cut his hair. So from then on, whenever Andrew made haircut appointments with that certain barber, he made the appointment under the name "Ian" just to avoid correcting the man. He even made a point to always pay with cash so the barber wouldn't see his real name on a check or credit card. It was so ridiculous! It sounds to me like something straight out of a *Seinfeld* episode.

INSECURITY CAN KEEP YOU FROM . . . FROM . . . WELL, FROM EXPRESSING YOURSELF.
I'll just go and say it — I can't pee if anyone can hear. You want specifics? At work I used to go to the restroom sometimes three or four times before I found one empty so I could go. One day when I was heading for the bathroom, I heard a flush inside, so I turned around before I got to the door. A guy was coming that way and said, "Change your mind?"

Many women have exactly the same hang-up in public restrooms. Isn't it interesting that insecurity can make a person unable to naturally do what is perfectly natural?

INSECURITY CAN BE A RELENTLESS ROBBER.

I have had so many foolish situations due to insecurity. Insecurity led me to make bad choices sexually and relationally, bad choices with food and in how I've dressed. But the greatest regret I have is that insecurity has kept me from so many things. It has kept me from instigating friendships that I desperately needed, kept me from pursuing career goals that I know God planted in my heart, and kept me from trying new things that would have been good for me.

One woman described with these moving words how insecurity robs us:

Insecurity makes us settle. Insecurity makes us distracted. Insecurity robs our confidence in our rich inheritance from God. Insecurity makes us put our gifts on a shelf to gather demonic dust. Insecurity disturbs our sleep. Insecurity derails our life.

The next and final story got me. I won't bother giving it a label. It speaks for itself.

My father left my mom when she was

pregnant with me. He only came to visit my sister and me two or three times a year. When he came, I had a strong need to hold his hand . . . and I held it and held it and held it. He would take us out for dinner, and I remember holding that hand and thinking to myself, *Look, look everybody! This is my daddy!* I was very insecure in my relationship with this stranger/father of mine. I'm thirty-eight years old, and this is still one of my strongest childhood memories. But praise God I've got an Abba Father who is no stranger to me at all. Not only does He hold my hand, but at times He carries me. He never leaves, and I'm definitely not insecure in my relationship with Him. But I must say, I still have that childlike longing to say to the world, "Look, look everybody! *This* is *my daddy!*"

What might surprise you is to know that God, too, delights in being able to say, "Look, look, everybody! This is My child!" Yep. Even after all the foolishness. David, a veritable emotional volcano constantly threatening to erupt and a man after God's own heart who, incidentally, also made a

fool of himself, inscribed these words on a
scroll:

> As a father has compassion on his chil-
> dren, so the LORD has compassion on
> those who fear him; for he knows how
> we are formed.
>
> PSALM 103:13–14

God Himself formed human emotions. He
knows how easily the heart can be broken.
The mind can be marred. He knows life
hurts . . . because people hurt . . . and then
hurt people. He also knows the resilience
with which He made us and the innate
capacity within each one of us to be restored. Remade. He knows we are capable
of loving even when we feel unloved because
He loves us enough to cover those who
don't. He knows we are not nearly as fragile
as we think we are, but we will act like who
we believe ourselves to be. He knows we
have the capacity to be astoundingly extraordinary, and not just in spite of where
we've been, but *because* of it.

God knows we're insecure. But we do not
need to be. And He will not leave well
enough alone. He has enough security for
both of us, and for those of us who call
Christ Savior, He slipped His own secure

Spirit within our simple jars of clay. It is in you to be secure, dear one. Do you hear what I'm saying to you? You have it in you.

Jesus is not ashamed to call them brothers.

HEBREWS 2:11

Or sisters.

And again He says, "Here am I, and the children the Lord has given me" (Isaiah 8:18).

Look, look everybody!

CHAPTER 8
A BEAUTIFUL PRIZE
CALLED DIGNITY

It's time we got our dignity back. Even if you're among the few who managed not to see yourself in the mirror of the last chapter, the fact that you're still reading this book suggests that insecurity has at least taken some kind of toll on you. After considerable research and a half century of experience, I've come to the conclusion that one of insecurity's biggest disservices is the pure loss of dignity. Follow me here for a minute.

When we allow a root of insecurity to reside within us and we don't let God deal dramatically with it, we will either

give way to it continually or
try to stifle it.

If (a) is the case, let me just spit this out lest we waste valuable time: you're a walking mess. A veritable train wreck. Don't feel condemned if that's you right now. I've certainly spent some very unpleasant seasons there myself. Persevere through this journey, and if you're willing, you will find tremendous relief.

If (b) is the case, you live at constant risk of your stifled insecurities getting triggered. This is exactly where I've lived most of my life. I go along successfully, knowing this unhealthy part of me is still present but currently dormant, then something happens to jar it, and in a second flat, it shoots from a root into Jack's bean stalk. That "something" that happens is what we're calling a trigger. Let's look at a few examples, big and small, keeping in mind that what triggers one person to a rush of insecurity may not affect another at all.

Your boss calls you into his office and shuts the door behind you.

You get an offhanded comment from a person who has a teeny stench of superiority about her/him.

Out of the corner of your eye, you catch your man looking at another woman. Maybe she's a stranger. Maybe she's your friend.

Your mom gets that disapproving look on her face over how you parent her grandchildren.

You get an e-mail from somebody you expected to hear from ages ago, and it sounds forced. Or you get a three-line response to an e-mail that took you a solid hour to write.

Somebody makes a presentation in class right before yours. And it's fabulous.

The guy you used to date walks into your church with a gorgeous girl.

You met someone you really admire and said something stupid.

Your guy has seemed distracted and disinterested for a solid week. You get that feeling in your gut that something's up, but you don't know what it is.

Your best friend of five years introduces you to a new friend from work. They laugh about people you don't know and talk over dinner like you're not there.

You have a new haircut. And it's hideous.

Your husband's on a business trip, and you can't get ahold of him.

You poured out your heart to someone and she/he didn't get it. You're pretty sure you told the person way too much.

You finally mustered the courage to reconcile with a friend after a hurtful fissure in the relationship. You can tell within thirty seconds that she doesn't feel the same way. In fact, she acts like the whole thing never even bothered her.

Triggers. Sometimes we don't bite the bait. Other times we do. On occasion we're able to get our game on instantly and not let our insecurity put on a show. Far too often, however, in that sudden, unwanted rush of unhealthy emotion, good sense and sound thinking temporarily fly out the window and head for the nearest hornets' nest. I don't know about you, but there have been times when I've totally embarrassed myself by saying something or acting some way that instantly exposed my fears and uncertainties. Trust me on this one: no matter how big a fool we make of ourselves on the outside, we feel like a bigger one on the inside. Even if what I've done or said wasn't a big deal to another person, I inevitably feel like an idiot. Even if I didn't say a word and completely kept my cool, I worry that my expression gave me away. Am I alone here, or do I have some company?

This chain reaction is not just about feeling foolish. It has a much greater spiritual and emotional implication than that. Insecurity is about losing our God-given dignity.

The enemy of our souls loves that. He knows that people who don't value themselves won't think they deserve any dignity. He knows that only the person who really believes God will insist on having her dignity back. Our enemy is hoping we'll get caught in a pitiful cycle of reacting to a sudden rush of insecurity with foolishness, feeling even more insecure, acting even more foolish, and then feeling vastly more insecure. He wants us to keep digging ourselves deeper and deeper into a hole until we feel completely stuck in this miserable corkscrew of self-hatred.

Listen carefully to me: we can begin to break this cycle *this very day.* Healing something as innate as chronic insecurity takes a little time as God helps us to see where we're broken and why. We can start recognizing triggers and responding to them differently today, however. I did say *today.* The cycle begins to break when even though we may still *feel* insecure, we make a very deliberate choice to not act on that feeling.

This isn't about getting your game on. It's about responding in a whole new way on the basis of a developing belief system that is making its way into our heads but is still en route to our hearts. Stay with me over the next couple of chapters, and I'll explain how these new responses work. I've been practicing them myself for the last several months, and I am astonished by how much progress I'm experiencing.

Those of us who have battled insecurity for years tend to have a couple of repetitive reactions to a trigger. In other words, we all have our patterns. Do any of the following look familiar?

Some get really defensive or display a false arrogance.

Some binge.

Some immediately retreat and withdraw.

Some drink. Or grab some medication to numb the feeling. (I'm not talking here about cases where medication may be appropriately prescribed by a good, solid physician. I'm talking about unhealthy and destructive coping mechanisms for sudden bouts of insecurity.)

Some shout and go into a rage.

Some subject their loved ones to excruciating interrogations.

Some grow completely cold and become punishing.

Some cry hysterically and beg for acceptance and love.

Some turn to compulsive self-gratification: pornography, danger, self-mutilation.

The list could go on and on, but as different as the reactions are, they all have one thing in common: they make you feel worse. More insecure. More prone to a bad reaction the next time. By the time a pattern is well established, you not only feel insecure and foolish, you also feel like a failure. After all, you keep doing the same thing again and again — with the same results. *Maybe,* you reason, *you're even crazy.* You need to know that a whole lot of people — including yours truly — have felt exactly like you are feeling, and some have experienced the exhilaration of overcoming it.

Over the course of the last year or so as God has graciously pinpointed this area of my life for healing, I've come to some stark revelations about the toll of my insecurity. I am convinced now that virtually every destructive behavior and addiction I battled off and on for years was rooted in my (well-earned) insecurity. Not only was I abused, I was also raised in a home where I constantly wondered if my parents loved each other. I was an emotional wreck even as a young child, fearful and tearful. I developed the disturbing impression, whether or not it was accurate, that no one was emotionally healthy enough to carry the heavy psychological load of us five children. By the time I reached early adolescence, those impressions gave way to new and dangerous "freedoms."

While the cats were distracted, the mice were destructive. I was crawling out of the bedroom window with my older sister when I should have still been playing with dolls.

As God took me through the journey that became the Bible study *Breaking Free,* He taught me to look for a common denominator among the things that triggered my destructive habits. Even then I came up with insecurity as the dominant answer. Christ performed a miracle on my heart and my mind through His Word and brought a decisive end to some behaviors and addictive tendencies I had battled almost all my life. It wasn't until the last few years though that I realized we had somehow never gotten all the way down to the deepest root of all: my persisting insecurity. Sometimes you have to shove all the surface stuff to the side in order to see what's underneath. Keep in mind that it took me a while to identify my ongoing problem because it only reared its head in certain select areas of my life. I was completely secure in others. Finally, those select areas caused me enough misery to make this pivotal God-fed decision: *I don't have to live this way anymore.*

You see, I had an advantage. I already knew Jesus could set a person free from absolutely anything. Insecurity did not have the right to be my exception, even if it had been with me from toddlerhood. Though I was no longer reacting to insecurity the way the enemy wanted me to, I had not yet begun to react in the way that God wanted me to. All too often, insecurity still left me feeling overexposed, foolish, and as if I had somehow lost my dignity.

Okay, Lord, so how do we begin? How are we going to attack this thing?

I've long since learned that God uses truth to set a person free, and since I was willing to be truthful about my own condition, I knew that God's truth was going to come to me next — probably in the form of Scripture. The only question was which one He would use.

She is clothed with strength and dignity.

No, He didn't say it out loud. This verse came to me from out of the blue, from the recesses of my memory, blinking like a red neon "Vacancy" sign. Significantly, this is a description drawn from the portrait of Proverbs' "woman of valor." You've probably more commonly heard her called "the virtuous woman" or "the woman of noble character." I wholeheartedly want to be a virtuous woman and possess noble character, but in reality, the Hebrew term is most often used to convey valor. In fact, the same word is translated "mighty" in God's reference to Gideon in Judges 6:12.

The LORD is with you, mighty warrior.

Why must it be translated differently in Proverbs 31 just because she was a woman? Is it because it doesn't take as much courage to be a woman as it takes to be a man? I don't know what kind of courage it took thousands of years ago, but I know how courageous women need to be today. Even in the context of this woman's rich role in the family, can't the home be a fierce battlefield too? *Word Biblical Commentary* translates this word using its most common meaning:

A woman of valor, who can find? Her value is beyond rubies.[11]

And right there in the portrait of this courageous, effective woman, we find the words

206

that scrolled through my head at the Holy Spirit's bidding: *She is clothed with strength and dignity.* I repeated the words over and over, then said them aloud, pausing this time with each word.

SHE. IS. CLOTHED. WITH. STRENGTH. AND. DIGNITY.

I stopped dead in my tracks on the word *dignity.* Weeks prior, God had already brought me to the conclusion that part of any woman's healing from insecurity inevitably involves reclaiming her God-given dignity. I had not thought, however, that the process could be found in this verse. It was a passage that had never really spoken to me before. But I'd never stopped long enough to really consider the implications of it. With your indulgence, I'd like to unpack the verse in hopes that you, too, will see why it is significant in our journey.

She . . .

Scripture's strong leaning toward male gender references never has bothered me. For instance, when the Bible refers to all of us who believe in Christ as the "sons of God," I'm perfectly at home with the generalization including females as well as males.

Anyway, the way I see it, we women get a big turn on the reference to believers as "the bride of Christ." Still, when a superbly rich verse with a refreshingly positive spin on it speaks of a "she," I bask in it like a hot bubble bath. That God would highlight this passage for our decidedly female journey was tremendously touching to me. His Word is never beyond our reach, but sometimes He seems to go out of His way to set it squarely in the palm of our hands.

. . . Is Clothed . . .
The word picture sketched by the reference of clothing speaks volumes. I don't know about you, but if I had to nail down the most common feeling I get when I've let my insecurity surface, it is the sense of being overexposed. I'm comfortable with the unhindered gaze of God on vulnerable places in my soul because I've come to trust Him so much and know how deeply He loves and accepts me. I'm not crazy about human eyes having that same kind of access, however. Obviously, part of that is my own pride. We'll deal with that issue soon enough. I have some broken, malformed areas deep down inside of me that I'd just as soon only allow God to see — at least until I receive a little healing. Make sense?

Someone might reason that any semblance of hiding is unhealthy, but I'm not so sure about that. Our first reaction when we have a wound is to cover it with our hand. It is only when someone we trust comes to us with a bandage that we're willing to take our hand away and let that person see it. And even then, the first step toward healing is to clean and *dress* the wound.

I have come to a place where I'm willing to be transparent with my insecurity, but I find great relief that human eyes have to see it through the filter — the clothing — of my God-given strength and dignity. I don't have to stand before you or anybody else in total emotional nakedness. I have a scriptural covering that gives me the courage to expose my most personal self. That's the only thing that makes the disclosure this book requires bearable for me. When you and I are triggered to expose the most vulnerable, broken parts of ourselves through a rush of insecurity, we can train ourselves to immediately recite this truth to our souls: "It's okay. I'm completely clothed." And oddly, that very thought all by itself begins the healing. We are not nearly as likely to react with the same level of insecurity when we remember how well covered we are by God. I so hope that makes sense to you, because it resonates so strongly with me that I could cry.

. . . With Strength . . .

Proverbs 31:25 tells us this "woman of valor" is clothed by two specific articles that become the perfect pair. The first is strength, and it has a tremendous bearing on our journey. Simply put, nothing makes a woman feel weaker than insecurity. When a wave of it hits us, don't we despise ourselves for not being able to handle the trigger better? Even if we didn't give our weakness away to the person nearest us, aren't we still painfully aware that insecurity got to us — *again?* Doesn't it have the most uncanny way of making us feel like wimps? Surely somebody else has said to herself the same thing I have: *I know better than this. I know this situation doesn't have the power to define or diminish me. Why on earth do I let it?* Because it makes me feel weak. And a little defenseless. And blast it, I'm not.

What would happen if, in the moment you feel hit by that miserable wave, you remind yourself emphatically that you are a God-clothed woman of valor and you have the privilege to wear divine strength like a garment? Let's not kid ourselves here. You and I are women. Nobody knows better than we

210

do that what we wear dramatically influences how we feel. When Scripture tells us to "put off your old self . . . and to put on the new self," it's inviting us to think in terms of taking off and putting on clothing (Ephesians 4:22, 24). We are all probably familiar with the process of standing in front of the closet, mulling over what to wear, and then changing two or three times before we head to work or church. Romans 13:14 tells us what frock we need to choose if we want to be successful: "Clothe yourselves with the Lord Jesus Christ." There is nothing weak about Him. Pure, unadulterated power resting on our very shoulders.

Oh, beloved, you are so much stronger than you give yourself credit for. If you are in Christ, you have divine power. In your gravest weakness, His strength is perfected. Sometimes it's imperative for a woman to give a good second look to what she's wearing out the door that day. If Christ is your Savior, sister, you are completely covered by a cloak of strength. But that's not all. You are clothed with strength. . . .

. . . And Dignity
Scripture doesn't say a woman of valor is clothed with strength and *masculinity*. It doesn't say she is clothed with strength and

211

inaccessibility. It doesn't say she is clothed with strength and *no humility.* It says she is clothed with strength and dignity. This is the perfect time to point out that the woman of valor painted in Proverbs 31 happens to be a really terrific wife. The word translated "wife" in most versions of Proverbs 31:10 (as in the New International Version: "A wife of noble character who can find?") is a word that also simply means "woman." The word could refer to one who is single as easily as one who has a husband. In the context of Proverbs 31:10–31, the woman was married, and therefore, the translation as "wife" instead of "woman" works well. I'll tell you why I'm making an issue out of it.

If we think that the means to security around men is our superiority, we're headed for a rude awakening. If we have to get mad at men in order to feel better about being women, we are no different than the feminists who erupted out of the sixties. Some women think that they can't be biblical wives *and* maintain their dignity too. To those women I say this: we don't have to hate ourselves to love a man or hate a man to love ourselves.

If she's got her head on straight and understands how to apply the biblical concepts correctly, a married woman who claims her dignity back is far more of a prize to her man than the one who doesn't. A marriage is never benefited by either partner's lack of dignity. In Proverbs 31:23, the fact that her husband was "respected at the city gate" wasn't in spite of the fact that his wife was clothed in strength and dignity, but at least in part because of it.

Pride is dignity's counterfeit. Never lose sight of that. We don't forfeit our humility in order to get over insecurity. That brings us to an important question: what exactly *is* dignity? The same Hebrew term translated "dignity" in the passage about the woman of valor's apparel is found in sublime words written by the psalmist to his Creator. Revel in the context.

When I consider your heavens, the work of your fingers, the moon and the stars, which you have set in place, what is man that you are mindful of him, the son of man that you care for him? You made him a little lower than the heavenly beings and crowned him with glory and honor.

PSALM 8:3–5

Here the word is translated "honor" in English instead of "dignity," but it is derived

213

from the same Hebrew term[12] and holds the identical meaning. We can insert our key word without damaging the meaning of the verse one iota:

> You made him a little lower than the heavenly beings and crowned him with glory and [dignity].

We have dignity precisely because God Himself gave it to us, His prized creation. You and I, along with every other human being on the planet, possess dignity because God Himself has it and He created us in His image. (The word is elsewhere translated as "splendor" in reference to Him.) God didn't just confer dignity to us. According to Psalm 8:5, He *crowned* us with it. We are wise to note that all people have God-given dignity even if they don't yet have eternal life through Jesus Christ.

To possess dignity is to be worthy of respect. Worthy of high esteem. Absorb this: you are worthy of respect. So am I. No matter how foolish insecurity has tried to make us feel, we have the right to dignity because God Himself gave it to us. If we really believed this truth, we wouldn't have to mask our insecurity with pride. If we knew who we were and what God has conferred upon us, what everybody else thought of us would grow less and less significant.

One last thing as we close this chapter. Notice that God didn't put this honor/dignity in our hands. He put it on our heads. He wrapped it as a crown right around our minds, just where we need it most. Our possession of dignity is not always something we feel. It's got to be something we know. Something we emphatically claim.

A few days ago I watched a debate on public television involving Dr. Deepak Chopra. I've thought and thought about the irony of something he said: "All belief is a cover-up for insecurity."

Quite the contrary, sir. All insecurity is a cover-up for unbelief.

She is clothed with strength and dignity.

Believe it, sister.

CHAPTER 9
A TIME AND PLACE TO HEAL

I don't have a scrap of interest in someone just reading this book. My determined goal and lofty hope is that every reader will find herself being loosed from the grip of insecurity, chapter by chapter. We've talked about how much we need our dignity back, but if the only thing we do is talk about it, we might be more informed, but we are no less insecure. To stir the pot we're drowning in doesn't do anything but intensify the under-current and draw us further down. In this book, we're going to do infinitely more than accrue information. We're about to make a soulful petition that we can date, document, and return to for years to come.

In the next few pages, we're going to present a pointed request to God, asking Him to help us reclaim our dignity and to prime our souls for security. Then we're going to actively and deliberately receive what He gives to us. If this kind of approach is new to you, don't freak out on me. I've purposely taken the guesswork out of the process and worded the concepts in ways that should resonate regardless of your background. Anyway, what do you have to lose but a little insecurity and indignity?

We're not waiting until the end of the book to do this because we need our God-given dignity if we ever hope to be empowered to make the decisions, exercise the reactions, and use the tools we'll discuss in the remaining chapters. We need something to happen *now* so we can be successful then. The beauty of having God in the picture is that we're not limited to learning a few helpful lessons that might lend occasional insight. We get to ask for a supernatural act of God Himself. We get to draw from the bottomless sea of divine strength. Even if you know very little about what the Bible says, I want you to lock your gaze upon these two verses and grasp their bearing on our journey.

This is the confidence we have in approaching God: that if we ask anything according to his will, he hears us. And if we know that he hears us — whatever we ask — we know that we have what we asked of him.

Hear this at a yell: it is God's will for you to have your dignity and security restored. You don't need to wrestle with this one. You don't need to read six more books. You don't need to ponder the subject matter until your next big disaster. This one is cut and dry. There are plenty of times when the precise will of God on a matter seems legitimately unclear. You may not know whether He's leading you to change jobs, marry a certain guy, or relocate, for instance, but other questions are answered before we ask them. After twenty-five years of study, if I know Genesis from Revelation, I can promise you that God wills for us to walk out the depth and breadth of our lives with dignity and security. Neither God nor you have anything to gain by your persistent insecurity.

When it comes to dignity and security, we have a golden opportunity to know in advance that we are praying the will of God for our lives. And we need to cash in that request post-haste. We can count on the answer being as sure as the appeal. In fact, if you're willing to exercise the kind of boldness that excites the heart of God, you can

218

go right ahead and thank Him in advance because you know that what you've asked is as good as done. Sometimes we see or sense the evidence immediately. Other times God lets it amass bit by bit.

So here's what I'm asking you to do. Find a private place where you can be undisturbed and undistracted for at least half an hour. If you can take a little longer to process the emotions with the meditations, the healing will be more substantial. Some of you may even have the means to get away overnight and have a retreat of sorts with God. That would be fantastic, but don't let complicated arrangements keep you from accomplishing the goal. Better to take that half hour now and get it done! Whatever block of time you choose, make a determined choice to let everything else go for that segment. Rest assured, what you are doing alone with God during those moments will also benefit every other relationship and circumstance in your life. Set all other priorities aside for a while so that a healthier soul can pick them back up.

Get in a comfortable posture before God, someplace where you can sit, kneel, or even lie facedown. Don't get antsy. We're not getting all mystical here. We're simply being mindful. You can find examples throughout

Scripture where people took on postures of prayer that reflected their sincerity. I want you to fully engage. Count on the absolute certainty that God will hear you and meet with you through the power of His Spirit.

When you've set aside your time, place, and posture, begin the prayer guide that follows. Read it slowly, thoughtfully, and *out loud* as if it were rising spontaneously from your own heart. This guide has not been written hastily or randomly. I've never before felt the leadership of God to put anything like this prayer journey in a book or a study. I am convinced it was His idea for this particular message, and if it was, I know He intends to make good use of it. God is incapable of wasting our time. I've asked Him to equip me with the supernatural wisdom and insight to compose a prayer that will receive His resounding "Yes!" And I have no other choice but to trust that He has answered my earnest request.

As a concept resonates, simply pray it to God with honesty from the depths of your heart. The only thing you have to do to make this petition your own is to *mean it.* When I word something that is different from how you feel or what you've experienced, take over that portion with your own words and record what you've said in the margin. You will see that I have given you space at various points in the prayer journey to finish sentences for yourself. Documenting and personalizing this experience will be the lifeblood of your journey. You will be able to reflect on this process for years to come, read back over the words, and remember where your release began. You will also be able to return to this guide and pray through it again when insecurity sneaks back up on you — and invariably, it will.

That said, pray on, dear one, and let God have complete access to your soul as you do.

Dear God,
I come to You this moment because I need some things only You can give me. I need restoration, Lord. I need my dignity back. You alone know what insecurity has cost me, what trouble — even torment — it has caused me. You are intimately acquainted with every time it's made a fool of me. You know how hard I've fought to play the game, but You also know that in the aftermath I've been defeated. I'm sick of faking. I'm sick of sulking. I desperately need and want to be delivered from my chronic insecurity. I am ready to discover what it means to be truly secure. I am will-

ing to do whatever it takes to be free and to allow You to do through me what I cannot do for myself. You are the all-powerful, all-knowing Maker of heaven and earth and the grand Weaver of every human soul. You alone know how we are made and who we're meant to be. I'm not asking for anything You're not willing to give me. You have not shortchanged me. I have shortchanged myself and allowed my culture to sell me short.

You know the way I'm formed. You know what motivates me. You know what shuts me down. You know how driven I am by fear and how exhausted I am from surrendering to it. Lord, in the most hidden places, I am so afraid that . . .

_____

_____

_____

Deliver me, Lord. You have not given me a spirit of fear but of power, love, and a sound mind. That's what Scripture says. I claim each of those priceless traits as mine this day. Your desire is for me to be free of every unhealthy motivation. Reveal any place they reside uncontested in me, and supply the courage I need to refuse to do their bidding. You have searched the deepest recesses of my heart and mind. I don't need to hide anything from You or act stronger or more together than I am. Help me to come before You with complete transparency, and grant me a supernatural confidence that I am safe with You and loved by You. I don't have to muster feelings I don't possess or hang my head in defeat and shame. Because of Your grace, I can come to You just as I am. This is the way I would describe myself to You right now:

_____

_____

_____

But Lord, You know me better than I know myself. You know why I think like I do and why I feel like I do. You know my every thought. My every disappointment. You know every ugly or ridiculous thing I've ever said or done out of insecurity. You see every fissure in my soul, and You look beyond the point of my failure to the depth of my need. As You reveal Yourself to me, I ask that You also mercifully reveal myself to me. Grant me insight into patterns I've developed, and give me answers that bring healing. Make me wholly unafraid of anything that I might see in myself in the light You provide. Help me to trust that You only shed light where You're willing to heal.

God, You know the complexities of my soul and that most of the time I can't even figure myself out. You know how I swing like a dizzy pendulum between self-loathing and self-exaltation. As I begin this prayer of restoration, I ask You, Lord, to help me take responsibility for the insecurity that is my own doing. My own fault. My own sin. I am painfully aware that I've created some of my own misery. I have tried to make a god of myself too many times, and it hasn't worked. It will never work. In calling me to this time of confession, Your desire is my freedom, not my self-condemnation, so with confidence, I welcome the one and reject the other. With these things in mind, hear my confessions:

_____

_____

_____

Please forgive me for my self-worship. For my relentless pursuit of control and for my futile attempts at doing Your job. Forgive me for my foolish pride. Forgive me for nursing my ego until it grows so fat that everything touching it bruises it. Forgive me for my miserable self-absorption. Forgive me for the jealousy and covetousness that feed my insecurity. Forgive me for turning too many things into competitions. For being so fixated on what I don't have that I leave the gifts You've given me undeveloped and much less effective than You intended them to be. Forgive me for thinking pitifully little of the person You've made me. Forgive me for committing the flagrant sin of despising myself and considering myself inferior to others. Forgive me equally for every time I've sighed with relief at the thought that I might be superior after all.

Forgive me for my unbelief. If I realized how valuable I am, my insatiable need for affirmation would be quieted. Forgive me for being such a perfectionist that I resist doing something good out of fear that it won't be great. Forgive me for the inordinate self-protection that has only managed to imprison me. Forgive me also for . . .

_____

_____

_____

This very moment I receive Your lavish forgiveness and Your complete cleansing and in Your name I release all the shame that has come from self-inflicted insecurity. From now on, Lord, and every day for the rest of my life, heighten my conviction until I'm instantly aware when insecurity is my own making. Help me to recognize any form of pride or unbelief and to refuse it immediately.

Now, Lord, I ask You to pull up the roots of insecurity that were not of my own doing, and usher in healing and restoration. You know every single place where instability has touched my life. You remember details that were long erased from my memory but are still inflicting insecurity. You know what first frightened me into believing that no one and nothing could be trusted and that I'm on my own out here in a very unsafe world. You know the rational origin of every irrational fear. You know where I developed a belief system based on the frailties of man instead of the bedrock of You. You have been with me every moment, even when I felt there was no one to take care of me. I give You my whole heart. Touch every broken and wounded place with Your healing hand.

Lord, empower me to forgive those who

have let me down, failed to protect me, or inflicted injury upon me. Help me to see them as needy, broken people in their own right, and Lord, where there is still life and opportunity, bring redemption to those relationships. Help me to understand the gravity of this juncture: that if I do not seek healing and wholeness, I will instead end up perpetuating the cycle of injury. Break the cycle with me, O Lord. Break the cycle with me.

Lord, come and treat my heart and soul where they have been shattered by loss. No one on earth can esteem the loss of something precious the way You can. You know the pain. You know the unbearable emptiness that can come with loss. You recognize my attempt to fill the void with things that never suffice. You know how my feelings frighten me and how the enemy of my soul would have me believe that I will never be okay. Make a liar out of him, Lord. Do not let him win. Do not let loss win. Be my gain, Lord. Flood my life with purpose and compassion. Be my strength in weakness.

Please do not let me confuse healing with betrayal. Help me to see any place in my life where I'm hanging on to my grief or anger in an attempt to hang on to what

I've lost. Grant me the gift of healthy grief that does not fight the pain or the process of healing. Lord, please help me to see where I have suffered a substantial loss that I've never regarded. Where I lost innocence, grant me integrity. Where I lost a relationship, grant me true intimacy. Where I lost a home, grant me an internal, unshakable sense of belonging. Where I've held someone responsible for my loss, grant me the ability to forgive. Don't stop until You've made a miracle of me.

Lord, help me to learn how to hang on tight to You when my life is rocked by dramatic change. Empower me to trust You and not to panic or fight for control. Help me to stop confusing a change in my circumstances with a change in my security status. You are my security, O God. You are the one sure thing. When everything around me shakes, You are unshakable. Nothing has the propensity to reveal false gods to me like a sudden change in my circumstances. Help me to see them and surrender them instantaneously. Use change to provoke what needs changing in me, Lord, and to increase my appreciation of the only One who is the same yesterday, today, and forever.

Lord, I now ask You to single out everything You entrusted to me as part of my physical and psychological makeup: personal limitations, my appearance, and my God-given disposition. You knew what You were doing when You formed me in my mother's womb. Nothing is without purpose. Nothing has thrown off the plan. Every gift, challenge, and obstacle is meant to shape the specific destiny You ordained for me before time began. Your intent is to make a wonder out of me and show what You can do through me. You mean to increase the praise that comes to You because of my life. You want to defy the odds in order to make Yourself conspicuous in me. Please deliver me from self-pity and a life of excuses and rationalizations. And Lord, where I've otherwise lapsed into self-adoration and self-centeredness instead, help me to recognize my narcissism and no longer tolerate it. Of all things, please don't let it be said that I loved myself too much to fully love anybody else. Please don't let me gain the world but lose my soul.

Father, help me to see where I am overly sensitive and where I put too much pressure on relationships. Help me to see where I insist on making a situation all about me. I really want to change. Help me to quit saying, "This is the way I am," and remind me that I am capable of tremendous transformation with You. Deliver me from insecurity in my relationships. Help me to cease being so easily wounded, but at the same time, keep me from growing hardened. Help me to resign my position as a game player and manipulator without resigning myself to a life of misuse. Help me to realize that it's pointless to demand that others love me more or love me better. Real affection cannot be coerced. I cannot put a human in charge of my security without setting him or her up for certain failure. Help me to stop using a person as my mirror and start seeing myself as You alone see me.

Lord, even in the midst of all these requests, I thank You with my whole heart for working so diligently in my life. Yes, there have been people who have hurt me and have done a very poor job of taking Your place, but there have also been people who have shown me glimpses of You. Not perfect people, but genuine people. In particular, I thank You for . . .

_____

_____

_____

I thank You for all You have done to get me to this place and for the plan You have ahead for me. I come now, Lord, to the apex of my petition: please restore to my soul all that insecurity has stolen from me. Overturn every single thing the enemy meant for evil into something good. Perform a miracle on me, Lord. Cover me with Your trustworthy hand. Clothe me with strength and dignity. Transform what drives me. Quell what triggers me. Make me a courageous woman in this harrowing culture. One who refuses to be reduced and defined by the media. Help me to make conscious decisions about whether or not the cost of what they're selling is worth buying. Give me the discernment to call a lie a lie.

Make me the kind of woman a little girl could follow to dignity and security. I actively and deliberately receive — and vow to keep receiving — everything that I have requested in Your will this day. Let this statement reverberate into every corner of my life and invade the bone marrow of my belief system: Today on _____ [date], I receive my dignity back. No one and nothing can take it from me because You are the One who gave it. Help me to recognize that I've lost my dignity only because I have surrendered it. Empower me to claim it back and hang on to it with all my might. Because of Your mercy, Lord, I am no fool. Only a wise woman shifts her trust to You.

In Jesus' saving and delivering name, Amen.

CHAPTER 10
NEITHER GODS NOR DEVILS

We're now barreling forward into my favorite part of our journey toward wholeness. We're transitioning from the problem to the real, live, doable solutions. Before we can move toward healing, we first need to talk about men, their insecurities, and the role they play in ours. It may seem like we're backtracking a bit, but if you will persevere with me, I promise you will see where we are going.

I thought of you recently as I sat in the waiting room of a prominent surgeon's office. My right knee keeps testifying to all the trouble it's seen. Truth be told, it's been through a lot. I was an eighties aerobics queen at the summit of high impact, and for years I held the time record at my gym on the StairMaster. I've jogged a thousand miles along the way and hiked a hundred more. I have done some hard living on that knee and the one next to it. A hyperactive writer is left to a life of extremes. I'm either sitting dead still or trying to work up a sweat — in jogging shoes or spiked heels.

When I started getting concerned that my kneecap was about to rebel, my intention was to tend to it at a suburban hospital. My buddies would hear nothing of it. In their persuasive estimation, I needed to head to Houston's renowned medical center and see the best orthopedic surgeon in town, who incidentally was also a friend of ours. He's worth it, but his office is at least twenty miles from my part of the city and right off the most congested freeway in the entire area. I'd rather have taken a beating than go to all that extra trouble for one small body part. But once I arrived and saw the Starbucks on the first floor of the high-rise, I rested in God's perfect will. I pushed the elevator button for the sixteenth floor, made a split-second ascent, and stepped through the doors to a hopping state-of-the-art sports medicine facility. I hear that many of Houston's professional athletes seek medical treatment here, but the best I could tell, it was mostly me and the University of Houston football team. I felt a bit awkward, but perhaps it appeared that I was their trainer. Okay, one of their mothers.

Finally a nurse called me back to an

examining room and told me they would need to take X-rays first. "Put these on," she said and kindly pitched me a one-size-fits-all pair of bright blue paper shorts with an elastic band, turned on her heels, and shut the door. At least a minute passed before I made so much as a twitch. *Do I have to? I mean, is it a rule that you can't get an X-ray without putting these on? Why can't I just roll up my jeans? It's just one knee, for crying out loud.* After a short, slightly annoyed sigh, I dropped my cute brown purse on the floor, picked up the shorts, and commenced getting changed. There, all by myself in the examining room, I got so tickled I could barely balance enough to get my second foot through a leg of the shorts, and trust me when I tell you it was not for lack of room. That was the moment I knew the rumors were true. The Houston Rockets' seven-foot-six-inch shooting star, Yao Ming, had undoubtedly been treated in this office, and I'll tell you something else: these were clearly his shorts.

Every now and then something so discomfiting happens to you that it doesn't matter if no one else sees it. Civilized creatures that we are, we are fully capable of being embarrassed for our own pitiful selves. In moments like these, I have half a mind to wonder if a hidden camera is on me or if my practical-joker friends are thinking they're hilarious again. As I sat on the edge of the examining table waiting for the nurse, I kept crossing and uncrossing my legs, trying to decide which looked less absurd. About the time I decided to go with crossing them and, out of sheer boredom, had begun to swing my top leg in and out like a high-kicker in a chair, she breezed through the door.

"Come this way, Mrs. Moore. Oh, and you'll want to put your shoes back on." No, really, I won't. I'll put them back on, but make no mistake, I won't want to. Yao Ming would not be caught dead wearing heels with these shorts. God must love me too much to let me off the hook from a good humbling, so as you might guess, the X-ray room was occupied and, rather than return me to my room, the nurse seated me squarely in the waiting area . . . with people in it. People, incidentally, who were wearing their real clothes and not paper shorts and high heels. I was so glad I had shaved my legs, but by sheer devotion to the Hippocratic oath, someone should have rushed me by ambulance to a tanning bed.

Then again, maybe people weren't staring at me. Maybe it was my imagination. Maybe a television I could neither see nor hear was an inch over my head, and everyone in the room was fixated on it. First I broke out in a sweat. Then I did what my family tends to do at inappropriate times. I got tickled. The snorting kind of tickled. Then I slipped out my cell phone and tried as inconspicuously as possible to hold it out in front of me and take a picture of myself from the waist down. I knew a few folks who would appreciate receiving it, and they did not disappoint.

I don't care what anyone says or what any store sells, men and women don't wear the same shorts. Not well, anyway, and whoever is responsible for elastic waistbands on paper pants should turn himself in to the authorities. Men and women are equally wonderful, equally eye catching, and equally competent, but in all our equality of value, we are *not* the same. We both have insecurities, but they often don't surface the same way. Take, for instance, a story I recently heard about Abraham Lincoln. A fellow lawyer, Edwin M. Stanton, called him "a gawky, long-armed ape," yet upon becoming president, Lincoln turned around and made Stanton his secretary of war. I'd like to propose to you that Lincoln's wife never would have done that. She more likely would have spent her life savings on an arm reduction and a thorough waxing, then held the man, pardon the pun, at arm's length for the rest of her fitful life. Believe you me, Stanton wouldn't have known the meaning of the word *war* until he ran into that woman in a dark alley.

Women aren't nearly as likely as men to respect someone who insulted them. And yet we brace ourselves constantly for the offense. Knowing I was compiling research on the differences between women's and men's insecurities, one woman offered a near-perfect illustration from the hallowed halls of middle school. In order to keep the story in its cultural context, permit me to leave the wording exactly as she wrote it:

After fifteen years of coaching basketball, for the first time my husband is coaching a team of junior high girls. He has coached a lot of boys' teams and a few young coed teams, but this is our first experience with the "group mind" of teenage girls. At practice yesterday, he called them together as a group to tell them two things. In their nervousness, the girls tried to guess what he was going to tell them. One girl guessed, "We're going to lose!" Another chimed in,

"You're going to tell us we suck."

My husband was baffled. None of the other teams he had ever coached had suffered from such blatant insecurity. He looked at me and laughed. "This is the difference in coaching girls, and I see how you got started!" (I suffer from the insecurity pit.) By the way, the two things he told the girls were that (1) it was okay to be aggressive and (2) they should not be afraid to shoot more.

But don't think for one moment that guys don't have insecurities. I owe a great debt of gratitude to 150 of them who were willing to lend me a little insight through a short survey I posted on my blog. The group was comprised of men — married and single — ranging in age from twenty to seventy. Though I did not request locations, you can almost certainly picture them coming from all over the United States. Because the goal for that particular survey was to gain cultural rather than spiritual insights, I didn't require that people post their religious affiliation or ages, and all comments were posted anonymously. Knowing how few words the average man speaks a day compared to the average woman, I thought I'd get the best responses if I kept the number of questions short and sweet:

1. What are your primary areas of insecurity, and how do they tend to act on you? (In other words, how do you normally act when you're feeling insecure?)
2. What is the most common way you notice insecurity in women?

Some of the answers to the second question will come up in later chapters. For now, let's sit tight on the first one. A handful of the guys claimed not to have any insecurity at all, and three or four of them built pretty convincing cases. One flatly stated, "I am not insecure . . . I just don't understand what there is to be insecure about." Personally, I don't think he's getting out of the house enough, but on the other hand, he honestly may not struggle with a single insecurity nor comprehend why anybody else would. Out of respect, I'll give him the benefit of the doubt.

Most of the men claimed to be in the same general boat we are in, even if their side of the ship is painted a different shade. They were refreshingly open with fears and self-doubts, even in short form, and ultimately gave women a pretty fair shake. You might be relieved to know that many areas of insecurity leap the gender gap and keep company on both continents. A number of the men in the survey grapple with their self-worth and self-image just like many of us do. They also described social and sexual awkwardness, as well as ongoing fears of rejection and scars from past relationships. You can hear pain and uncertainty in their words much like you hear in ours. Listen for yourself as you thumb through their comments:

I want most to be loved even if I am wrong or fail. I fear unforgiveness. So I forgive, knowing at least God will forgive me then. I want only a faithful love. I fear being ignored, abandoned, and abused. So I pay attention to those who are present to love, even in silence. I want a last love, never a first. I fear it is too late for me. So I love those put before me today and look for tomorrow.

I'm very insecure about whether or not my wife is happy. This isn't because of anything she does; I just get more and more convinced every day that she could do so much better than me. She deserves more.

241

I'm most insecure about whether others will love me back if I don't love them well. Deep down, I wonder who will love me back if I don't do more for them than they do for me.

Listen to the throb of fear in this one:

I am thirty-six, and my most common area of insecurity is being worried that my wife is cheating on me. I have actually had this happen a couple of times, and so when I don't hear from my wife when I expect to or sometimes even if she is just out, my mind starts to "What if?" Then I work out how I will react when she finally tells me or I find out for sure. This is crazy, as I trust my wife and have no reason to doubt her — just past baggage rearing its head.

Countless women know exactly what he's talking about. Half the time we don't know if we're discerning something real or making something up. Our similarities go far beyond matters of the heart. Don't think for a second that guys don't care about how they look. Plenty of them fret over their weight, about being out of shape, and about whether or not their mates or members of the opposite sex will find them desirable.

They may be less obvious about their appearance insecurities, but those fears are present and accounted for. We'll let the men speak for themselves:

The biggest area [of my insecurity] would be my over-forty body. I want to look good for my wife and to others, but I got behind on the ole physical fitness routine. . . . For my appearance I started a new diet and workout routine and try clothes that look better.

Are you quick to assume it's just an age thing with men? Think again.

I am twenty-seven years old, and I am most insecure about my height and weight (or at least lack of the physical tone I once had).

Sound familiar? This one might too.

I'm insecure about my weight. I shy away from doing things that other people do, like water sports.

We feel your pain, sir. At one time or another every woman, no matter how young and darling, has glanced at her bloated self in the mirror and thought she'd rather take a sharp stick in the eye than put on her two-piece and go skiing. Then again, men don't just worry about being overweight. They also worry about being underweight:

> I am not generally insecure. I have a wife who often gives me strong affirmations, and I have a secure job despite the economy. We have an amazing marriage that we continue to work on, and we are on the same page on most issues. I'm most insecure about my physical appearance. I am thinner than most and genetically predisposed to stay that way. I tend to wear layers and like that we live in a northern area that has long winters requiring bulkier clothes.

Granted, few women in our culture would scribble excessive thinness in their top-ten list of insecurities, but none would argue that physical appearance is not a huge factor in the insecurity struggle. Here are a couple more to make sure we've hammered down the point. Interestingly, both of them come from thirty-four-year-old husbands.

> I don't think guys are much different than girls these days. My insecurities are that my wife won't always love me — or

find me attractive — that she'll leave me someday. (Though there's zero evidence that that would be the case. We have a great relationship. It's an internal struggle for me.) I wish I was a better lover.

I still struggle with thoughts that if I am the "perfect husband," then she will love me more. Even though I know the truth, Satan uses doubt to make me believe the lack of physical intimacy in our marriage is because I am unattractive, unlovable, and undesirable.

In so many ways, men are just like women. Each gender was created in God's spectacular and multifaceted image. Each of us houses a human soul that craves love, acceptance, and affirmation and fears anonymity and rejection nearly to the panic point. The insecurities mentioned so far from the survey were not at the top of the food chain for what eats a man alive, however. Ask the men in your life, and most of them will come up with the same answer even if they state it a dozen different ways. I tried it just last night when my oldest daughter, Amanda, and her family were at our house. While we chatted in the den after dinner, I asked my son-in-law Curtis if he'd had a chance to look at the men's answers to the two questions I'd posted on insecurity. He's a stellar guy with an uncanny knack for the bottom line, and his input on virtually any subject proves noteworthy. He responded, "No, I haven't stopped long enough to read them yet, but I bet I know what turned out to be the number one insecurity of men." And he was dead on.

Fear of failure.

Failure of what, you ask? Based on the explanations, it could be failure of any kind and of anything. It depends on each man's reference point and what he perceives as valuable in his environment. One respondent represented the broad potential for failure with a fill-in-the-blank:

[My biggest insecurities come from a fear of] not being able to _____.
[In other words:] Failure to deliver on whatever. Failure to . . . provide for my family, protect my family, complete work projects thoroughly and quickly enough, disciple my children, be the spiritual head of my home, show strength without dominance or anger or frustration, love my wife in such a way that she knows it and draws strength from it.

246

Many others conveyed the same broad, sweeping fear that feeds a demoralizing sense of insecurity. Two areas of potential failure floated to the top among the responses. In uncontested first place: failure to provide. The fear was so raw and so real that it stirred up significant compassion in me, shook loose a few preconceptions, and gave me a new appreciation for what men face. Don't get me wrong. I still think women got the short end of the cultural stick in several ways, but our gender is far from alone in facing monumental areas of self-doubt. Listen to this guy's heart:

I worry that I'm not good enough to rise to the top of my field — and that I'll someday be cast aside. So what then? I'm insecure about being able to provide for our family financially. I feel a lot of pressure about money long term. I sometimes feel insignificant — like I was born for something great but that I wasted it and I'll never get there now. I wonder if God gave my resources to somebody else like the parable of the talents.

If the men who answered the questionnaire were even the smallest representation of adult males in North America, the temptation to confuse who they are with what they make is astronomical. Add economic meltdowns, foreclosures, pay cuts, and layoffs to the landscape, and you've got yourself a serious breeding ground for insecurity. The thought occurred to me that the same culture that makes so many women feel inadequate physically makes just as many men feel inadequate financially. Multimillions are spent annually on marketing in our western hemisphere toward one specific goal: to convince us that we don't yet have enough. To have more, we need to make more. To make more, we need to be more. That's some substantial pressure, sister.

Let's rush to state that many women also carry tremendous financial burdens and feel some of the same pressures to provide. This is true of no one more than single moms. While financial insecurity came up often enough in the women's survey I offered, I can't remember a single one saying that her biggest insecurity of all was her fear of failing as a provider. The difference in nuance between basic insecurity about finances (which many women feel) and failure as a provider (which many men feel) may seem subtle, but the internal ramifications could be severe. One feels frightened by it, but the other feels defined by it.

Fear of failing as a provider was the first of two potential failures that floated to the top in the survey with the guys. The second was failure to prove himself a man. At first glance, the two may seem redundant, but the more I thought about it, the more I got the feeling that this one deserved a category all by itself. Without minimizing the minefield of women's insecurities, our gender could stand to have our eyes pried open to the fierce battlefield men occupy in the fight for their own souls. In all these years, I can't remember ever hearing a female say that she feels the need to prove that she's a woman. We tend to consider it a fact that was settled at conception. We may want to prove that we are *desirable* women, *capable* women, *intelligent* women, or even *real* women, but there's still a subtle difference. Men aren't tagging their gender with an adjective. They want to prove to be *men*.

And that's when it really occurred to me. They feel a truckload of pressure to be what we would consider them to already be. Girls become women when they reach a certain age. Boys become men when they attain and conquer. A male doesn't become a man just by growing up. Apparently most guys feel like they have to prove something in order to be men. If they don't, they're just over-age, awkward, acne-faced boys without a hair on their chests. And it's not just about being manly. It's about being what they consider to be a *man.* Maybe that doesn't seem like a big deal to you, but I think it's huge. Whether we're married or single, moms or not, women tend to be more confident (dare I say it?) of their basic womanhood. I didn't say we were more confident *in* our womanhood but *of* our womanhood. There's a difference. Even with the ravages of cancer leaving breastless chests, hairless heads, and total emotional upheaval, most females still tick and tock like women until their time is finally up. They may not feel like *whole* women, *sensual* women, or *happy* women, but underneath that fragile skin they are still woman-to-the-bone.

Men in this society, on the other hand, feel they have to earn their manhood. To make matters more complicated, the ultimate judgment is often left up to one individual's scrutiny: their own father. And God help them both if the father didn't prove his own manhood to his son. His word can become their lifelong bond whether it was affirming or searing. If every person on the planet acknowledges that a man is a man but his own father does not, the fight to earn his stripes is twice as bloody. Needless to say, you and I have a host of other issues with our moms, but oddly we tend to know we are women whether or not they affirm it and give us their blessing. I can't really tell you that my mother relished being a woman, but *I've* loved being one nonetheless. I'm not sure many men could say the same regarding their fathers. As it turns out, perhaps life is as complicated for them as it is for us.

As you read the following comments from five grown men, don't just skim their concise words. Look beneath the expressions to the broader human struggles.

[I am] insecure about my acceptability to other men (not validated by my father much); I struggle with whether I measure up . . . whatever that means (income, athletic prowess, professional standing, academic credentials, etc.). This gets in the way of building healthy friendships with other men of God.

I am twenty-eight years old. The things that I'm most insecure about are usually the things that I'm naturally not good at. Since I'm naturally introverted and quiet, people have a tendency to question my traits as a "strong" man. Since this bothers me most, I tend to get defensive and explain why I acted in that manner and try to prove my actions to the other person.

I am thirty-three years old, and my primary areas of insecurity are the fear of failure (or being viewed in this way), that I will not be viewed as an honorable man due to my actions, and that I will not be viewed as a "man's man." I do not enjoy talking about or dwelling on my insecurities. The way I typically deal with these insecurities is by acting proud and lashing out.

My primary area of insecurity is in being around other men I feel are more apt at being a man than I am, whether it is career, income, social status, or educational background.

I can find myself insecure when I speak with my dad. I feel that I have to justify my decisions and often seek his approval.

So why on earth do we need to know all this about men? Are we supposed to feel sorry for them or something? After all that our culture has put us through as a gender, are we expected to pull out our violins and play a tragic ode to the male race? No, they would probably tell us we could save our pity. But I do think it would do us a world of good to develop some compassion. A dab of understanding. A peek of recognition that they aren't getting off easy in this culture either.

If you and I are going to develop into real, live secure women, it is absolutely imperative that we realign our mentalities toward men. We've got to get it through our thick skulls that men are neither gods nor devils. They are neither to be adored nor abhorred. As you stare at those opposing terms, I ask you to consider your own tendency as I consider mine. Maybe like me you vacillate between the two, but this is the news flash: either extreme — adoration or abhorrence — always betrays the depth of our own insecurity.

Men are human flesh and blood caught up in the conflict between the sacred and the crude, just like we are. They also waver miserably between what they really need and what they think they want. They have been hurt by women just like we have been hurt by men. They have felt overpowered and undervalued by women just like we have by men. They have felt under our spell just like we've felt under theirs. All of us have a human nature that is selfish and depraved, yet by Christ's touch, is also graced with wonder and good. We are fellow sojourners here with feet of clay, and neither man nor woman is immune to broken hearts, chipped minds, and crumbled lives.

And we all, to whatever degree and for whatever reason, battle insecurities. Part of our perception that women are the only ones fraught with them may come from the differences in how they surface in each gender. Thanks to the humble men who responded to the survey, we're about to get a glimpse into the ways they tend to act when they feel insecure. These, from their own mouths:

When I feel insecure, I clam up and turn inward, and depending on the situation, I might be snippy or depressed. Sometimes I pretend like there's no problem at all so she won't see what I'm feeling and thinking.

I find myself turning inward and/or becoming defensive when my insecurities flare up. At the end of the day, once I've dealt with the emotional aspects, I just try to work harder to make those things better, and I try to remind myself that those things really have very little significance on my self-worth.

I get very edgy and sometimes respond more angrily to my family than I should.

I look for people and things that make me feel secure.

My insecurities show up in my relationship with my wife. As I get out of balance and put my expectations on her instead of God, my security of who I am is more fragile when she doesn't react in the way I am expecting. My most common reaction is self-pity.

Anger, frustration, melancholy, fatigue/ exhaustion . . . increased need for solitude (prayer, reflection, decompression). Sometimes a desire to just leave, run, evacuate, escape.

I usually boast in myself or try to make

myself look better than others.

I find myself avoiding eye contact or telling better stories that aren't always truthful in order to gain respect.

I react by withdrawing and waiting for someone to draw me into the conversation, and I often wonder how I am being judged.

As a man, I feel like I ought to know how to do the things that present themselves to me. I usually respond to these feelings by either ignoring the issue altogether or acting as if I know what I'm doing.

I usually am more anxious, easily agitated.

I divide the events of my day into wins and losses, and a series of losses can send me into a mood or grumpy period where I try to run off to a cave and sulk.

Lastly, this one from a single twenty-five-year-old:

I can act out and rebel and try my hardest to do everything opposite of what society expects, or I can isolate myself from . . . family and friends. I'm extremely uncomfortable with change in my environment; I usually put out a standoffish, don't-talk-to-me, don't-mess-with-me vibe. I will go off by myself.

Overwhelmingly, the men used one word to describe what they do when they feel insecure: *withdraw.* If they don't overtly withdraw, they will probably behave in a way, whether consciously or unconsciously, that will make their loved ones withdraw. One way or the other, a man who feels insecure will often force space. (And as my son-in-law interjected, deny that he's doing it.) If quietness doesn't work, excessive irritation, agitation, or anger can usually do the job. We're not talking about mean-spiritedness here. We're talking about human nature. If we'd let it, the concept of withdrawal could explain so much to us. We think we're the only gender that gets eaten alive with insecurity because we don't recognize the opposite gender's signals. Leaving room in our minds for obvious exceptions, let's throw a couple of common tendencies on the table. Generally speaking, men withdraw when they feel insecure — and women cling. Men give off the don't-mess-with-me vibe. Women give off the please-mess-with-me vibe. Hence, from all familiar indications, women assume we're the only ones who ever deal with insecurity. And we're mistaken.

Tucked unassumingly in the folds of Mark's Gospel, you can find a brief and often overlooked encounter that is marvelously baffling. You won't find anything like it in the rest of the Bible from Genesis to Revelation. Take a good look at it:

> [Jesus] came to Bethsaida; and they brought a blind man to Him, and begged Him to touch him. So He took the blind man by the hand and led him out of the town. And when He had spit on his eyes and put His hands on him, He asked him if he saw anything. And he looked up and said, "I see men like trees, walking." Then He put His hands on his eyes again and made him look up. And he was restored and saw everyone clearly.
>
> MARK 8:22–25, NKJV

No, it's not the spit that makes the encounter weird, although if you're not very familiar with Jesus, His method here could admittedly seem bizarre. What puts the interaction in a class by itself is that it suggests a partial healing. In every other Gospel account, and for that matter, in virtually every other Scriptural account, if a physical healing took place, it was complete. The person would ultimately die just like all humans do, but for the time being, the man or woman was completely restored and made whole.

Not this time. The man brought to Jesus in Mark 8 was as blind as a bat. Christ used the saliva from His own mouth as the healing salve. (In terms that are common to us today, you might think of it as Christ slathering the blind man's eyes with His own DNA.) After dousing his eyes, Christ placed His hands on the man. All four Gospels burst at the happy seams with stories of healings, so thus far nothing out of the extraordinary-ordinary of Jesus Christ has happened. Then comes the tricky part. Christ asked the man if he saw anything.

I see men like trees, walking.

Hmmmm. That's not good enough. Christ didn't want to improve the man's vision. He wanted to fix it.

> He put His hands on his eyes again and made him look up. And he was restored and saw everyone clearly.

I doubt that the brightest scholars could tell you for certain what point God intended to make in this encounter or why He rolled it up so tightly in the sacred scroll. One of the most fascinating things about God is that He reserves the right to retain His mystery. Several elements about this scene in Mark 8 make my theological head spin, but I'll tell you one thing that screams at me loudly in terms of our journey. The first result of the encounter between Jesus and the blind man represents exactly what can happen to you and me on an emotional level. We can "see men like trees, walking." Not as fellow human beings. Not as peers on planet Earth. Our female eyes have a strange way of viewing the opposite sex as something more or vastly less than they really are. Nothing would do us more good right this moment than to realize that our vision is impaired and it doesn't have to stay that way.

Blurry vision toward men can develop in a couple of different ways. On one hand, maybe we've elevated them so high in our thinking and given them so much credit for our soul's animation that we can't see their frailties. The notion is not far-fetched, and neither is it necessarily conscious. The only way you might know if this is the case is to take an honest appraisal of your preoccupation with men. Are you wholly unable to imagine being fulfilled without a man in pursuit or one in your clutches? We're particularly vulnerable to this brand of impaired vision if most of the affirmation we've received along the way has come from men. Maybe all your best friends are guys, and truth be told, it's girls you don't trust. If all your hopes are in men and all your dreams are spun around them like silver crowns on kings, you are not seeing clearly. And if the reverse is true and men hang their hopes on women, they're not seeing clearly either. At the end of a disappointing day, we do men a disservice when we refuse to see them as regular people like us, with weaknesses and strengths, self-doubts and second guesses. When our vision is blurred with distorted images, we can let the entire gender grow out of proportion in our romantic imaginations until we've begun to see them, you might say, as trees: towering, mighty, muscular trees.

A few days ago Amanda and I had a conversation about her husband, Curtis, and it keeps churning in my head. It was perfect timing for this chapter. I had just said what a great guy he is and how much respect I have for him. "Honey, it must really be something to have a man who has such a priority relationship with God and is so incredibly devoted to Him and to his own wife and kids." So you'll get the picture, allow me to interject that he's the kind of husband who gets out of bed and goes straight into prayer and Bible study every morning of his life. Seems to me, a woman could be pretty secure with a man like that. My very wise daughter responded with these words: "I am so blessed, Mom. He only gains my respect as time goes on. I've seen him grow like crazy, but it also occurs to me that the devil doesn't want to trip up any man on earth more than a man like Curtis. He's a great guy, but he's flesh and blood just like the rest of us. God has taught me not to put any confidence in the flesh." It was profound. She chooses to see him like the wonderful man he is, so worthy of respect, but she refuses to see him as a mighty, invincible tree, walking.

On the other hand, our vision of men could be even more impaired by disdain. Maybe you've sustained considerable injury from them along the way. Life can set us up

for some pretty devastating disappointments, especially those of us who were told
in an unending stream of bedtime stories,
books, and movies that someday our prince
would come. For some of us, men were
involved in our hardest blows and deepest
heart breaks. Or maybe it was just one man.
Maybe then we shoved him up on a high
hill as the icon of his entire gender and
systematically sought out like individuals to
confirm our suspicions. Once we compiled
enough evidence to convict the lot, perhaps
we bunched them all together until we
could no longer see the forest for the trees.

I see men like trees, walking.

Big, monstrous, ugly, gnarly trees.
Strangely, women who have been seriously
injured by men don't always respond by
loathing them or avoiding them. Perhaps
more often they become emotionally en-
slaved to them. Remember, we don't have
to love something for it to become a god to
us. All we have to do is devote our most
valuable mental attentions to it. In its most
basic essence, worship is simple focus.
Voluntary preoccupation. People bow under
the weight of anger and unforgiveness just
as prostrate as they bow under the weight

of adoration. The same hurts that make some women despise or disrespect men make other women idolize, crave, and obsess over men. Countless women keep searching for a do-over in the deferring hope that something will turn out differently this time. And sometimes it does.

It happened to me with Jesus. Then it happened by the power and plan of Jesus through one man after another who didn't prove to be any more perfect than I was — but who proved to be honorable. Authentic. Worthy of respect. And over time, a touch of healing came to my heart. It was real, all right. But it was only partial. You see, I still placed a little too much of my personal value and status of wholeness into the hands of a few men: my dad, my husband, and probably even my two brothers. Somewhere deep inside, I still believed that I was at their mercy — but none of them could handle that kind of pressure. As long as I saw men as anything above or below what God created them to be, my vision might have improved, but I was not yet restored.

He asked [her] if [she] saw anything. And [she] looked up and said, "I see men like trees, walking." Then He put His hands on [her] eyes again and made [her] look up.

Make no mistake. Christ can use all manner of circumstances, unmet expectations, and disappointments to make us look up. Oh, that we would not fight the touch of that healing hand on our chins, urging us to lift our faces to the sky. We are bereft of clear vision toward man — or woman — until we look up steadfastly at our wise and one and only Savior.

And [she] was restored and saw everyone clearly.

Well, maybe I'm not completely restored, but the Lord and I have gone a mighty long way in the process. And maybe I don't see everyone clearly, but I can tell you that my vision is clearer by a long shot than ever before. Men mostly look like men to me these days. No longer like trees, walking. I don't need to minimize them, feminize them, or idolize them anymore. On a good day when my head is on straight, I can just walk next to them, respect them, and intercede for them as those who need God as desperately as I do.

When you've stared at the face of Christ long enough through the lens of Scripture, you will begin to look around you and see men clearly. No longer like trees, walking. No longer like gods or devils. Just fellow sojourners with God-given dignity — and feet of clay.

CHAPTER 11
EATING FROM
THE WRONG TREE

Never let anybody tell you that sustainable victory in this flesh-and-blood existence is not possible. A secure woman exists inside of every one of us, and she's begging to come out. In this next section, we're going to learn practical ways to bring her to the surface. We want her to stick her soles in our sweet shoes and make herself comfortable in our skin.

Depending on how much you've tied your insecurities to men, some of you may have taken a decisive step forward in the last chapter by recognizing that your vision is badly distorted. You may have realized that if you look *up* at Jesus before you look *out* at men, He will joyfully restore your sight. The eyes of a healthy feminine soul see men as men — inestimably valuable yet very fallible, just like their counterparts. They are not devils to us. They are not gods to us.

In this chapter, we're going to flip those

statements in order to gain a new perspective, one that has equal capacity to curtail our insecurity:

They are not devils to us, and we've got to stop playing the devil with them. They are not gods to us, and we've got to stop playing God with them.

At first I was sorely tempted to skip over the part about playing the devil and go straight to our propensity to play God, but I know better and surely have a better memory than that. I can remember as far back as my teenage years the surge of power that came from messing with a guy's mind. To give you a snapshot of the selfishness involved, I'll put myself out there and make a confession that does not come without shame: much of the time I didn't even want the guy. I just liked to see if he was interested in me. Once I got my answer, the game was over. Just knowing I could have him if I wanted him was enough. If, on the other hand, I realized that I *couldn't* have him, the stakes went up as my self-image spiraled down.

That's not only the mark of a messed-up woman, it's also the mark of an insecure woman. And if she doesn't bother to change, she becomes the devil with a blue dress on. Before somebody trips over her doctrinal skirt, let's be clear that I'm speaking meta-phorically here. Women who have received Christ are sealed by God, inhabited by the Holy Spirit, and can't be possessed by demons. But trust me when I tell you that we can still run their errands.

So how does a woman play the devil with a man? She tries to shake him from his convictions. Perhaps you've been so burned by guys that you are cynical; if so, you could probably use the reminder that plenty of men with strong convictions and deep commitments do exist. Unfortunately, you can also find a host of women who get a kick out of testing those men. I hate to have to tattle on my own gender, but the truth is, some women adore nothing more than unsteadying a steady man. It's that whole Samson and Delilah thing. Left to our basest nature, women love the power of making a strong man weak. If he seems happily married, some want to see if he can be enticed away from his wife. If he seems aloof, some want to see if they can make him reach for the proverbial carrot. And if he's a pastor, some would love to give him a sermon illustration he'll never forget.

There's something about a man of conviction — whether he belongs to us or not — that makes the most dangerous kind of unhealthy women want to break him. It's a sad admission that sometimes women simply aren't satisfied unless they think a man would choose them over God.

Of course, it's the devil who is ultimately scheming to destroy godly men, but he's particularly adept at enlisting female puppets to play his part. A woman may not necessarily be looking for an affair, but whether she realizes it or not, she's definitely looking for a little salve for her excruciating insecurity. Just looking for a little company. Trying to have a little fun. Playing the harmless flirt. But that's when the gates of hell start quaking. Don't kid yourself into thinking that any woman is so secure that she won't go after somebody else's man to boost her ailing ego.

After all, how would she know she's still got it unless she gets him? Ironically, the pursuit is often as much about the woman she's trying to rob as it is about the man. It's her reckless way of proving that she measures up to the woman who currently has him. Perhaps her worst fear is that she doesn't — and she's trying to prove herself wrong at everybody else's expense.

Sometimes the guy stands firm. Sometimes he sees through it and is turned off by it. Other times he tumbles into a full-fledged affair or, perhaps even scarier, a one-time encounter that ends up becoming a "fatal attraction." The second the dust settles, the man realizes he has made the worst mistake of his life and he's now tangled up with somebody who is not going to go away quietly. He wanted a moment. She wanted a man. And she's taking no prisoners. Whether he fell (or jumped) into the affair, a guy can end up losing a wife and family he genuinely adored. Don't misunderstand my sympathies. Of course, he's guilty too, but if we pitch aside the insidious power of seduction, we're missing the magnitude of what has taken place.

This scenario can as easily happen in reverse. Neither sex holds the patent on this one. Seducers and seductresses alike operate out of warped souls, insatiable selfishness, and spiritual brokenness, and they can show up anywhere normal life takes place. Even church. Some people cannot keep destruction to themselves. They spew it everywhere they go.

The last thing we want to do is become paranoid and suspicious, but we could stand to wise up and develop some discernment. Far more important, however, we'd better make dead sure we're not the ones playing the devil. Insecure people have a head start

271

at doing foolish things in order to feel better about themselves. Because I had the makings of a woman who could wreak havoc, maybe I'm on to her more quickly than someone who has the luxury of being naive. When Keith occasionally accompanies me to a women's event, many of the attendees are so intrigued by their teacher's handsome husband that they flock to him like hummingbirds to a red feeder. I'm amused and blessed by the attention he receives because I'm proud of him and I know it's innocent. He's also right there in the open air where things don't get out of hand. Knowing the darker side of my gender, however, I've also had to warn him not to let someone corner him alone or ask for his private counsel. (They're liable to get my private counsel instead, and it won't be pretty.) I love women and have devoted my life to serving God through them, but I'm not nuts enough to trust a woman who can't trust herself. My man's not going to be her trophy if I can help it.

Capitalizing on her sensuality isn't the only way a woman can play the devil with a man and try to shake him from his convictions. It's just the most famous one. The devil wants to challenge men's convictions in any number of areas ranging from work ethics to child rearing to what they do for amusement. If those convictions seem bizarre, out of kilter, or plainly unbiblical, I'm not suggesting a wife or a girlfriend shouldn't question them. They should. But when a woman sweet-talks or badgers a man out of what he holds as a genuine, God-given conviction simply because she finds it inconvenient, she is playing the devil.

By the time a woman gets a hold of a man and makes him less principled than he was when she found him, she's the one who probably could use a dose of conviction. I've seen it with my own eyes a number of times. I'll think something like, *Girlfriend, I know a hundred women who would beg, borrow, or steal to have a man like yours. Why do you constantly tear him down or make fun of him? And when you've accomplished what you were after, will you be happy with what you have left?* Nothing brings out the rebellion in a woman like a man who's trying to be righteous. And vice versa.

Okay, so enough of that. Now you know why I was tempted to skip that part. Maybe you would never dream of playing the devil to a man, and you don't hang out with those who do. On the other hand, maybe the idea of playing God to a man has a decidedly greater appeal to you, just like it does to

273

me. Now we're talking. Women who struggle with insecurity are particularly taken with two divine attributes: omnipotence and omniscience.

Let's give omnipotence a shot first. The word means all (*omni*) powerful (*potent*). Needless to say, although humans can't attain total power, knowing that fact hasn't kept us from trying. The most we can successfully achieve is excessive control. Right about now you may be inclined to picture someone you know who is unbearably controlling and battles insecurity.

People who are chronically insecure often have an overwhelming tendency to become control freaks. Upon serious consideration, that inclination makes perfect sense. We feel most secure when our environment is in control, and since no one is able to control it to our satisfaction, we decide we have to do it ourselves. If someone would do it and do it right, we wouldn't have to take over, so it's not really our fault, we reason. It's our responsibility.

At first glance, you may think this shoe doesn't really fit because you don't have a desire to control *everyone* around you. I'm the same way. There are just those few individuals who bring it out in me. Have you ever wondered, *Why them?* I had never connected the dots until preparing for this book, but here's what I discovered: an insecure person's greatest need for control is directed toward those who have the most potential to either threaten her security *or* strengthen it. That is why women choose boyfriends or husbands as the primary candidates for control. These men have the greatest capacity to affect our sense of personal well-being and security, and they pose the biggest threat. Children also have the power to rock a woman's world, so the more insecure a mother is, the more she fights to control her children. By the time a controlling mother's strong-willed child reaches adolescence, it's a family free-for-all. Let's take care not to confuse proper authority and much-needed discipline with excessive control. The former teaches the child to choose certain paths and behave in certain ways. The latter tries to *make* the child.

Controlling relationships go well beyond the front door of our homes, flowing into friendships and workplaces. You can pinpoint your own natural targets by tracing the insecurity tie. Begin by searching for the spots where you either derive the most security or perceive that it's most threatened. That's where you'll be most prone to wield excessive control. If you're like me, that's also where you most often volunteer to fill in for God.

Sometimes our answers may be wrong, but our hearts are right. I believe our greatest challenge as women is to avoid trying to control someone toward what we're genuinely convinced is a better life. The more insecure we are, the more tempting it is because something is in it for us, too. In other words, if my loved one would _____, then I'd be _____. The more blanks you can fill in, the more conditional your security and the more it is associated with flesh and blood. The *If he– then I (If she–then I)* thought process isn't hard to comprehend because by nature, human beings are egocentric. It's natural to have thoughts like this sometimes. But if we let it convince us instead of tempt us, we're liable to develop a God complex. It can start with something as healthy as accountability, but before we know it, we've turned into sheriffs who arrest rather than invest in our loved ones. We hold them up and put them in emotional jail, where everybody gets punished.

There has never been a soul on earth I wanted to control more than Keith Moore. He is my beautiful and unpredictable loose cannon. God has used him more powerfully in my life than anyone on the planet, precisely because he refuses to be managed. If he feels strong-armed into doing something, he suddenly develops a voracious appetite to do the exact opposite. The good side of it is that I can rest assured that Keith has loved me and spent his entire adult life with me because he wanted to and not because anybody told him to. He wouldn't mind me telling you that he has a rebellious root so deep that to pull it up could cause a tremor all over the state of Texas. I've nearly thrown my back out trying.

Honestly, I just wanted him to be happy, and he seemed to have such unnecessary ups and downs. (Does that sound familiar?) I knew what worked for me, and I wanted it to work for him. (Also sound familiar?) The way I saw it, the man had so much potential if he would just do things God's way. But since he wasn't really listening to God, maybe my way was close enough. (Is this getting on your nerves like it's getting on mine?) If he would just have a regular prayer time or memorize a few Scriptures or listen to Christian music or be more jovial or more compliant or less free with his opinions but more talkative about his feelings or more selective about what he watched and more careful about what he ate, he'd be so much happier. Clearly, I needed to take control of the situation and try to shove Keith to his happy place.

I bought men's devotional and inspirational books, but he used them for coasters for his Route 44 cherry limeades from Sonic. I got him so many great CDs that you can hardly get the glove compartment open in his car to put one in his player. I got audiobooks by the actual authors, and he has taken such good care of them that they're still in the cellophane. I purchased enough vitamins and supplements to keep a whole football team healthy, but the bottles still have the safety seals on them. When he complained that he was looking older, I bought him a skin regimen complete with toner and lip balm. At least I know it's there in the bathroom drawer when I run out of my own.

Goodness knows I tried not to nag. I hate people who nag. I tried pep talks that would have won a professional team a national championship. Still nothing. I tried rationale after rationale to no avail. Only when all else failed did I turn ugly. Is it my fault that all else kept failing? Sometimes I resorted to record keeping. I would try to keep score on how long it had been since he had been

278

to church and how many times that day he had said that word or how much time had lapsed since he had opened a bill. No effect whatsoever. In fact, sometimes he just laughed and asked me if I knew how cute I was. Cute? Are you kidding me? You think I'm trying to be *cute?*

I'm much better about it now than I used to be. Now I vacillate somewhere between giving up altogether and giving it one more tiny little try. I live in neither place, but this much has become remarkably clear: we cannot control people. Goodness knows I wish we could, but we can't. It doesn't work. It will never work. And here's the worst part: the insecurity that drove the desire in the first place only deepens with each failure.

Most of my control issues with Keith are fairly benign these days, but that's not the way it always goes. Our attempts to control can take us all sorts of places we never meant to travel. Sometimes we impose ourselves on our controllee, but other times we're invited there. Even dragged there. When was the last time somebody put you in charge of his or her problem? Has anybody besides me ever had an addict make you responsible for keeping him or her away from the substance in question? Ever been in charge of an alcoholic's liquor cabinet?

279

Ever heard the words, "If I could live with you, I'd do so much better" or gotten the feeling that somebody was thinking, *If you're going to tell me what to do, why don't you do it for me?* The misleading part of our pursuit of omnipotence is that the setup actually appears to work for a while, particularly if you're dealing with someone who is passive-aggressive. Eventually that person is going to start kicking out of the confines, however. Sooner or later, all false gods get fired. Or tired.

The tricky part is that God blatantly instructs us in Scripture to help one another, so how do we know when help has morphed into a quest for control? The first clue is when the helper is the one doing all the work. Simultaneously, the one being helped lazily lapses into the mentality of a victim of his or her own weakness and all the while gets to be the center of a strong person's attentions. What a deal.

It's frustrating though, isn't it? Some of us know from personal experience that joy really is possible, that victory really is possible, that freedom really is possible, that meaning really is possible. So why are there so many people who talk a big talk about what they need to do but then won't do what it takes?

Sometimes it's because there's something about unhappiness that is working for them. It could be the attention they're getting or the excuse they're milking. Some won't do what it takes to liberate themselves because their particular form of bondage provides a momentary respite from real life. It took me forty years in the wilderness to realize that at the end of the day, people do what they want to do. You can't make them do something else. You can't force them. You can't change them. You can't deliver them. Only God can. And that's why He's omnipotent and we're not.

We are not in charge. Somewhere along the way, we each have to acknowledge that our loved one is a separate person from us — someone God loves, pursues, and when necessary, chastises. When we try to do God's job, we get in God's way. We are called to cherish, support, and pray for others, but tying our security to them is a lost cause. That knot we keep tightening is no more fair to them than it is to us. Hand that rope over to God. Let Him undo that tangled-up mess and retie your security to Himself. He's the One with all the power.

The second divine attribute that insecure people find most appealing is omniscience: the ability to know it all and see it all. Of course, only God is omniscient, but boy, do we want it — and for good reason. If we're trying to play God, we need an ample dose of omniscience to fire up our omnipotence. We can't control what we don't know, and we can't secure what we can't see. It is dangerous to play God, and the minefield is never more fully loaded than when we covet His omniscience. I'd like to share with you how God opened my eyes to the trap of thinking I had to know everything. Sometimes I learn a divine concept over a stretch of time, study, and experience. Other times I seem to get an instantaneous revelation that nearly takes my breath away. This was one of those times.

It happened just recently. A young woman I've come to know and love came to me with a serious confession. I knew she had been through the wringer over a broken engagement, and the trauma was heightened by her absolute certainty a year earlier that she had found the godly man of her dreams. Over time, however, something had begun to go awry, and several of us began to wonder if they might not be such a perfect match. They were both wonderful people, but perhaps not such a wonderful pair. I had hoped that she was healing somewhat, but from the expression on her face, I could tell that her emotional entanglement with him had only grown tighter. They hadn't been in touch for months, so the intensity of her turmoil was bewildering.

"I've got to tell you something, Beth, so you can hold me accountable, or I don't think I'll ever stop."

"Stop what, sweetheart? Tell me what you're talking about."

And so she did. Apparently while they were dating and then planning their wedding, she had become increasingly convinced that something about her fiancé was not quite what it seemed. He had appeared to be a steadfast young man of faith with strong ministry intentions. A catch if you'd ever find one. However, she constantly caught him ogling other women. At first she thought she was imagining it, but after a while she found it maddening. When she confronted him, he always denied it. In the aftermath of a fight, she would second-guess and condemn herself for being so suspicious and insecure. After all, he was such a great guy. Such a *spiritual* guy. Still, she couldn't shake that feeling. Though she had never caught him red-handed in a single serious infraction, her suspicion spun out of control until the fabric of the relationship began to unravel. He emotionally retreated and came just short of calling her unstable.

As painful as the breakup was, she knew God providentially accomplished what was best for both of them. Even through her tears, she had said to several of us, "This is the right thing. I know it is. I know God stopped it." But alas, trusting His providence wasn't enough. She became obsessed with whether or not her suspicions were founded. She got on his e-mail account and tried to figure out his password. Smart girl that she is, it was only a matter of time until she broke in with a cheer. Thankfully, she did not discover pornography, but she read e-mail after e-mail where he had crossed the boundaries of familiarity with a number of girls. He was a flirt at best and a fraud at worst.

He was not the man she would have wanted to marry, but of course, God had already told her that. Instead of coming to peace with His protective will, she became completely fixated on her ex-fiancé's e-mail account. She got on numerous times a day, reading every piece of correspondence he sent and received and then thought about them all night. She had her proof, but strangely she didn't feel better. Not only did she get angrier by the minute, she also grew less secure. After all, what did those girls have that she didn't? My friend knew that what she was doing was wrong, and she promised herself over and over that this would be the last time. *I'll know all I need to know after this.* Actually, she already knew *more* than she needed to know. Months had passed, and she was now utterly miserable. Her fixation glued her to the very person she needed to forget.

Imagine the quandary. My young friend had a stack of incriminating evidence but could do nothing with it because of the fraudulent way she had attained it. The information was exploding in her head, and she was at her wit's end trying to figure out what to do with what she knew. I listened carefully to her story, and when she finished, something came out of my mouth that I've never said and never thought about before.

"Darling, you have fooled around and eaten from the tree of the knowledge of good and evil."

"What? Beth, what do you mean?"

"I mean you have done what Eve did. You've eaten from the tree of the knowledge of good and evil. You wanted to know what God knew. Think about it!"

Do you remember the story? The serpent used powerfully shrewd and deceptive reasoning to tempt the woman to disregard

285

divine instruction and eat from the one forbidden tree: "God knows that when you eat of it your eyes will be opened, and you will be like God, knowing good and evil" (Genesis 3:5). There you have it. The first human pursuit of omniscience. Eve wanted to know what only God was meant to know. And so did my young friend. The parallel was as plain as day to me.

God had already told her what she needed to know and what her heart and mind could tolerate without self-destruction. But she insisted on knowing something she was wholly incapable of handling. We talked a little more, and then we came up with a plan to help her stay out of the trap of too much information. As I placed my head on the pillow that night, I thought of the times I've done something similar. Times I also insisted on biting into a piece of information that I couldn't swallow after all. It happens every time I beg to know what I end up wishing I never knew.

Surely we've walked together on this journey long enough for you to know that I'm not a proponent of ignorance or denial. The pursuit of knowledge for the edification of soul and community is a priority passion. But that kind of positive result comes from eating from the "tree of life," metaphorically speaking, not from "the tree of the knowledge of good and evil" (Genesis 2:9, 17).

There is an enlightening knowledge that builds up and fortifies the human psyche, but there is also darker knowledge that rips it to shreds. There is *knowing.* And there is *knowing too much.*

I believe those two trees in humanity's first garden were living symbols of these very concepts. One promoted life. The other promoted death. Because God is complete perfection and immutable holiness, He can handle omniscience. He can know all things — good and evil — without responding with sin, weakness, horror, or despair. We, on the other hand, don't have that luxury. Think how many times we've begged someone to tell us something and sworn we could handle it only to flip like a flapjack the second it was out of the person's mouth.

What God initiates, He equips us to handle. This is true even when emotional assimilation requires a process. Have you ever come upon information that was shocking, disheartening, or difficult, yet you somehow found that because God insisted on that discovery, He also provided you with the grace to handle it? Even though the unsolicited information might have caused pain and great conflict, if God initiated the revelation, He had a goal in mind that was steeped in great love. Even if He used a messenger you didn't like, He worked through His sovereignty to open your eyes to something vital. Perhaps God knew that the discovery was necessary for an area of healing or deliverance to take place. Maybe He knew it would shake you from your slumber.

When we scratch and claw to dig information out of the dirt, however, we don't get the same kind of grace that accompanies divine revelation. God graciously forgives, restores, and even resurrects as we bring Him our needs, but the pursuit of omniscience costs us dearly in the meantime.

> You must not eat from the tree of the knowledge of good and evil, for when you eat of it you will surely die.
> GENESIS 2:17

Since the concept is figurative and spiritual in our regard, we don't experience a physical death after eating from that tree, but make no mistake. Something in us does die, and usually it's our security. Let's put a few examples on the table.

We can insist on knowing more about our

mate's past relationships than we end up being able to handle. What is it about women that makes us so intent on knowing the gritty details of our men's histories? I think it's that whole omniscience-omnipotence complex. We feel like we can't control what we don't know. Don't get me wrong. We need to know vital basics like whether or not they've been married or engaged, slept around, been in jail, battled an addiction, had a track record of unfaithfulness, or left a string of shattered hearts. We'd also better be crystal clear on where they stand spiritually. By all means, let's seek to know their hearts inside and out, but must we force ourselves into the closets of their minds as well?

Details like what he did with whom and how can paint vivid murals on the walls of your mind that jump to life every time you close your eyes. Inordinate curiosity can kill more than the cat. We ask until we harass, then one day we're told. Most of the time the information emerging from our persistent, prurient interest proves very harmful. What's most baffling is the cycle of insecurity it causes. We pry because we are insecure, and then we are more insecure because we pried. God is the only one who can know a person's every thought, every motive, every temptation, and every flaw yet still feel good about Himself. If we want to become secure women of God, we must cease asking questions we can't handle the answers to.

We can discover a pornographic Web site our mate has visited and then stay on it. Instead of knowing what we need to know so that we can confront it factually, we insist on going through those images one by one to see exactly what he saw. That, beloved, is eating from "the tree of the knowledge of good and evil." Long after he's sorry (assuming that he is) and the hard drive of the computer has been swept clean, those pictures will still play like broken records on the screens of our minds. God will equip us with the grace to deal with the initial discovery. Indeed, He may have even plotted it in order to bring eventual deliverance. But in order to receive His grace, we must halt with what we need to know rather than moving from "the tree of life" to "the tree of the knowledge of good and evil" and insisting on seeing more than we can handle. God will grant us the grace to heal if we seek Him, but our memories will bear unnecessary scars for years to come.

We can go beyond the bounds of sound doctrine on demonology and open a door to the occult. Once again, God protects what He directs, but when our curiosity takes us beyond a knowledge that edifies and fortifies to a knowledge that exposes and terrifies, we might find that we are in for the psychological and spiritual battle of our lives. Don't kid yourself. There is a very real and deadly demonic world in the unseen realm that we need to stand against, not stand amid. We can crack open a door, but by the time we realize what happened and cry out for help, an avalanche of evil could land in our laps.

How do you know when you're moving from one tree to the other in your pursuit of knowledge? Usually you will be able to feel it. Something inside of you says, *I know enough. I need to stop here.* Because the air around them can get foggy, make sure you're differentiating between the healthy pursuit of knowledge and what I'm calling the human pursuit of omniscience. Reflect for a moment on the young woman who became obsessed with reading her former fiancé's e-mails. Her colossal misstep was seeking knowledge in the dark rather than knowledge in the light. As Ephesians 4:18 says, she became "darkened in [her] understanding" instead of enlightened. She went where she did not belong and acquired what she could not confront. Remember, God had already conveyed that the young man was not the best choice for her. She already knew in her heart what she needed to know. When she insisted on a little slice of omniscience (knowing what God alone needed to know), she ended up with information she could not handle.

On the other hand, many smart husbands and wives leave their e-mail accounts wide open to one another's eyes. Keith can look in my in-box any time, just as I can look in his. None of our correspondence is off limits. Because we have that freedom, we often feel little need to act on it. Knowing that the other has access is enough to spur caution. At our house, we also have full access to Internet histories, and they're often right there on the margin of the screen. That's not an attempt at omniscience. That's just being open and honest.

Healthy access to information is important

in a marriage, but it can be a matter of life and death or safety and peril to our children. Parents would be out of their minds in this sketch of time not to be in their children's personal business. I would not only be all over my daughters' computers, I'd also get ahold of their cell phones. In this culture, making frequent spot checks of texts, pictures, and unfamiliar names and numbers is part of responsible parenting — and you shouldn't be bullied out of it by your children. If I happened on a pornographic site one of my daughters had accessed on a computer, I would react differently than I would if it were my husband. No matter how distasteful, I would likely glance through every image in order to see how far my child had gone and what kind of help might be warranted.

What may be the equivalent of eating from "the tree of the knowledge of good and evil" for a child could be the equivalent of eating from "the tree of life" for the parent if it leads to help, healing, and deliverance.

In matters of explosive information, these are the questions to ask: What is God showing me? Or what am I demanding to be shown?

Playing God is never more dangerous than when we seek to be omniscient. We toy at it every time we attempt to get all the way into somebody's head and credit ourselves for essentially reading his or her mind. All we've really accomplished is a speed-reading of our own skewed minds. A fool sticks her ostrich head in the sand about generalities that would help her understand her man better and closes her mind when he's begging to tell her something he desperately needs her to know. That's acceptance, not omniscience, and even when the disclosure stings, we can receive the grace of God to handle it like big girls. But we try our hands at omniscience every time we corner guys into oversharing too many details about their thought lives, temptations, attractions, and fantasies.

Keith and I somehow have our best conversations in the car, and since we're both road warriors, we get plenty of opportunities to have them. A few days ago while we were on our way home from West Texas, he grew very serious at the wheel and confessed several fears to me that I never realized he had. Both were fears that I could help quiet as his wife. I was so relieved he told me, and I loved him even more for his openness. That kind of free disclosure is the heart of true intimacy. It differs dramatically from drilling into the well of somebody's innermost thoughts, struggles, and imaginations and asking loaded questions we can't handle when they're answered. Guys would have similar difficulty dealing with some of the temptations, doubts, and dreams that run through most women's minds — though they're not as apt to beat that door down. In all fairness, our gender's propensity to want to look inside the hearts and minds of others comes from an admirable desire for true intimacy. This is its dangerous distortion.

From one woman to another, I cannot caution you strongly enough to tread carefully in the turbulent, deep water of another's mind lest you nearly drown. I've talked to too many women who can't get over it and on with it. Their security is slashed drastically, and they take personally and seriously what may have been neither. Unlike God's omnipotence and omniscience, no compulsory correlation exists between human knowledge and power. Our finite minds can insist on attaining far more information than we have power to affect — except through prayer.

For many of you reading this chapter, the warning may have come too late. Perhaps you've already opened Pandora's box, and tucked inside was a bomb that blew your security to bits. Jesus was a carpenter by trade. He can rebuild lives blown sky-high even by our own two hands. He is an artist by essence who can paint over the walls of a mind trafficked by torment. He is everything we need, inside and out, because He sees it all. And, yes, He can handle it.

The healing of the mind requires far more intimacy with Christ than the healing of mere bodies. He rarely snaps His fingers and whitewashes our thoughts because, were it so easy, we'd turn around and open them to destruction again. Instead, He chooses to transform our willing minds one reflection at a time. Start right now. Tell Him what keeps haunting you. Ask Him to grant you His own words to recite the moment you replay those old conversations and images. Then take all that insatiable desire to delve into the unknown and focus it right on His face.

[You] may know the mystery of God, namely, Christ, in whom are hidden all the treasures of wisdom and knowledge.
COLOSSIANS 2:2–3

That, sweet one, is knowledge with power.

CHAPTER 12
THROUGH THE EYES
OF THE GUYS

Remember that men's survey I told you about a couple of chapters ago? We purposely limited that inquiry to two basic questions in order to attract the most participation from men. The first targeted men's individual insecurities and the ways they surface. Their responses became the subject matter of chapter 10 and pried open the door for chapter 11. After asking the men to divulge their own insecurities, the second question turned the focus from their take on themselves to their take on women:

"What is the most common way you notice insecurity in women?"

After reading every syllable of every answer, I have three words to say to you: *they're on to us.* By the time I reached the 150th response, I knew they had us pegged, and frankly, it annoyed me to no end. I'm sure at this point you're probably feeling a little defensive and wondering why I bothered asking them and why we should care what they think. Never mind that they're the other half of the world's population. If you'll put up with a personal story, I'll explain why I sought their perspective.

Keith and I didn't make it to our first anniversary before we needed marriage counseling. Our start possessed all the tranquility of a pair of bottle rockets duct-taped together. By the time we'd been married a month, I had convinced myself that the whole thing was a huge mistake and we should back out just like we'd backed in. About the time my exit strategy was shaping up, I was hanging my head over the toilet, thinking about how sick marriage made me. As we stared at the positive sign on the home pregnancy test, we both nearly dropped dead on our brown-speckled linoleum. It was a classic case of good news and bad news. We were going to have a baby . . . but we were also going to have each other.

On rare occasions, foolish couples do smart things. We headed for professional help as fast as our feet could carry us. At our first appointment, the counselor gave us an assignment to complete before the next week. "I need to hear from both of your hearts. I want each of you to write me a letter telling me why you're here, what you're feeling, and what you don't like about your marriage partner. Tell me everything that's wrong from your perspective. Spit it out, stick the letter in an envelope, seal it, and turn it in to me next week."

So that's exactly what we did. With the green light to rat on one another, we wildly wrote out our grievances and complaints, as if the chance would never pass our way again. We returned the next week, clutching our big secret tells with no small satisfaction.

"Did you each write the letters I requested?"

Smug nods.

"Good. Now, hand them to each other, open them, and read them."

More sophisticated couples would have been on to the scheme the moment the psychologist requested the exercise. We, however, were barely in our twenties and never saw it coming. We had gotten some things off our chests all right, things we meant to say behind one another's backs, not to one another's faces. It was excruciating.

Don't take the story as a recommendation, but the end result accomplished something remarkable for us. We said some things that needed to be said, but in the process, we each looked at the other, saw the pain our harsh words caused, and grieved. At the same time, the confessions revealed things that neither of us could see in ourselves. The only way I could prove Keith wrong was to change.

That, beloved, is the primary reason we need to know how men perceive us and our insecurities. We may not realize the impact our insecurities have on our relationships — or the lack of them. Worse yet, we probably don't have a clue how obvious they are. We think we've got our game on more than we do, which brings us back to my story for a few seconds. As it turned out, Keith and I had not only written about our angry grievances, we had also confessed to our own mistakes and regrets — even without being asked to divulge them. Somehow, the more we got off our chests, the more our hearts were revealed.

The guys who participated in our survey were at no loss for words when it came to describing our insecurities, though their appraisals included far more than critiques. The majority spoke with affirmation and respect toward women, and many owned significant responsibility and regret for fueling the fire of female insecurity. This is an example:

We as men (me included) have failed to assure women they are God's most beautiful creation. A woman's insecurities could be drastically reduced if men would love like Jesus did.

There were a handful of spiteful ones to whom I will offer little space and a recommendation for counseling. My objective is to mention only the comments that hold constructive value. As you read them, you'll notice the beginning of our transition from men-related insecurities to insecurities we have with other women. We will fuse the two for a while and then move decisively to dealing with our own gender.

Overwhelmingly, survey participants noticed that women seemed most insecure in the area of appearance. No contest. Over and over, the men asked questions to this effect: "Why do you have to worry so much about how you look all the time? Why can't you realize how beautiful you are to us?"

Granted, we didn't drum up insecurities about our appearance all by ourselves or out of pride alone. Our culture places such a high premium on looks that we almost can't help but feel the backbreaking pressure. My man is big on looks, and especially at this point in my life, I'm squirming under that microscope. At the same time, the fact that the male respondents wished we weren't so self-conscious and *weak* about our appearance is noteworthy. We'll delve deeper into that element toward the close of the chapter. For now, let's look further at our survey results.

In tandem with our insecurities about appearance, many of the men mentioned our painfully obvious propensity to compare ourselves to other women. They catch us literally sizing each other "up one side and down the other," especially if we feel threatened. I was appalled, not because we compare ourselves to other women, but because men *know* we compare ourselves to other women.

One guy summed it up this way:

Most obvious is when women are around other women; they try to size each other up and look for reasons to not get along rather than to get along. They seem easily intimidated, whether by physical beauty, character status, or whatever makes them feel that the other woman has more going for her, and a barrier goes up.

Annoying, but too often true. Guys no

doubt compare themselves to one another too, but generally speaking, they seem secure enough not to be quite so obvious. Maybe they also limit their self-comparison to someone really intimidating. On the other hand, women tend to do it automatically and even unintentionally. One survey respondent mentioned that he wasn't sure his wife recognized that her habit of changing outfits five times before she walked out the door to Bible study was rooted in insecurity. (A man may try to get into our minds, but he'd be wise indeed to stay out of our closets. He crossed the line there, didn't he?) Then, as if a light came on for him, he wrote:

Maybe that's it! I realize when I am not feeling very secure, but women face insecurity everywhere they go, so perhaps it has become second nature.

He's probably right, but if he is, we need to dump that second nature. If we're in Christ, we already have a second nature that is not remotely insecure. In a few chapters we're going to learn ways we can break the habit of constantly sizing ourselves up against other women.

According to the male respondents in the

survey, another telltale sign that a woman is feeling insecure is incessant talking. You need look no further than the book you hold in your hand for exhibit A. Needless to say, some women clam up when they're hit by a wave of insecurity, but many of us do exactly the opposite. In the words of one of our men, we "babble." When I first read that, I reacted the same way you're probably reacting right now. I wanted one solid hour to give him a piece of my mind. Then again, I suppose that would just prove his point. Simply being aware of the tendency to talk too much is enough to help me exercise some verbal restraint when I feel insecure. That's the only reason I shared it with you. Remember, we're only discussing the comments with constructive value.

The next one reveals not only female insecurity, it also suggests male duplicity. Many men enjoy ogling a woman who is sensually or immodestly dressed, but over and over again, the respondents claimed that guys perceive this as a sign of insecurity. In fact, a twenty-nine-year-old respondent used one lonely word to describe the most common way women demonstrate insecurity:

Cleavage.

Here's another one who says the same

thing with a few additional terms:

> [They show their insecurity by] how they dress; the more skin they show, the more insecure they are.

The criticism is particularly fascinating since we women generally assume that men want us to look sexy. Perhaps many do. But they also think we're a little pathetic. That kind of duplicity — if not hypocrisy — was maddening to me until I realized that men have their own lockers full of trash, just like we do. When we apply what we learned about not seeing men as gods or devils, we understand that men are not one blink healthier than women are emotionally. A person can be on target about something, however, without necessarily being healthy. If what these men say *could* be true, then we would do well to listen to them — regardless of whether they have their own acts together or not. Of course, they would do well to listen to us, too, but we'll leave that to them. And anyway, men are not alone in their duplicity. We fight the same tendency when we strive to control our guys, and then when we finally get them to submit to us like whipped dogs, we think *they're* a little pathetic.

You're probably going to want to hit this next guy with a table lamp, but let's hear him out anyway, keeping in mind that he's twenty-three:

I don't know of any girls who don't act insecure. They are all up on guys, and they sleep with anybody. They look hot, but everybody says stuff about them later. There aren't any girls out there who you would want to marry and be your kids' mom. Sad.

The dude has a severe problem with stereotyping. He obviously isn't getting out enough. Many women have similar sentiments about men. Listen to one guy's frustration:

I hear so many women complain they can't find good men. They're all over the place, but they don't necessarily fit your idealized standard of the tall, strong, good-looking knight on a white horse who is featured in various forms in the overdramatized, unrealistic romance novels so many ladies crave. No wonder we can't please you. I can't even ride a horse!

Let's overlook the romance novel dig unless you habitually read the kind he's insinu-ating. I don't think he's talking about Jane Austen's *Pride and Prejudice* or Shake-speare's *Romeo and Juliet,* although a steady diet of either one could probably skew your relational capacities a bit. I'm pretty sure he's referring to the kind of romance novel that is all lust and zero literature. Let's do each other a favor and not let this guy be right about us. I hate being stereotyped as an airheaded, superficial female. If you insist on a steady diet of books like that, for cry-ing out loud, quit taking them in public because you're giving us all a bad name. I mean that in the nicest way. That said, let's admit that this guy is right about many women who complain that they can't find a good man. That admission will help temper the fact that we just heard a twenty-three-year-old say there are no good women out there. Stereotypes are never fair.

Guys in our survey listed a number of other top-ranking insecurities in women:

irrational jealousies
full-blown emotional episodes (whatever
    could he mean?)
an obsession with what people think
an insatiable need for affirmation

One man suggested that insecure women ask a lot of "Am I?" questions, either directly or indirectly: "Am I beautiful? Am I loved? Am I a good mom?"

In my estimation, the most intriguing part of the whole survey was this: across the board, regardless of age or marital status, the men who responded did not want women to feel insecure. Given the nature of the blog post and the willingness of the participants to help, many of them were clearly terrific guys and maybe even the cream of the crop. Some men relish an insecure woman, but I didn't sense that tendency from a single one of these men. They didn't even like to see insecurity in women when it offered them the upper hand. By the time I had pored over every response, I got the distinct impression that men would rather have a secure woman any day over one they could completely dominate and exploit.

The men seemed resistant to female insecurity both for our sakes and their own. They hated to see us so miserable and openly vulnerable, and they also seemed to find the evidence a little repulsive. Consider the following comment:

As far as female insecurities, no offense,

ladies, but you have us trumped on just about all fronts (and that includes the "front"). Typical, common, widespread insecurities include looks, body shapes, lack of education or perceived intelligence, neediness, and many others. It manifests itself in nagging, self-doubt, self-loathing, seeking approval/validation, and the need for constant reassurance. It gets quite tiring for men who, as we get older, just love *you* for exactly the way you are. Can you not understand that? We are not lying if we tell you we love you, you are beautiful and appealing, and we enjoy being with you immensely. When women's insecurities are vividly displayed to us, it turns us off, frustrates us to no extent, and perplexes us. Get over it!

Whether or not you agree with everything he said, the last portion is definitely worth pondering. Men *are* repelled by open displays of female insecurity. In the long run, it does not make them more tender to us, more careful with us, more loving toward us, or more attached to us. It makes them, in the words of another guy, want to "run for [their] lives." It may not be fair, but it is a fact.

After months of research, I'm convinced that men are indeed more intrigued by a confident woman who carries herself well and knows who she is than a picture-perfect beauty who seems little more than that. Some men might be tempted to take the latter to bed, but when all is said and done, they would more likely take the former to *heart.* When the average guy sees the woman in his life hold her own in the face of intimidation, he is impressed. At the end of the day, both men and women want to be with someone they can respect.

Early in our journey together I told you how much I hoped we would find a deeper motivation for saying so long to our insecurity than for the sake of pleasing men. The only definitive and enduring motivation for a true transformation in our security will be God Himself. The Creator of heaven and earth assigned us dignity and immeasurable value, and only when we finally accept those inalienable truths will we discover authentic security. I know a little bit about how the human mind works, however, and I know that some of you will require time and concerted effort to transfer your motivations. Call me naive, but I'm holding out hope that, on the way to divine revelation, we can all learn to trash the tactics that keep us insecure.

Insecurities do not attract. They repel. Insecurities do not invite intimacy. They invite uncertainty. They do not work for us on any level at all, except to open our hearts and minds to the healing, securing strength of Christ. Through Him we have acquired the human unction upon which every life pivots: the power to choose.

CHAPTER 13
THE POWER TO CHOOSE

The most prized possession God gave humankind when He formed Adam from the dust of the earth was the power to choose. Nowhere do we bear the image of our Creator more forthrightly than in the ability to exercise our free will. Before God ever spoke the words, "Let there be light," He had determined to let there be choice. God knew every implication of the human will in advance and that the gift would enable us to accept or reject the very One who gave it to us. But He sought relationships, not robots. He designed our intricate souls to flourish where they are free and to recoil where they are forced.

The power to choose takes precedence in our relentless fight for security. No matter how hard we work to improve our circumstances, our spirituality, and our associations, merely walking through daily life is enough to till the soil and sow insecurity into our souls. The point of this chapter is to suggest that we really can say, "No, thanks." We can make a deliberate choice to refuse insecurity the space to seed. Every person created in the image of God has the right to choose, but those of us who have received Christ's own Spirit also possess the concentrated strength to exercise that right.

Flip back to chapter 8 in the pages of your memory where we talked about triggers of insecurity. Recall what we said about our tendency to stifle insecurities rather than allow God to flagrantly tend to them. Things that aren't dead don't stay buried. If we suppress our insecurities rather than inviting specific truth to supplant them, we leave ourselves wide open to the next onslaught. The result is a constant psychological roller coaster. We can feel generally secure and on the right track one moment and get completely derailed and go off the cliff the next.

We also discussed the downward spiral of reacting badly to the trigger and then, out of humiliation or self-condemnation, feeling even more insecure than we did in the first place. The next time around our reaction is even worse. The cycle can perpetuate until we spiral into a chasm of self-hatred, the last ounce of our security circling the drain.

Here's the good news: we can spiral up

instead. By choosing to have a different reaction *even prior to having a different emotion,* we can effect an immediate sense of heightened security. The reaction leads to a new feeling, and the new feeling leads to more consistent reactions. The result? We spiral up.

One of the most common human claims is that we can't change the way we feel. That may be true, but we *can* change the way we think, which will change the way we act. And as we change the way we act, the way we feel also begins to change. In the breaking of every habit, someone wills it first and feels it later. Whatever you do, don't shrug your shoulders and decide the prospect is too hard to do and too much to ask. What could be harder than fighting a lifelong battle with insecurity? Thank God we don't have to wait until we feel more secure to start acting more secure. That's the heart of living by faith until we live by sight. We act on the basis of scriptural fact and supernatural power rather than mercurial feelings.

If a woman doesn't have the Spirit of Christ within her enabling her to do what she can't, the pressure will prove too much and her strength too small. A tenacious countercultural mind-set will be impossible to maintain in the long run because she's limited to her own current mood and the ebb and flow of verve. Hear me out for just a moment. If you do not have a personal relationship with Christ, I'm not trying to manipulate you, pressure you, or worm you into some kind of cult. My life's passion is to see women like you really live and truly thrive. No matter how our beliefs may differ, you were created in the image of God and therefore possess a dignity that deserves my respect. I joyfully and unhesitatingly give it. You also possess the God-given free will to choose Christ or not, and regardless of what you decide, I'm grateful you came along on this journey.

I need to shoot straight with you though, lest you find yourself exasperated with another book that makes a promise it can't keep. The human spirit on its own is not strong enough long enough to keep its security afloat in the shark-infested waters of our current society. You can still find help within these pages, and I encourage you to see it to the end. Some of our most practical applications lie ahead. The thing is, we don't just need help with our insecurity. We need healing.

Grant me one chance to say this. If you're not a believer in Christ, you can ask Him to come into your life this moment as your Lord and Savior, and you will instantly and permanently possess the divine power inside of you that I'm talking about — and eternal life besides. If you're interested, look in the back of this book for the page entitled "So, You're Considering Christ" and I'll walk you through several simple steps. It will take all of five minutes. What happens if you do? The moment you receive Him, His Spirit takes up residency inside and you possess what the Bible calls "all-surpassing power" in "jars of clay" (2 Corinthians 4:7). I've encountered this supernatural unction countless times, knowing even in the moment that God was enabling me to do something that I was totally incapable of doing in my natural strength. It's a high like no other high. It has also made my lows so very less low.

Here's what this enablement looks like wearing human flesh: this inner source of inexhaustible force means that the next time a situation arises that would normally set off an internal security alarm, you have the wherewithal to react like a totally different person. A very secure person, as a matter of fact. You can stop in your tracks and first ask yourself how a secure person would respond. Then, by the power inside of you,

you can do what that secure person would do. Your new actions are the way you call that deeply entrenched security to the surface. By faith, you summon what is inside to the outside.

But we don't just want these kinds of results on rare occasions. We want to live here. That's why it starts with one new action but ends with a whole new attitude. The action gets the security to the surface. The attitude *keeps* the security at the surface. Make sense? If not, I think it will over the next couple of paragraphs.

We will always have triggers of insecurity, but *we* get to decide whether or not we're going to take the bait. I don't recommend having no reaction. We are human beings with God-given emotions and visceral responses that don't always show up politely. One reason God wrapped our souls in limber flesh was to give our emotions a means of expression. I recommend that you refuse insecurity the right to stalk every other reaction. If you're like me, these may be refreshing new revelations for you:

We can be hurt without also being insecure.
We can be disappointed without also being insecure.

We can be shocked without also being insecure.
We can be unsure without also being insecure.
We can even be humbled without also being insecure.

Insecurity is more than a complex emotion. It is a lie about our God-sanctioned condition. While something may cause us to feel sad, confused, angry, or threatened, we have the power to choose whether or not it gets to assault our security. When we decide to be strong willed about what God strongly wills, that, beloved, is the epitome of empowerment. The next time someone says or does something to you that has the capacity to dent your security, instantly think one of these thoughts toward that person:

You can hurt my feelings, but you cannot have my security. I won't let you. It's mine to keep. You cannot have it.
You can criticize me and even be right about what I did wrong, but you do not get to damage my security. It's mine to keep. You cannot have it.
You might have embarrassed me, but I refuse to let it fall on me so heavily that it smothers my security. It's mine

to keep. You cannot have it.

You may be so intimidating and threatening that I feel I have to hand a lot of things to you, but I refuse to hand over my security. Who you are doesn't get to dwarf who I am. My security is mine to keep. You cannot have it.

Just a few days ago I got a letter from a woman who had no idea I was writing this book. She just wanted me to know how my Bible study had helped her through a harsh time. She said that ever since cancer caused her to require a double mastectomy, she feels like she sees nothing but breasts everywhere she looks. While checking out her groceries in front of glossy magazine covers with summer swimsuit editions, she silently testifies to God, *Nothing has the power to make me less of a woman. I'm not going to let a pair of breasts tell me who I'm not.* That's what I'm talking about, sister.

Maybe some of you are too sophisticated to have deliberate thoughts as cheesy as those I suggested, but don't knock it until you've tried it. Give it one week, and you won't believe how divinely empowered you feel. Two days ago someone I love said something to me that would shoot a poison arrow straight to the heart of any woman.

Just as my soul was about to wilt like a weed, I steadied myself and remembered our journey. Then I thought these words toward the person: *You don't get to go that deep. I refuse to let your words go all the way from my ears to the core of who I am. Nope. I'm not doing it.* Do you want to know something? Later I still cried about the hurtful words, but I didn't feel insecure. Injured? Yes, but I still had my dignity, and because I did, I bounced back twice as fast as I would have otherwise.

You see, somebody may take that proverbial pound of flesh from you, but you get to decide whether or not they get your security, too. Those of us who have struggled with chronic insecurity have made a life practice out of attaching it to every other negative emotion we feel. We never let hurt happen by itself. We attach insecurity to our hurt like a conjoined twin. We never let humiliation happen by itself. We attach insecurity to our humiliation like a twin. We can never just feel like we look subpar that day. We attach insecurity to our appearance like a twin. We can never just deal with those ten extra pounds. We attach insecurity to our weight like a twin.

Let's stop playing matchmaker with our insecurity. Let's learn how to process something negative without automatically allowing it to keep company with our insecurity. Those other emotions are hard enough to deal with. Make them go solo. God gave you your security, and nobody gets to force it from you. You must make up your mind that the only way someone can take it from you is for you to hand it over. You have the right to hold on to security for dear life in every situation and every relationship. It's the power of choice.

The power to choose is so inherently God-given that Scripture raises a gigantic red flag over people who make us feel so weak we can't make a sound decision. Second Timothy 3:6 spits the truth right out on the page: "They are the kind [of people] who worm their way into homes and gain control over weak-willed women, who are loaded down with sins and are swayed by all kinds of evil desires." I totally resonate with Paul's warning to Timothy. I remember being in relationships where my will was consistently weak and I felt almost powerless. I would determine in advance what decision I would make when the opportunity arose, only to lose all resolve once I was in the person's company. In one case, I was head over heels in love but still felt an odd sense of relief mixed with grief when the association ended. A person cannot be whole in a relationship where he or she feels powerless to make healthy choices.

I'd like to suggest that what the Bible describes as a person who worms his or her way into lives and gains control over weak-willed people, one secular psychologist calls an "emotional predator."[13] Remember when I pointed out in the last chapter that none of the men answering the survey preferred insecurity in a woman even if it could give them the upper hand? That's how remotely healthy people are supposed to think. Unfortunately, we're sharing space on this planet with a number of individuals who are neither healthy nor remote. In fact, one of them may live in your house. Whether male or female, any person who enjoys and exploits another's insecurity and sensitivity is an emotional predator. See if this description makes your skin crawl like it does mine:

> Emotional predators learn that being aggressive often gets them their way. They rely on others' anxiety as the key to getting their way. Naturally, physical abuse should not be tolerated at all. That should be grounds for any sensible person to leave. However, many emotional predators use verbal aggression as

opposed to physical aggression to dominate a relationship.[14]

The emotional predator sometimes has redeeming qualities that complicate things considerably because they allow us to make excuses for the person and avoid drawing solid boundaries. Paul describes such a predator as having "a form of godliness but denying its power" (2 Timothy 3:5). Please hear this part with both ears: we are also explicitly told to "have nothing to do with them." I want to be as clear in the next statement as absolutely possible: if you are single, I implore you not to marry an emotional predator. If you struggle with sizable insecurity, you could be a sitting duck for one. Rethink any relationship where you tend to be remarkably and consistently weak willed.

The power to stand at a crossroad and make a good, sound choice based on a solid sense of security is a gift from God straight to the souls of His image bearers. If you often feel unable to exercise that power in your current relationship, it is most likely not God's will for you. If you can't ease out of it gracefully and safely, please seek assistance and then do what I had to do: get to the bottom of that weak will and find out why you're so easily swayed by emotionally dangerous people.

If you're already married to an emotional predator, your obstacles are sky-high but not utterly impossible to jump. That's one of the most beautiful things about God. Nothing is too difficult for Him. Please seek godly counsel and know that your insecurity and consistently weak will are not doing anybody — including your emotional predator — any favors. Secular psychology calls that being an enabler. Scripture would more likely describe it as a grace abuser. There is no greater form of extortion than the slow-bleed robbery of our sense of security. By all means, let's not open the front door and invite the thief in. Or worse yet, take him to bed. Lord, help us.

Sometimes we don't have an emotional predator on our hands. We just have an emotional wreck. I've been one and lived near more than one, so I'm not talking theoretically. At one time or another, we've all handed over our security to a person who doesn't have enough of his or her own to stay up on two wobbly feet. How we think those individuals are going to carry us too is one of life's mysteries. Whether the damage we sustain from an emotionally unhealthy person is intentional or not, we have the right to refuse people open access to our security and our dignity. We can also draw a few boundaries.

I'd like to single out one challenging area in particular where we must jealously guard our security before we conclude our segment on man-related insecurities. The threat of pornography has surfaced several times in this journey, but now we're going to practice applying our new response to it. I have received countless letters through the years from women whose men are dealing with pornography issues and addictions. Ages and ethnicities vary, but from the tone of their letters, these women have at least two understandable characteristics in common: their self-esteem is shot, and their security is trashed. As if the feelings of betrayal and inadequacy aren't enough, most of them decided to own the loved one's problem. Certainly staggering numbers of women share the same sexual stronghold, so the things I'm about to share are just as valid in reverse gender.

Not long ago I got home from work a little early, poured a cup of coffee, and plopped down on the couch to let my mind rest for a few minutes. I grabbed the remote and tuned in to a show I've enjoyed no less than a hundred times. That particular day I listened to the very likable and persuasive host voice approval over the use of pornography to spice up a couple's sex life. I had to rewind it to make sure I had heard correctly, and then I paced around my den for half an hour at my wit's end and with my jaw dragging behind me. I wondered how many doors to a spicy new life would swing open that very night. What I didn't have to wonder was whether or not the approach would instantly deliver what it promised. It was the thought of what else it would deliver that scared me half to death.

Like few other developing appetites on the human palate, a taste for pornography has an uncanny way of morphing into a binge with lightning speed. And this is one binge that's terrifically hard to purge. No matter what your spiritual beliefs may be or whether or not they concur with a moral law, an addiction to pornography will eat a soul alive. Even if experts were to shove every spiritual and moral ramification aside as archaic and outdated, they would still have a hard time denying the long-term erosive effects on the individual. Anything that keeps our relational lives in a whimsical world and requires absolutely nothing from us but further self-absorption is a severe detriment to our security. The human psyche was designed for real relationships and cannot flourish amid nothing but fantasy. The plan to keep pornography at bay and not allow it to affect relationships is a bigger fantasy than the one on the screen or the page. Countless pornography addicts reach a point where they can no longer have sexual intimacy with a spouse. That *sustained* inability is often the first tip-off that something or someone else has entered the picture.

A pornography addiction severely blocks personal development, and if unstopped, eventually stunts productivity in every area of life. It is as insatiable as the grave. It cannot get enough. It will not maintain. It constantly demands something more. Something deeper. Something further. It catches you and then eventually it gets you caught. Pornography also turns the lock ever so quietly on the cell of solitary confinement. The irony is that it promises company but ultimately leaves its victim with all the psychological fulfillment of caressing a ghost. Contrary to the claims of our sensual culture, we were not created merely for sexual gratification. We were created for affection, and that requires another person.

I'm pounding the point in case your man has an ongoing issue with pornography and you've decided one of three things: (1) If you can't beat it, you might as well join it. (2) Since he keeps doing it, you might as well look the other way and act like you have no clue what to do. (3) If he has rejected you for something or someone else, you are not worth having. Just look at yourself. Who would want you anyway? You're pathetic. It's all your fault. And if not, it's at least all your responsibility. You convince yourself it's all about you, then spend every last ounce of your security owning his problem.

Does any of that sound familiar? Do not think for a split second that I'm minimizing the pain and confusion of this issue or the natural viability of any one of those three options. This one is tough. It is also torturous to our security, so there's no way we can avoid talking about it. If you are in this position, the first thing I want to tell you is this: there really is life after pornography for many couples. I am pro-marriage, pro-forgiveness, and pro-doing what it takes to work things out. One of the reasons Keith Moore and I have been married for thirty-one years is because we're willing to sweat our way through a crisis. I believe that with God's help and centrality, a couple can move through almost anything and flourish once again. Perhaps the couple will even come to a healthier, happier place than before. To state the obvious, however, doing nothing will never accomplish anything.

The second thing I want to tell you is to seek face-to-face counsel from someone you know to be wise and discreet. No book can ever take the place of good, solid, sound-minded counseling, because it lacks the framework of individuality and account-ability. I cannot emphasize strongly enough that you need to find a safe place to tell the secret, or you'll never get your ankle out of that trap and neither will he. If the two of you could fix it by yourselves, you probably already would have. Get help for yourself whether or not your spouse or fiancé accompanies you.

The third thing I beg you to hear is that you are not doing your man any favors by letting him continue to get away with something so destructive to him and to your relationship. So often when we women claim that we don't know what to do, the truth is, we *do* know what we need to do. We're just scared to do it. Again, I'm not minimizing the difficulty of facing a problem this serious and intimate head-on; if you don't know how to go about it, seek good advice and assistance from someone you respect. Confronting someone is hard, and the risk of discovering something worse than you suspect can be enough to paralyze you until the whole relationship goes up in smoke. The alternative to practicing what Scripture calls "speaking the truth in love" is continuing to communicate a lie in fear (Ephesians 4:15). That's no way to live.

If you're like me, you can't imagine calmly or even civilly confronting something that feels so personally threatening and betraying. That's where accountability comes into very important play. Knowing that we're going to report back to an adviser or even a trustworthy friend helps us behave in a way that we might not otherwise.

Here's some advice from Rob Jackson, a licensed professional counselor who specializes in intimacy disorders like these:

You confront because you care. Armed with knowledge that your spouse is acting out sexually, you have no other responsible option. Your information may be incomplete, but any verifiable evidence of illicit sex is enough. This could include but is not limited to viewing pornographic materials, visiting sexually explicit chat rooms, browsing adult bookstores or going to strip clubs, frequenting prostitutes, engaging in voyeurism, exhibitionism, or sexual behavior with others. Indecisiveness won't do — not if you hope to save your marriage.

When done correctly and motivated by love, confrontation becomes an act of profound compassion. Frankly, it's easier in the short run to look the other way. If you intend, however, for your marriage to overcome adultery of any type, you must confront if your spouse fails to confess. To quote Dr. Dobson, "love must be tough" — and consistent.

Further in the article he sets a vital balance:

In addition to love, confrontation must be centered on principle. The dialogue should never degenerate into who is right, but should focus on what is right.[15]

Confronting an offense and setting a boundary is never trickier than it is for a woman who is trying with all her might to be a godly wife. I know the struggle because I've felt the strain. We can misunderstand submission to be an invitation to oppression rather than order. When my man has taken enough leash in a particular area to nearly hang himself and I'm wrestling with whether or not to let him off the hook, I try to check my heart by giving serious thought to what is best for him. I'll offer you a nice, benign example in the midst of this hard subject matter. Keith is an avid outdoorsman and spends a fair amount of time away from home. From October through January his schedule escalates and he's gone for a week at a time, home a few days, and gone again. Until late December, I tend to remain congenial and cooperative. After all, he's doing what he loves. About the time I start feeling like I could probably make it without him, however, I know it's time to jerk that leash he's on. At that point, when I call him on his cell and he answers with a chipper, "Hey, darling!" I might be overheard saying something like this: "Get your tail home, and boy, am I not kidding."

And he does. Do you want to know something else? He never fails to say, "Thank you for telling me to come home, baby. I knew I was getting out of control." Keith and I have both said many times that if either of us had a spouse we could run over, we'd each be married to a flapjack. I'd like to share one major biblical element that, when I'm thinking clearly, helps me decide whether to let something go or reel it in.

The Greek lexical term most commonly translated "love" in the New Testament is *agape.* It means all the things you would probably imagine, but it also involves an element that is crucial as we wrestle with our current subject matter. *Agape* is a kind of love that is in another person's best interest. To stand back and watch a spouse spin further and further out of control without ever attempting to confront, set a boundary, or permit consequences is not in his (or your) best interest.

Throughout this chapter, we've talked about the power of choice. Nowhere is the concept more challenging, vital, and emotionally lifesaving than when a mate is caught up in a sexually illicit activity or relationship. By human nature, women tend to take that kind of offense at the deepest personal level. Even though experts continue to tell us that a man's sexual problem is not about us (and I believe them), it still affects us. We feel betrayed, replaced, rejected, and inadequate. We picture the women in those perfectly lit images, or we romanticize the one who has stolen his gaze, and we lose heart that we can't compete. After all, the other women aren't the ones doing laundry and spraying Lysol in the bathroom. But this is the news flash: we don't have to compete. In fact, we must refuse to compete. God's Word tells us:

The LORD gives his people strength; the LORD grants his people security.

This is the very moment we must head straight to the throne of an all-powerful God and Father, rehearsing over and over who He says we are and what He says we're worth. We must call on Him to fight our battles for us and through us and to stand us on steady feet in a confidence only He can supply. We must ask Him to bring forth the women in us that we didn't even know we were — women of substance and confidence with whom an image or adulteress cannot compete. We don't have to compete with them. Let them compete with us if anyone must. After all, "if God is for us, who can be against us?" (Romans 8:31). This is exactly the crisis point when we must say over and over in our thoughts toward our mate:

You may have broken my heart and shaken me up, but you cannot have my security. I will not give it up to you or to anyone else. I am a woman of God, clothed in strength and dignity, and no one gets to take those things from me.

Then say it again:
I am clothed with strength and dignity!
And again:
In Jesus' name, I am clothed with strength and dignity!

Don't just repeat these kinds of thoughts first thing in the morning when you are in crisis. Say them all day long and as often as you must in order to set your mind on truth. You may think this is a battle of the body, but it's not. This war will be won or lost on the battlefield of your mind. Write those truths on index cards if necessary and take them with you everywhere you go. For crying out loud, write "Proverbs 31:25" with a Sharpie on your hand if you have to. Get yourself immediately surrounded by supportive people of sound faith. Dive into a group Bible study that requires homework so you're forced to fix your mind on soul-patching truth. This is no time for indecisiveness. This is no time for doing the same old thing the same old way. Determine with the divine power invested in you that you will not give up your security and your dignity no matter what transpires.

Even if your mate doesn't end up choosing you, God has chosen you, girlfriend. Believe it. Invest that truth in your emotional bank, and it will earn interest for the rest of your life. Your confidence will either draw your man back to you or hold you steady if he heads the other direction. In Christ, you are so much stronger than you think you are. Second Corinthians 12 says that even in our weakness we are strong and that His power is made perfect. Wear your God-given strength. Throw on your God-given dignity. Walk with your head up in your God-given security.

LOL

Then humbly duck so God can lovingly, compassionately, and redemptively hit your husband — for his own good.

Listen, if melting into a puddle of spinelessness or flying into a fit of hysteria would save our relationships and honor God, I'd recommend nothing faster. The fact is, they do neither. Flee from arrogance, but whatever you do:

> Do not throw away your confidence; it will be richly rewarded. You need to persevere so that when you have done the will of God, you will receive what he has promised.
>
> HEBREWS 10:35–36

I think you should know that I just wrote that Scripture from memory. It has lived in my head for the last eighteen months so that

I could call it from the back of my mind to the front of my conscious thinking at any time. Rest assured, you're not being asked to consider something this author is not willing to practice. I have a low tolerance for hypocrisy, especially in myself. There are certain parts of my story that I choose to keep private out of respect to my beloved family, but you can know that I don't shoot untested principles at you. I might not have experienced your exact set of circumstances, but I promise you the devil has tried on countless occasions to steal, kill, and destroy my family and everything we stand for (John 10:10). Those of us who are still intact under the Moore roof testify to the power of God and the victory of truth.

The enemy of your soul will never have to worry about what kind of damage you could do the kingdom of darkness if he can get you to buy the lie that you are incompetent, weak, and inadequate. But you're not. Neither are the men in your life. You may be "struck down, but [you are] not destroyed" (2 Corinthians 4:9). As we wrap up the segment of this book dealing with men-related strongholds, let's pray for our husbands, sons, brothers, nephews, friends, and fathers. Thank God for each one of them by name, and ask Him to make them courageous and mighty in His strength in their spheres of influence. Ask Him to be a shield around them, to be their glory and the lifter of their heads (Psalm 3:3). While we're at it, let's ask Him to make us the kind of women with whom they can be His kind of men. Let's stop kidding ourselves. This culture is as brutal on a man as it is on a woman.

We all need God.

CHAPTER 14
CAN WE DO IT FOR THEM?

Five months ago today, my man and I huddled over the hospital bed of our older daughter and whispered a quivery hello to her brand-new baby girl. Weighing in at a whopping six pounds and six ounces, she established a position that no future progeny can displace. She is the first granddaughter on both sides. With her inky eyes squinting in the unwelcomed light, Baby Girl couldn't make heads or tails of us that day. These days she recognizes us all the way from the front door to the den, and she lights up like the dawn at the sound of our voices. Just moments ago I rocked her in my arms, sang her to sleep with made-up songs, tucked her in her crib, and stared at her with wonder. I wasn't planning to write today, but suddenly I'm feeling inspired.

I am a blessed woman indeed. I have the tremendous joy of living only fifteen minutes from my daughter Amanda and her family

ur. She and her husband, Curtis, are
mom and dad to the other star of our
extended tribe, my three-year-old grandson,
Jackson.

Jackson is the biggest ham bone flavoring
our family stew, and until five months ago,
the uncontested center of copious attention.
When Amanda and Curtis announced they
were expecting their first baby, I wanted a
man-child in the worst way. After raising
daughters, I thought it was high time for a
healthy dose of testosterone. We certainly
got it. He could make car sounds by the
time he could sit up and could say "monster
truck" almost before he could say
"Mommy." Born competitive, when he was
first potty trained, every time he tinkled in
the potty, he would pump his fist in the air
and say, "I win!"

To Jackson, I am Bibby. We were going for
Bee-Bee, but he chose a short *i* over those
long *e*'s, and who were we to argue? If we're
together, he says my name every other
minute, even if his head is dropped down
toward a two-inch car on a bright orange
track. Much of the time he doesn't need
anything in particular. He's just taking roll
to make sure I'm close by in case he should
need me to top off his juice or race a couple
of Hot Wheels (and lose). A month or so

before his tiny sister was born, Jackson spent the weekend with me while his parents were on a "baby-moon" and Keith was out of town. He had outgrown the crib at my house, so I tried tucking him in one of the twin beds in the kids' room while I slept on the other. At some point during the early hours long before dawn, he sat up disoriented in that enormous bed, slid down the side, and whined to get in the one with me. "Of course, baby. Come on up here." I lifted him onto the mattress and laid him down right beside me.

Over and over in the remaining hours before daylight, I felt his little plump hands patting me on the underside of my arm to make sure I was there. We both finally fell asleep for the better part of an hour, and when I awoke, I had the sweetest cherub face an inch from mine. Blue eyes puffy and cheeks bright pink, he chirped, "Bibby! It's time to say good morning to Mr. Sun!" So we did our usual routine. I picked him up, held him at the bedroom window, and opened the blinds. He was so warm and cuddly. It was one of those perfect moments in life when you are so happy, your heart aches. There's just nothing more adorable than a toddler in his jammies, especially one who happens to love you. With great enthusiasm we both looked through the blinds and voiced our greeting in perfect unison, "Good morning, Mr. Sun!"

Then we headed downstairs, where Bibby made pancakes and turned on cartoons. Don't start with me about kids and too much TV. One of us needed a quiet moment with some strong coffee while the other one was happily distracted. As I sipped liquid consciousness from my favorite cup, I watched that darling man-child and wondered how many times in the course of my life my heart had been so thoroughly slain. Only his mother and his aunt Melissa had ever left me so defenseless.

And now this: *a granddaughter.* A woman-child born into a family called to serve women. I didn't know if I could take it. I had also babysat Jackson two months earlier when Amanda and Curtis went to the doctor's appointment where they learned the sex of their second child. It was right after a hurricane ripped the Gulf Coast to shreds and left most of Houston without power. Since babies don't keep, their OB clinic was up and running well before most area businesses, enabling Amanda and Curtis to keep their appointment. None of the traffic lights worked, however, so it took an eternity for them to get to the doctor's office and back. I walked to the front door to look for their white Jeep Cherokee at least one hundred times. Amanda had convinced herself she was having another boy, and goodness knows we would have been happy, but Keith and I thought it would be so fun to have pink this time around. We knew that our firstborn secretly hoped the same.

After nearly four hours, Amanda and Curtis sauntered through the front door like they'd been on a leisurely Sunday afternoon stroll. I was ready to strangle them. I couldn't tell a solitary thing from their expressions, but thankfully they determined to put me out of my misery quickly. Amanda handed me a genderless lemon yellow and lime green gift bag stuffed with matching tissue. I wasted no time, digging right down the middle of it until my head was awash in lemon-lime. Then there it was. Pink, pink, glorious pink! "They are 100 percent sure," she quickly added. We squealed like schoolgirls and as my grandmother would have said, haven't been worth killing since. Curtis doesn't yet know what hit him. All he knows is that their cost of living has escalated considerably.

Keith was beside himself. Being a father of daughters, he loved the idea of a little girl, which had nothing but pure, unadulterated gladness attached to it. The whole family was ecstatic. A few days after the big news, Amanda, Curtis, and Jackson stopped by the house. The boy went straight for his box of monster trucks, and our daughter and son-in-law asked us to sit down so they could tell us something.

"We've chosen her name."

"You *have?* What in the world is it?"

For a split second time stood still, and I poised myself, shifting in the chair, to learn the name of someone who would soon become one of the most important people in my entire life. How many times, after all, would I call this name in the course of my days?

"Annabeth. Her name will be Annabeth."

There's something about a name. Instantly, the baby has an identity. Instantly, it's no longer a pregnancy. Nor even just a baby. It's a person. A person with a name. A person you'd now miss should anything, God help you, happen to her. You don't really give your heart away to something until you know its name. You can feel affection and anticipation, but created in the image of God, you simply cannot surrender to something nameless. In fact, sometimes I've been known to make up a name for someone I've seen but not met just to ease the craving for intimacy. Even in the introduction of two adults, learning what to call each other is the first step to getting to know a real, live God-stamped individual. Identity as the introduction to intimacy is the whole idea behind God telling Moses in Exodus 33 that He knew him by name. The same was true when Christ called Himself the Good Shepherd in John 10 and told His disciples that "he calls his own sheep *by name*" (emphasis mine).

Then, as if learning a baby's name isn't big enough, there's that titanic something about hearing your own name tossed in the middle of it. I could hardly sleep that night for one word rolling around in my head like a tricycle tire. *Annabeth. Annabeth. Annabeth. Annabeth.* Occasionally my own tormented soul broke in with questions like, "How much power does a name have?" And "Does the redemption of God diffuse the bad things attached to a name and leave only the good?" Boy, am I ever hoping so. I can't say I've ever hated my name, but I have wasted considerable time hating myself. Those days are mostly behind me now, but having someone named after you makes a soul think a lot about legacies: what you want someone to inherit with a name and what you decidedly do not. You'll never find anyone who has loved being a woman more than me. You'll find people who have done a better job at it but never a single one who has enjoyed it more. Furthermore, I love hanging out with a bunch of women better than most activities under heaven. But to tell you the road to womanhood has been rocky for me is like calling Mount Everest an anthill. I have such mixed thoughts about my childhood. The emotional toll of the sexual abuse I sustained early in life marred many memories of regular childhood experiences that in themselves weren't even bad. When I replay some of the good memories of that time of my life, feelings of sadness still force an unwelcome invasion. At least in my mental replays, it is strikingly clear that something had happened to me. I was anxious and afraid of some undisclosed thing all the time. Why couldn't someone figure it out and help me?

At the same time, I vividly remember being able to get lost in a pretend world where I felt strangely happy and secure. I would spin myself in circles on the burlap-bag swing hanging from one of our pine trees, holding my head all the way back and watching the limbs play tic-tac-toe on the blue sky. I'd play with my dolls, bathe them and powder them, dress them and rock them — sometimes without a care in the world. I remember feeling happy then. I'd sit in front of my teenage sister's vanity mirror, put on her lipstick, and pin up my hair. And for that moment, life felt right. Yet so much was wrong.

And I was six.

Most of the time I lived with an unidentifiable sense of foreboding. My big brother tells me that I often looked like I would burst into tears if someone glanced at me cross-eyed. But I can also remember moments of respite that fetched me to a place where I would feel light.

My love affair with Jesus began at that very point in my life, back in a Sunday school room in a small-town church with linoleum floors and black heel marks. I still cannot explain why someone sitting pretty for an ugly future believed the good press about God. Maybe I just had good teachers. When you're little, the teachers don't feel compelled to say, "Now, Jesus loves all of you but mostly just cares about what you boys will be when you grow up." Nope. There's none of that. And oddly there never was much of that in my path until I was grown and already knew better. The thought never occurred to me that Jesus didn't call girls to follow Him alongside the boys. I've been wrong about a lot of things but not that one. We might be commissioned to do different things, but Jesus ministers next to men and women alike.

Always has. In a culture where some sects of Pharisees started their day by thanking God they were not born a woman, Jesus had a passel of women right at His side. See for yourself:

> Jesus traveled about from one town and village to another, proclaiming the good news of the kingdom of God. The Twelve were with him, and also some women who had been cured of evil spirits and diseases: Mary (called Magdalene) from whom seven demons had come out; Joanna the wife of Cuza, the manager of Herod's household; Susanna; and many others. These women were helping to support them out of their own means.
>
> LUKE 8:1–3

I'm not trying to make too much of this. I'm certainly not suggesting a point of doctrine; rather, I'm simply pointing out some wording that resonated with this former pit dweller. Though the Gospels present "the Twelve" as following Jesus closely after having been called, these women followed Jesus closely after having been *cured.* Don't let me confuse you. To be called is a wondrous thing indeed. In fact, that very word is used in reference to the way every Christian, regardless of gender, first comes to Christ (Romans 8:30). But here in this portion of Luke's eloquent Gospel, alongside "the Twelve" were "also some women who had been cured." I know the feeling.

I am so taken with Jesus and so convinced that abundance is in His wake alone precisely because He has done so much to heal me. I should be nothing more than a casualty of sexual abuse and perpetual family dysfunction. My past gave me ample permission to make disastrous decisions, and to prove it I made at least a thousand of them. Despite my own determination to reconfirm how worthless and filthy I was, Jesus just would not let me be.

He would pull me out of the slime, and I would slink right back into it. He'd pull me out again, and there I'd go again . . . and all the while as saved as that old preacher in my childhood church who dunked my mixed-up head in baptism. I rededicated my life at least fifty times, and still the soles of my feet stuck to the mud like a rat to the goo of a trap. Every time Keith tucks one of those merciless contraptions between the washer and dryer at our place in the woods, I wonder why we don't kill the poor rodent quickly rather than let it stick there till it dies. I guess I've taken it too personally and projected myself right onto its mangy gray coat. There was a time in my life when I was sure I would stick there in the slime till I died. Honestly, I wished someone would just put me out of my misery.

Then, in His great and wise mercy, God let me see how much my determination to hang on to my messed-up self was going to cost me. Jesus did not scare me to death. He let me scare myself to death. My heart and my mind were sick. Like Paul, I had the desire to do what was good, but for the life of me, I could not seem to carry it out. Mark my words. All the invitation Satan needs to bring destruction to any life is a half inch of duplicity. If we don't stop feeding that unhealthy part of us — that beast within — over time it will develop the strength of a grizzly and drag the rest of us off as its kill. Nothing tells the enemy that it's time to wage an attack like that little gap of space between us knowing what we need to do and us doing it. I needed more than a commissioning. Girlfriend, I needed a cure.

And I got one. In Hosea 14:4 the Lord says, "I will cure them of their unfaithfulness. I will love them freely."[16] That's what happened to me. God cured me of my own gross unfaithfulness. He healed my unloveliness with His own love. As I live and breathe, I am not the woman I used to be, but the fact is, I started this journey because I wasn't yet the woman that I wanted to be. Somehow I don't picture her sitting around fixating on all the delicacies of her inadequacies like I too often have. Surely she feels too good about God to wonder why she doesn't feel better about herself. I have a suspicion she's never going to be as perfect as I picture, but the woman I want to become is still a long shot from the one who wrote the first chapter of this book. That's why I thought I'd better get on with it. God was right to bring me here. He and I have wrestled some things out and won some big victories in the last six months as my insides spilled out all over this subject matter. This has been one of the most vulnerable journeys of my life, but I'm the better for it. And there's better still.

As long as we're here in these human bodies on the topsoil of planet Earth instead of six feet under shoving up weeds, we'll always have a few places that could use some curing. And we won't need curing just for our own sakes.

"What's your baby sister's name going to be, Jackson?" I was making conversation with the boy while his parents were away and he tumbled Hot Wheels down Bibby's stairs like he never could if they were there. I just wanted to hear him say it. I was dying to know again that it was real. I needed to know if the woman-child we were expecting in four short weeks really would be a namesake. I would know his parents hadn't changed their minds if they were serious enough to tell him, too, because once you've told Jackson Jones anything, there's no untelling it. He can make an elephant look like it had dementia.

I waited a second or two for him to answer me.

Nothing.

Not a single word.

Just the sound of cars bouncing down the hardwood stairs.

"Jackson, listen to Bibby. I'm asking you what your baby sister's name is going to be."

"Alphabet," he answered drily. *Authoritatively.* His tone was tinged with insult like I had asked something everyone on earth already knew. I hid myself from him and laughed my head off. I could hardly wait to tell his mommy when she came to pick him up.

Miss Alphabet Jones. I have a feeling she has come to change the way we spell a few labels that dangle from the limbs of our family tree. That's okay with me. Come on, little girl, and mess with this woman's life. I did things for your mother and your aunt that I never would have done for myself. They were somehow worth changing for when I wasn't worth the effort myself. I will do for you, baby girl, what I've yet to do even for them.

Change has come. Annabeth's mother knows it too. I'll never forget what Amanda said the very day she and Curtis learned they were having a girl. I'm not sure if she was saying it to me, to herself, to no one in particular, or to God. "A girl. *A girl.* Oh, man. I'm going to have to deal with some of my stuff. I sure don't want to give it to her." You see, there were certain things she could get away with as the mom of a boy without worrying that he'd take it on. Mothers and daughters don't have that luxury. Neither do fathers and sons.

One of my bloggers expressed the gender

connection vividly in a comment to a post about women and insecurity.

> I had just had a pretty emotional talk with my middle school girl. [A little while later I] was praying about our conversation that pretty much revolved around insecurities, and my comment to God was, "She is saying everything that I say to myself still! As a thirtysomething married mother to three! How am I supposed to help her with her insecurities when I can't get over my own . . . which are awfully close sounding to a preteen girl's?! How pathetic am I?" Then I came to my computer and went to your blog . . . and I read the post and started sobbing. I want to be free from my insecurities; I fear they are tearing me apart from true friendships and putting a wedge between me and God. *And* I want to be strong for my daughters. Thanks for listening to me.

Darling, I wasn't just listening to you. I've been you. But this I know. Just because we have estrogen milking up our bloodstream doesn't mean we have to carry on the insecurities of a preteen girl. We really can grow up. As hard as it is, we really can take responsibility. We really can find freedom. We can sit around and think about how pathetic we are, or we really can pursue some healing — for ourselves and for that preteen girl. You and I, just like the woman who wrote that comment, have got to make a definitive decision to be strong for our daughters. And don't even try handing me the excuse that you're not a mom so this doesn't apply to you. The entire generation of adult women in any culture is systematically raising the next, whether they mean to be or not. Every acne-faced middle school girl you pass in the mall, texting on her cell phone or checking out that older guy in the food court, is your daughter. What are you going to do about her? What would you be willing to do *for* her?

Next time you're in a public place and a stroller rolls by with a baby girl in tow, know for certain that the woman who's pushing those wheels isn't the only one who will teach that child who to become. You will do your part in her life too. And if she just happens to have on a monogrammed pink jacket that says "Annabeth," I'm going to hope like crazy that she sees in you somebody who thought little girls like her were worth doing what it took.

It's time we girls helped each other out.

CHAPTER 15
LOOKING OUT FOR
EACH OTHER

So how can we women start helping each other out? How can we be part of the insecurity solution rather than an embarrassingly large part of the problem? That's what we're throwing on the table in this chapter. Remember the guy from the survey who called us out about our insecurities toward one another? I quoted him in chapter 12, and his comments echoed what plenty of other men implied about women and their insecurities:

Most obvious is when women are around other women; they try to size each other up and look for reasons to not get along rather than to get along. They seem easily intimidated, whether by physical beauty, character status, or whatever makes them feel that the other woman has more going for her, and a barrier goes up.

Before we talk about this, I do think it's safe to say that women don't *always* throw up barriers; many of us have long-term, genuine friendships that would be impossible to maintain under those conditions. To be sure, intimidation suffocates the life out of intimacy. But this guy certainly pegged us on too many occasions and encounters. To our relief, what might have been less obvious to him is that women don't necessarily have open discord with others who intimidate them or make them feel like they don't measure up. Sometimes we muster or feign confidence or contentment because we are honest enough with ourselves to know that our reaction is inane and self-absorbed. Many of us are well aware that our insecurities, given full sway, would dictate if not utterly destroy every female friendship on the horizon.

The loss would be incalculable. My good girlfriends are some of the dearest treasures in life to me. They are bright, gifted, hilarious, opinionated, and delightfully different from one another and from me. They make me think and rethink all sorts of decisions and probably deserve as much congratulations on my wedding anniversary as Keith and I. The best of friends talk each other out of the worst of plans. My good friends and I all have some sizable scars on our feet from this thorny sod, so we're incapable of walking indefinitely in perfect harmony. In the host of words shared between women friends, especially amid colliding hormones, sometimes something gets said that leaves the other pondering the old familiar question: "What in the world was that supposed to mean?" The lure to assume offense becomes a long-handled spoon stirring our hidden insecurities.

But that's one of those times when we get to exercise the power of choice. Will I think the best of her or the worst? Will I focus on this exact moment of offense, or will I remember a faithful, long-term friendship? The camaraderie my closest female companions bring to my life is well worth having to occasionally whisper to myself, "What you're feeling right this minute is stupid. Stop it."

Insecurity will rob us of some of the richest woman-to-woman relationships of our lives. It turns potential friends into competitors. It can also cause us to pursue associations out of unwell or impure motives. I'll pitch out a few examples. Some women completely avoid being around other women who make them feel even slightly inferior, only making friends with those they can successfully look down on. Sick but true. If no one in her closest social circle is remotely as cute as she is, you're probably staring a perfect example in the pretty face. Others do something just as extreme but on the opposite coast. They attach themselves to women they perceive as superior because they feel like they can at least share a small measure of status by association with them. The plan has its advantages for both parties for a while, but eventually it backfires. Living in a constant shadow has a conspicuous way of turning icy cold.

Most of us live somewhere between these two extremes. We don't feel threatened all the time. Just too much of the time. We're up to our ears in social networking (I like it too), in touch with a hundred women yet especially close to none. We can't figure out for the life of us why we fight this looming cloud of loneliness. We know we should be happier and wonder why we're not. Most of the time we have no idea we are scrambling to play our part in a make-believe world. The high-definition images surrounding us at every turn and screen look so real that we forget we're being vacuumed into a matrix. A constant stream of media and celebrities pressures real women to either try to measure up to pretend lives or admit to failure. We end up feeling like we're on a runway in our old underwear. Nobody's clapping, and everybody's a competitor.

I have a buddy who is a very popular DJ at a contemporary radio station in Houston. A few months ago, when we had a chance to catch up after an on-the-air interview, she asked me what I was presently researching. When I told her it was women and the honest-to-God pursuit of security, she made a quick and clever comment that I haven't been able to get out of my head since:

"Let's see. Hmmmmm. Secure women. Isn't that an oxymoron?"

It doesn't have to be. The insecurities of women have gone viral, and as if our culture is not host enough, now we're catching it from one another. Call me an optimist, but I have to believe that security could be just as contagious. We've talked at serious length about becoming healthier and more secure in our relationships with men. I learned from my survey of over nine hundred women, however, that many females struggle more intensely and frequently with insecurities toward their own gender.

In this chapter, we're going to fasten our attention to several ways we can jump-start substantial security in our relationships with other women. Should we choose to adopt it, this kind of perspective could be unique and refreshing enough in our spheres of influence to cause practically any woman near us to notice. She may not be able to define the difference at first, but she'll know we possess assurance, strength, and grace that she is missing and craves.

Let's look at a few things we could do to develop a case of infectious security with our own gender.

Stop Making Comparisons

Our constant propensity to compare ourselves to the women around us is wrecking our perceptions of both ourselves and them. Most of us aren't in a public place for five minutes before we peruse the female players in the room and judge where we rank. Human nature rarely balances itself on the tightrope of equality, despite our noble claims. Far more often in our comparisons to other women, we fall headlong to one side with inferiority or swan-dive to the other side with superiority. A bloody tumble is inevitable either way.

The nature of our competition depends to a large extent on what we tend to value. If intelligence is high on the list, given the opportunity, we will try to assess whether or not the people around us seem smarter than we are. If appearance is a personal premium, we have the tendency to rate ourselves according to the looks of those in eyeshot. The same is true of talent, giftedness, spirituality, and success. We tend to make our toughest comparisons according to our top priorities.

But we can stop playing the game even if no one else in our environment signs the no-compete. If we don't think we can, we're not giving ourselves enough credit. When we work from an activated mentality of God-given security, we are fully capable of thinking another woman is beautiful without concluding we are ugly. We can esteem another woman's achievements without feeling like an idiot. We can admire another woman's terrific shape without feeling like a slob. Where on earth did we come up with the idea that we have to subtract value from ourselves in order to give credit to someone else? You see, it's our insecurity that makes us so poor at math. It constantly leads us to draw the wrong conclusions.

If security says $2 + 2 = 4$, insecurity says $2 + 2 = 9$. In other words, she is this + I am that = I'm a loser. Or just as often we might come to the opposite conclusion: she is this + I am that = she's a loser. The insecurity equation can play out any number of ways. Consider a few others:

I tried to talk to her + she seemed really distracted = she hates me

She's really gorgeous + she gets a lot of attention that I don't = she must be really conceited

She's got this + she's got that = I've got nothing

She doesn't have this problem + I've got that problem = she doesn't have a care in the world

Look what she's got on + look what I've got on = I have the fashion taste of a tsetse fly

Do any of those equations sound vaguely familiar? That's exactly why we need to start catching ourselves in the act of comparison and tell ourselves to stop. We need to roll our eyes at ourselves and think, *There you go with the bad math again.* Even when we're convinced our facts are straight, if insecurity entered a single digit into the equation, we can't trust our summation. $2 + 2 = 5$ is still wrong even if it's closer than $2 + 2 = 9$. Let's learn to call ourselves out before we ever make it from plus to equals.

You may not know what to think about the art of talking to yourself. Actually though, we do it all the time. I'm only recommending that we become deliberate about what we say. I've suggested several statements so far to whisper in our own heads when we need to summon forth some healthy activity from that secure person God has placed within us. Here are a few of the most vital ones:

"I am clothed with strength and dignity."

"My security is mine to keep. God gave it to me. No one gets to take it from me."

You might be relieved to know that the psalmists addressed their own souls on any number of occasions. One asked himself, "Why are you downcast, O my soul? Why so disturbed within me?" (Psalm 42:11). Another called himself to a summit of focus: "Praise the LORD, O my soul; all my inmost being, praise his holy name. Praise the LORD, O my soul, and forget not all his benefits" (Psalm 103:1–2). The psalmist likely didn't command his soul to praise because that's what he felt like doing anyway. I believe he caught himself in the act of destructive or distracted thinking and intended to change the course of his thoughts. That's exactly what you and I must do if we want to start living like the secure people God created us to be. We must catch ourselves in the act of unhealthy thinking and call our souls to switch tracks.

Needless to say, the power of talking to our own souls pales in comparison to pouring out our hearts to God through prayer and requesting His all-glorious intervention. That's why we equipped ourselves with an intense prayer journey in chapter 9. We can turn back to it at any time. By the last page of this book, we'll also have a brief prayer we can say every single morning of our lives, if necessary, to stand our secure ground. This self-talk I'm suggesting is designed to replace the destructive statements and poor equations we're already replaying.

In Galatians 5:26, we can find some great words straight off the sacred page to whisper to ourselves when we're tempted to enter the competition our culture has cast between women:

We will not compare ourselves with each other as if one of us were better and another worse. We have far more interesting things to do with our lives. Each of us is an original.

THE MESSAGE

So that's the first one: we're going to start catching ourselves in the act of comparison and call ourselves out. Now let's look at a second way we can develop a case of infectious security with our own gender.

Start Personalizing Other Women

When we feel threatened by another woman, we need to personalize her. This point never would have occurred to me without happening on the wording recently from Eugene Peterson's translation of Galatians 5. It spoke so clearly to our present subject matter, I almost pole-vaulted ahead of myself to write this chapter. In a segment of Scripture dedicated to drawing a stark contrast between natural living (us on our own) and supernatural living (us empowered by the Spirit of Christ), we're implored to drop . . .

> . . . the vicious habit of depersonalizing everyone into a rival.
>
> GALATIANS 5:21

Read those words a couple of times and start analyzing the concept in your own experiences. That's what I did. I began to test the indictment on every rising temptation I had to feel either *threatened by* or *competitive toward* another woman, even if for only a moment. In no time at all, I knew

Peterson's translation was right on target. In order to successfully view someone as a rival, we have to depersonalize her to a measurable extent. And make no mistake, it's a vicious habit. In order to nurse a rival mentality, we almost always view our competitor through a one-dimensional lens. She is not a person. She is a contender. If she got the guy we wanted, we don't see her in terms of a multilayered life of ups and downs, self-doubts, and second guesses. We depersonalize her into a manipulator or a relationship wrecker. It's easier to despise her that way. If she got the promotion we sought, she's the embodiment of selfish ambition in tan hose and black pumps. If she's more attractive than we feel, she's only skin deep. We can't fathom that she's ever been betrayed or brokenhearted. The list goes on and on, and the concept remains intact.

When we go against the grain of our human nature and determine to personalize someone instead, rivalry loses its bedding ground. My oldest daughter attended junior high and high school with a total phenomenon. Her friend Brittney was not only beautiful. She was smart. That wasn't all. She was so incredibly gifted at sports that her name made the *Houston Chronicle* numerous times. She was just the kind of girl so threatening that none of her female classmates and team members should have liked her. The problem was, they couldn't help it. Brittney was also one of those rarities as endearing as she was talented and as gracious as she was attractive. Amanda was crazy about her. Still is, as a matter off act, and the feeling has always been mutual. If my much shier girl was ever jealous of the friend that couldn't shake a spotlight, I never caught a glimpse of it. Amanda simply never could depersonalize Brittney enough to feel rivaled by her.

Now let's raise the stakes and go from a sweet example to one where the odds are beyond every fair player. A dear friend of mine lost her young husband years ago to an ugly affair that turned into a wedding. My friend didn't have the luxury of running from every reminder because their unsuccessful marriage had resulted in two beloved children. This meant that she came face-to-face with the happy couple at least every other weekend and at every school and sporting event. By anyone's standard, she had every right to hate the woman who had taken up with her man, and granted, she did allow herself to bask in disdain for a couple of long and miserable years. Then one day while we chatted on the phone, she mentioned something in passing about some advice her ex-husband's wife had given her. I was flabbergasted.

"Hold up," I said. "Are you telling me you two are talking? Like, casually?"

"Oh, Beth," she said, "she's got so many problems. I feel for her. I wouldn't be in her position for anything on earth. I don't feel threatened by her anymore."

I wanted to tell her she was nuts, but I couldn't deny her pervading sense of peace and liberty. What had shifted my friend's mind-set? She could no longer get away with depersonalizing the other woman. In the process of seeing her competitor trying to navigate life's inevitable challenges, my friend became less and less fixated on her as a rival. I'm not suggesting we all buddy up to our betrayers or make friends with a spouse's mistress. I do, however, think that if we view potential contenders as equally broken people with real problems, pain, hopes, dreams, and disappointments, we will have taken the first step toward unraveling a rivalry. No one lives on this planet long without scars. The woman who hurt you — whoever she may be and whatever the circumstance — has also been hurt. Either we can keep stabbing each other back or we can lay down the sword.

In Jesus' name.

Incidentally, I've also found it difficult to keep despising someone I consistently pray for. I won't kid you. The process is really hard at first, especially if betrayal was involved. But consistent and humble prayer eventually has a way of changing our feelings and paving a way through the dirt so that the favor of God can flow when the dam breaks. And it will. When I humble myself enough to pray for someone I feel threatened by — and especially when I muster up the courage to ask God to profoundly bless that person — I end up blessed every single time, and the rivalry gets diffused. I keep 1 Peter 3:9 in the recesses of my mind so I can recall how God can work in a harsh conflict:

Do not repay evil with evil or insult with insult, but with blessing, because to this you were called *so that you may inherit a blessing.* (emphasis mine)

It's how we take the high road when somebody is begging us to mud wrestle with her in the potholes of the low road. The very day I stop praying, the toxins return to my emotions.

How about a third way we can develop a case of infectious security with our own gender?

Don't Trip Another Woman's Insecurity Switch

Listen, sister, in a culture this torturous on our gender, we need to be friends, not competitors. We need one another's help, and often when we give it, the benefits that come back to us in terms of our own security are definitely worth the effort. Glance at a handful of examples that illustrate this concept:

If you have the money for a great wardrobe, or even if you have especially great taste on a budget, you don't always have to outdress the rest of your friends. Only avid competitors always feel the need to win.

If you have a fabulous figure, you don't always have to wear a skimpy bathing suit when you and your husband are going boating or to the beach with several other couples. By all means, wear it for him in a less public place, but take caution before you parade it in front of all the other husbands and their wives. You could end up ruining another woman's time or causing a serious altercation between her and her man.

The same suggestion goes for provocative dress when a group of couples is going out to a movie, a restaurant, or an event. Sometimes women dress sensually around other men because they want their husbands to wake up and notice them. But they have no idea how they could be making the other wives feel. Let's exercise a little sensitivity and deal with our insecurities and cravings for attention in ways that don't minimize the women around us. You'll especially want to avoid sensuous dress if you and your mate are being taken out by an employer and his or her spouse, especially if they are older. I assure you it will not serve you well. You will never gain the genuine favor of anyone who perceives you as a threat.

If you know there are certain areas that trip a sister's switch, you can avoid intentionally steering discussions toward those subjects. Years ago when I was a young bride, Keith's Grandma Pereira told me a story I've never forgotten. She and Keith's grandfather lived on a farm with a pond where she had practically domesticated a gaggle of geese. They followed her around like a litter of puppies. On one Saturday afternoon while she and I were on a walk, I spotted a goose hopping behind us that had only one leg.

"What happened to that poor little guy?" I asked.

"I don't know," she said, "but he's my favorite — I guess because I have to keep an eye on him all the time. The others peck at him constantly because they know he's weak."

It really disturbed me. In fact, I nearly cried. I've seen that same syndrome a thousand times with gaggles of humans. We all have just enough meanness in us to occasionally enjoy a peck or two at somebody we know to be weak. Maybe we're usually compassionate, but every now and then we're in a mischievous or terse mood or maybe just tired of tiptoeing around a person who needs to deal with her issues. No matter what's driving us to pick at somebody, let's keep in mind that only insecure people enjoying tripping another person's insecurity switch. Every time we're tempted to do it, we're probably having an attack of our own and trying to build up our wounded selves at somebody else's expense. I've noticed along the way that mean girls grow up to be mean women if they never catch an ugly glimpse of themselves. Let's take a good, long look in the mirror and make absolutely sure we don't see a mean woman staring back at us.

Mind you, some women are so insecure, there's not enough you can do, wear, or say to shield them, and to be honest, they're the ones who need to get the big grip. Try this for the balance when you can't decide if your sensitivity is helping them or hurting them: the goal in our female relationships should be to encourage one another's security. Not enable one another's *in*security. If we simply help each other stay chronically insecure, we've accomplished nothing. I want my closest female associates to offer me a relatively safe place to grow in my security, not wear themselves out over my lack of it.

If we want to develop a case of infectious security with our own gender, here's what we've learned so far: we should start catching ourselves making comparisons and tell ourselves to stop; we should start personalizing the women who feel threatening to us; and when possible, we should avoid tripping another woman's insecurity switch.

We Must Be Examples of Secure Women

For most of us, to see is to believe. The thought never crossed my mind that I could come to love Jesus more than any other living soul on the planet until I saw someone cloaked in flesh and blood actually do it. Her name was Marge Caldwell. Until then, the whole idea was nothing more than a lofty theory we had sung about at church but hung on the coatrack when we headed to the car. The thought also never crossed my mind that I could love the study of Scripture and get the thrill of my life out of hearing God speak through the pages of the Bible until I saw someone else do it. His name was Buddy Walters. Both of these living, breathing examples proved to me that something most Christians believed was theoretical was indeed really possible. And for normal people just like me. I wanted what they had, and bless God, I found it.

Most women will likewise never believe that a secure woman is a real, live possibility until they see one face-to-face. Problem-to-problem. Threat-to-threat. Chase-to-grace. If you'll become the first example in your sphere of influence, you won't be the last. You may pop up all by your lonely self in the beginning, but soon another will pop up close by, then another, because it's as contagious as its counterpart. Wouldn't it be wonderful if a few of those girls who popped up around you were twelve or thirteen years old, with their whole adolescence and adulthood ahead of them? Anybody can be like everybody else. Only those who are exceptional choose to believe the possible over the probable. You, beloved, were created to be exceptional.

Like my friend Stacy. She's a thirtysomething I've known since her college days, a devoted follower of Christ and a fabulous makeup artist by trade. A few weeks ago she was at my office to help me get ready for a photo shoot for this book's cover. When I told her what the book was about, she nearly flipped.

"Beth, I've been obsessed with this subject lately," she said. "I'm so concerned about it. I'm concerned for myself. I'm concerned for my six-year-old daughter and the one on the way. You can imagine in my line of work that I see insecurity everywhere. It's epidemic."

Then Stacy told me a story right in the middle of applying my eye makeup. Through the years she's done her magic on a very attractive socialite for various events in a large, metropolitan city. Because my friend is so adorable and lovable (my description, not hers), she soon won the unsolicited favor of the socialite and found herself on the guest list of a prestigious annual event where fashion is queen. Because she's convinced God orchestrated the relationship, she attends every year. But every year she also stresses. What's a social stepsister supposed to wear to a ball filled with rich Cinderellas? What should she do with her hair? We'll pick up the story in her own words.

I've done makeup on women in those kinds of circles so many times, and I know the kind of insecurity they battle. No matter who they are, how they look, or what they have, their world is filled with so much pressure to be perfect that it's unbearable. And I, a woman who has walked with Christ all these years and ought to know better, found myself feeling all the same things every time I got ready for that event. I was acting no different than a woman wholly *without* the indwelling Christ . . . until this year. All of a sudden I stopped myself in the middle of a panicked frenzy and said to myself . . .

Before she finished her sentence, she put down the makeup brush and patted her heart passionately, confidently, and almost tearfully. She hit each word slowly and deliberately like a hammer on a nail until it pierced my granite head and penetrated all the way to my heart.

But . . . I . . . have . . . this . . . Treasure!

Chills instantly covered my arms. I knew exactly what she was talking about because I was familiar with the passage. It's from 2 Corinthians 4:

> God, who said, "Let light shine out of darkness," made his light shine in our hearts to give us the light of the knowledge of the glory of God in the face of Christ. But we have this treasure in jars of clay to show that this all-surpassing power is from God and not from us.

Did you hear that? We have this treasure! We are aflame with God's glory and radiating with the light of His knowledge in the exquisite face of His Son, Jesus Christ. And we're *insecure?* What kind of lies have we believed all this time? We, of all people on the earth, possess the reason, the residence, and the ongoing revelation to be, of all things, most secure.

By the time my friend was finished testifying, I was nearly on my feet, and my heart was a flood of fresh faith. That's the way women are meant to build one another up in God-given security.

And it doesn't always have to be in person either. We can help each other out from across the planet if that's what it takes. A few days ago I was working on a Bible study by my friend Jennifer Rothschild as part of my early-morning time with God. She told a story about listening to the Bible on tape while she worked out on her treadmill. Here's the part of it that speaks so clearly to you and me at our present juncture:

In between verses, my mind would wander to other things, like my flabby arms. I began to scold myself for not being more diligent with exercise. Then I followed my thoughts down a path of how disappointed I was that I let my weight fluctuate. I would veer off my miserable mental path every few seconds to tune back into the Bible that was still reading in my ear. I remember distinctively tuning in just in time to hear

Psalm 84:1.[17]

Sit back and absorb the verse she's talking about:

How lovely is your dwelling place, O LORD Almighty!

I memorized that wonderful pilgrim psalm many years ago, but not once have I ever seen the opening verse in light of believers as the current dwelling places of God's Spirit. A few quick glances in the New Testament would tell you that my friend had her doctrinal ducks in a row (1 Corinthians 3:16; 6:19). Imagine how different our days would be if we woke up every morning and, before putting on a stitch of makeup or flat-ironing our hair, we confessed out loud to God: "How lovely is your dwelling place, O LORD Almighty!" And what if we said it with the enthusiasm conveyed by the exclamation point playing pogo at the end of it? Actually, I don't have to imagine what it would be like, because I've been trying it. I say it in the early-morning darkness on my way from the coffeepot to the place where I sit with my Bible, and I smile every time. I think God does too. If you are a believer in Jesus Christ, I dare you to say this out loud right this minute no matter where you are:

I am lovely.

One more time with a little more enthusiasm.

I AM LOVELY!

Yep, I think you are too. A well-meaning man asked me not long ago if I was scared a book like this would tempt women to pride. Are you kidding me? This culture is so brutal on a woman that my fear is not talking long enough and hammering hard enough on her value. Girlfriend, the fact that you've made it this far in this journey means that you needed it as much as I did. We can't even check out our groceries without looking at the covers of magazines and feeling ugly — even if we have on our favorite jeans and the cutest top in our closet. Arrogance comes from a whole different place than God-confidence. If somebody walks away from this book with pride, she missed the whole point. We simply want some dignity back.

Because we happen to be lovely — but, these days, it's a beast to believe it.

CHAPTER 16
A PASSION TO
LOOK PAST OURSELVES

Well, my sister, we are only three chapters from our journey's end. Before we know it, we'll each be on our own with a faithful God, challenged to live steadfastly as secure women in the rough-and-tumble of a grossly insecure world. It will not suddenly cease shouting deceptive words to us about our identity, our dignity, and the fast track to security. If the roar of the world were unconvincing and illogical, books like this one would be unnecessary. We're together on this page because we're in a battle that can't be won timidly or accidentally. We need to be ready to discern the difference between the truth and a lie, especially when the lie is proclaimed at high volume while the truth is only whispered through a still, small voice. In this chapter, let's reiterate what we can expect to hear shouted from the world and learn how to actively offset our addiction to listen.

After all, we still have to live here, and we might as well admit that the world has its appeals. I'm fairly certain my two daughters toddled their first strong steps while in a shopping mall. When you live in a stifling climate like ours with air so hot and wet you practically have to hack through it with a machete to get to the car, you either swim or shop for amusement with your children. By the end of June, the pool water feels like a hot tub without the jets, so if you're like me, you set your sights on the welcome corridors of the closest mall and start digging through your purse for Happy Meal money.

Amanda, Melissa, and I have bonded over the Formica tables of food courts for decades. We've often bought little more than lunch on our frequent shopping sprees, and we bowed our heads and thanked God for the joy of it. On the other hand, a few times we've blown so much cash that we've driven home on the fumes of frantic prayer because we didn't have a dime left for gas. Our saving grace was embodied in a woman of impressive stature and garlic-strong personality by the name of Mary Jo. Heads of state would have done well to hand Mary Jo the nation's checkbook. She was a math whiz with a hard-knocks degree in accounting who kept the books for my father-in-law's successful plumbing business for thirty years.

Seeing the handwriting on the wall with the birth of a second daughter, Keith put Mary Jo in charge of our family finances while he and I were still in our twenties. The girls and I were scared half to death of her — and with ample reason. She'd agreed to the position under one condition: her way or the highway. The fact that we aren't hitchhiking on that highway today is a testimony to her larger-than-life role in our lives. We mostly lived on a cash-only budget because she made us pay off our credit cards in full every single month, even if we had only four dollars left to last us from the twentieth to the first. Every month she issued us six envelopes with words like *groceries* and *gas* scribbled on the front of them. Each one contained the amount of cash she deemed we could afford to spend on each need. Let me interject that the woman saw no need for frivolity, and if my middle name was anything at all, it was frivolity. To say we were on a budget with no budge is putting it kindly. I felt she didn't understand our needs. She felt I didn't understand our balance.

Keith and I stood at her casket three days ago with such lumps in our throats we couldn't speak, but had we been able to utter a word, this is what we might have said:

Thank you, Mary Jo. We paid for two girls to go to college because of you. We narrowly avoided foreclosing on a home during the Texas oil crisis because of you. We're not in debt up to our eyeballs because of you. We always pay off our credit cards each month, even if it nearly breaks us, because (we're still scared) of you. We're holding out hope that you may be faking your demise because we honestly don't know what we'll do without you. And Mary Jo, one last thing: our girls are better women because of you. We'd have been in perpetual bankruptcy, and they'd have been perpetually spoiled rotten. After all, our name is Moore. To us, if a little is good, more is better. We were blessed with a little bit less all because of you.

At least for now, Keith and I can pay our bills every month. Our house of twenty-five years is paid off, and so are our cars. I mention these facts because we are all so very tempted to think that financial solidity would make us secure. That's why a fresh reminder might be in order: though this book's poster child (please see cover) possessed financial stability when she wrote the first chapter of this book, she was still absolutely desperate to be free of the albatross of insecurity. Money helped pay our bills. It did not assuage my chronic insecurity. Maybe, in fact, it was the last straw. The final proof that nothing I could hold in my hands or put on my body would ever do the trick. No amount of stuff and no amount of money can soothe the savage beast of insecurity within all of us. The sustained hope that we will someday have enough only increases the pressure, decreases the time off, and delays the inevitable disillusionment.

Thousands of years ago, an old prophet spoke words that would be frighteningly consistent with many of the headlines we're seeing on news magazines during this nation's current economic crisis:

> You believe your wealth will buy security, putting your family's nest beyond the reach of danger.
>
> HABAKKUK 2:9, NLT

No amount of wealth can buy security. Every rich man and woman in the world is squirming in that reality right now. You and I have learned along the way that our need is far deeper than our circumstances and more cavernous than our pockets can plunge. Our world system has made finan-

386

cial promises it can't keep, and though its confessions are made only in whispers, if we'll listen closely, it's finally admitting the lie. A fat bank account is still entirely dependent upon the dollar retaining some value. The red flag is waving. Though we had all better get serious about making wiser financial decisions and learning the science of saving, no bank under heaven can promise complete immunity from economic disaster. Even if, God forbid, we withdrew every dime from our accounts and buried them in airtight chests in the family grave-yard, the question would still remain: what will the dollar be worth when we dig it up? People who have placed their trust in money are shaking in their boots on slippery sand right now.

There are other deceptions that this world system doesn't have any intention of own-ing. There's too much at stake to even whisper these lies. We've hammered one of them over and over because it's such a huge investor in female insecurity, but as we start drawing our journey to a close, we're going to hit it one more time. In order to sketch a familiar concept in a fresh framework, permit me a quick return to the shopping mall with both of my daughters.

Since much of the time when we're together both girls are attached to me like a fifth and sixth limb, I always know something is up when they try to lose me at the mall. If either one of them asks, "Why don't we go our separate directions for a few minutes and meet back up?" it ordinarily indicates one thing: one of them needs to grab a new undergarment at a certain infamous store, and the last thing on earth she wants is for me to accompany her in there. All this fuss because on the rarest occasion I've voiced the meekest opinion about said store. I'd like to be clear. I believe wholeheartedly in underwear, so my issue is not with the merchandise per se. My objection is the gigantic, hypersexual posters in the storefront for every prepubescent girl and boy in the entire mall to see. That's what I find particularly appalling.

A couple of years ago I waited and waited to no avail at the spot in the mall where we three were supposed to meet after going "our separate directions." Finally, I headed to where I knew I would find them. Sure enough, they were both standing in the checkout line at the store in question, and I suppose it's only fair to add that both girls were well into adulthood and could purchase what they pleased without my permission. Both of their faces turned as white as

388

bleached sheets when I joined them in line. The ensuing conversation went like this:

Amanda: "Mom, why don't you go out there and sit on one of those benches till we're done? This could take a little while."

Me: "Do I look seventy to you? I can still outrun both of you. I don't mind waiting right here."

Checkout girl: "How are you today, ma'am?"

Melissa: "Please, miss, don't ask her any questions. It's better if she doesn't talk. She's fine, and she's on her way out of the store."

I received a firm nudge but remained impressively stalwart. After all, the young woman at the checkout asked me a question and how rude would I be to ignore her?

Me: "I'm well today. [Followed by something I, the pun queen, alone found amusing:] How is business here in the underworld?"

I glanced to my right and to my left for a little appreciation of my obvious quick wit, but Amanda and Melissa did not crack a smile. Both nearly bore a hole through my forehead with eyes like steel bullets. The checkout girl sensed something was amiss and wisely joined them in observing a moment of silence.

Me (trying to be reassuring): "Don't mind me. I'm just going to mind my own business and stand right here until you guys finish up."

I was feeling mature. Surprisingly unbothered. Both daughters resorted to nervous fidgeting and several unsuccessful attempts at line cutting. I pinched my lips pale while two women in front of us checked out, but I began to feel a certain itching sensation on my tongue as we stepped up for our turn. After a near eternity of waiting, both girls finally put their small (emphasis on small) purchases down on the counter. I stepped up right between them and received one last stern stare from each direction. I had planned to keep my mouth shut this time. I really had. Even when I loosed my lips, I meant to limit myself to a friendly repartee. Anyway, how can a person learn if she doesn't ask questions?

Me: "I was just wondering what makes a mint sexy."

Checkout girl, looking baffled: "Pardon me, ma'am?"

Amanda: "Oh, no. Here it comes."

Melissa: "Don't do it, Mom. We're almost done here. Thirty seconds, Mom. Thirty seconds!"

Me (ignoring them): "I was asking you

about these cute little containers here on the counter. The ones called 'Sexy Mints.' I wonder what qualifies a mint to be sexy. I mean, since they're food, really, and not even much of that, I'm just curious about the name. What makes one mint sexier than the other?"

The unsuspecting young woman looked at me like I'd looked at Mary Jo during one too many excruciating interrogations. In hindsight, the darling salesclerk was as sweet as she could be and awfully caught off guard. I was wrong to hold her responsible for an entire company's ad campaign. She was just trying to pay her rent and get a small discount on elastic bands. It was entirely my fault. My self-control took flight and fled, and mature reasoning followed it. Just as I was on the verge of becoming one of those people I can hardly stomach, Amanda and Melissa each did an about-face in perfect synchronization, hooked an arm through each of mine and literally dragged me out of the store. I was still facing the checkout counter as they headed toward the door, hauling the very woman who had walked through the valley of the shadow of death to birth them. As we finally crossed the sacred threshold back into the light, I got out my last few words: "I just don't get it! Why does a mint have to be sexy? Why can't it just give us fresh breath?"

The silence on the way home was deafening. The only words the girls said to me were these: "That's it. Never again." Thank goodness, they didn't mean shopping. They just meant that I never get to accompany them into a store like that again. They've kept their word. The problem is, it's not the inside of the store that bothers me so much. It's the outside. It's the involuntary visual assault on innocent passersby. You could be on your way to the Disney Store with your seven-year-old daughter to pick up a birthday gift and suddenly find her transfixed in front of a huge glossy poster of a gorgeous young woman in her underwear in a pose that ought to throw her back out.

Perhaps now is not the best time to try to convince you of this, but I really tried to pursue a semblance of balance in my parenting as I raised two daughters in this out-of-balance society. Keith and I were deliberate in our choice to protect our children within our culture rather than isolate them as the general rule. Our strategy didn't turn out perfectly, but parenting is too hard and too human a job to perform to perfection. To the grace and glory of God, the "four Moores," as we refer to ourselves, made it to our primary goal line without too many scars. Sometimes the process wasn't pretty because Keith and I had our own ugly baggage, but both daughters turned out to be gracious, God-seeking adults who seem to know that people are higher priorities than possessions.

Yes, I will admit that if we were raising them in today's culture, we would definitely have to make some adjustments for the snares that have multiplied in the jungles of childhood. Each set of parents has the responsibility to pray for wisdom, follow their own healthy convictions, and determine what works best for the individual child. As for Keith and me, we just never felt that social isolation was the ultimate answer.

With a mom in the annoying middle of their personal business, both girls were very involved in large public schools, had boyfriends, and participated in all sorts of extracurricular activities. We saw movies and watched television and kept up with current events. (These are not remotely offered to you as recommendations. They are simple facts and perhaps even confessions in hopes that they'll buy me some credibility on an impending issue.) One of my worst nightmares was that in trying to do the right thing, I would shape our children's theologies in such a way that they would see God as the Big Taker in the Sky instead of the Giver of "every good and perfect gift" (James 1:17). I never wanted them to think that the only word He had uttered since the conclusion of the sacred canon was no.

Thus saith the Lord: *No, you may not . . .*

That's not the way I saw Him. That's not the way I believed Scripture painted Him either. These are the kinds of things God has taken from me: a ton of guilt, a path of addiction, a string of bad relationships, and a future no different from my past. Every no God has issued to me was to keep me from missing a glorious and far greater yes. I wanted my children to know the God who had been the biggest joy and adventure of my entire life. In my attempt to choose battles carefully and balance some firm, immovable noes with plenty of yeses, we occasionally wobbled on a pretty fine line between worldliness and godliness. On a constant intravenous drip of grace, we eventually made it to the other side in one piece, and the girls knew without question what was important to us.

Why am I bothering to tell you this? Because I want you to know that I'm not one of those Christians with a phobia of everything vaguely enjoyable or superficial. I have no allergy to fun. I like cute clothes and pedicures, and I rarely have fewer than three colors in my hair at any given time. I do not live my believing life with my nose turned up in constant disapproval, nor do I ask every morning what this world's coming to. But make no mistake, there are a few things I genuinely hold in contempt. One is our culture's propensity to force our children to grow up too fast. Another sits in tandem beside it: teaching our daughters from the earliest age the high priority of sensuality. It's what author Cooper Lawrence calls "early hypersexualization" in her book *The Cult of Celebrity.* To any adult willing to listen, she writes:

It's not all in your head: There is a difference between celebrity and media images girls see now and what you were exposed to as a child. Highly sexualized images of younger and younger women are becoming the norm.[18]

That's why an illicit storefront in a mall with an otherwise family-friendly atmosphere is objectionable to me. As long as a boutique gives the consumer some accurate idea of what's inside, the responsibility is on our own heads once we walk through the door. Having images forced on our young children through storefronts or even billboards is another matter entirely. It's a full-throttle shout of twisted values that develop into all sorts of destructive beliefs and behaviors in the accidental buyer. No, I don't expect advertising to improve, but we'd better start saying a few things to ourselves and our girls at significantly higher volumes.

I've watched an unsettling trend develop over the last decade, and I'm convinced that it is the result of this "early hypersexualization." In previous generations, the girls who were the most insecure and desperate and the least likely to set boundaries and practice self-respect were normally those with a background of sexual abuse or misuse. We were the ones who settled for so much less in our relationships, caved to pressure, felt like we always had to have a boyfriend, and acted like *no* was all but missing from our list of multiple-choice answers. Over recent years, a growing number of middle and high school girls who have never been inappropriately touched have taken on these same characteristics. After watching the disturbing trend too long to shake it, I finally realized that our whole Western world is under sexual assault. Whether or not a girl is physically touched in sexually inappropriate ways, the visual impact of early hypersexualization is still significant enough to dramatically shape her self-concept and sexuality.

Our world system is shouting no louder lie to its female population than this: *To be desirable is to be valuable, and to be sensual is to be secure. These are the attributes that guarantee you will always be loved.*

Those buying the lie are getting younger and younger, and the emotional toll is getting higher and higher. This book is built on one major premise: try as we might, we are not likely to change our culture. But we can let God change us, and vital change will happen *within* our culture. We are surrounded by a superficial world making deceptive claims. That will not soon change. We find ourselves with three basic choices: (1) We can pull out of the world system entirely and isolate ourselves and our families. In this case, we will need a substantial amount of money to buy a remote farm where we'll need to drill a well and get a septic tank. Forget being light in the darkness. Just go hide it under a bushel of split peas. Don't get me wrong. I'm not bashing farming. It's our grocer, for Pete's sake. I'm bashing hiding. (2) We can immerse ourselves in superficiality and find it utterly insatiable. In this case, we'll need to make peace with self-loathing, because we will undoubtedly become our own worst enemies. (3) We can fend off the effects of superficiality with a deliberate devotion to the profound. We can fight to find purpose.

As long as we live, our self-absorption and our insecurity will walk together, holding hands and swinging them back and forth like two little girls on their way to a pretend playground they can never find. Human nature dictates that most often we will be as insecure as we are self-absorbed. The best possible way to keep from getting sucked into the superficial, narcissistic mentality that money, possessions, and sensuality can satisfy and secure us is to deliberately give ourselves to something much greater. We are under the constant indoctrination that getting is the way to receiving.

Christ, the Author of life more abundant, taught something totally different. He showed us that giving, rather than getting, is the means to receiving. I will say it again before our journey ends: to find yourself, your true, secure self, you must lose yourself in something larger.

With your permission, I'm going to ask

you some probing questions as our road narrows toward a close. What is your passion? Because we've been handcrafted in the very image of our Creator, we each have a cavernous need to live a life that matters. What matters to *you?* As you draw your last breath, what do you want your life to have been about? Don't feel condemned and shallow if you can't think of anything meaningful at the moment. Search your heart. Your vision may be buried somewhere beneath the cynicism you developed as a defense. Life is hard, but even the harshness of life points toward purpose. If you're willing, you can probably trace your passion all the way to the deepest point of your pain.

For many of us, God used painful experiences to birth our life passions. A fire burns in me to see women of all ages and colors freed and flourishing in Christ, because I've known the anguish of bondage and abuse. I have a friend who was profoundly affected by abandonment and now pours her life into helping couples adopt. I know of another woman who struggled in school and didn't get her GED until well into adulthood. She now helps children learn how to read. I know countless addicts freed by God who now live their lives to help others discover the same deliverance. I have so many friends involved in prison ministries because they know what it's like to feel trapped by terrible decisions. I know a former exotic dancer who gave her life to Christ but through His sanctifying presence kept her love for the innocent and beautiful side of dancing. She now teaches ballet to little girls and has never been happier. They don't know her past because there is no further trace of it, but those of us who are aware of where she has been are twice as impressed with where she is now. She is a miracle.

Please allow me, for the sake of emphasis, to repeat myself on issues so vital to our journey's success: you are meant to be a miracle too. Your past has not come full circle to its complete redemption until you allow Christ to not only defuse it, but also to use it. I'm not suggesting that you have to go public with all your sins and sorrows. I'm simply proposing that the only reason God allowed all that pain in your path, as much as He loved you, was to bring good from it. Have you offered Him the freedom to work all those hardships together for good as He promises in His Word to those who love Him and seek to fulfill His purposes?

Beloved, pursuing a life of purpose is one

of our strongest guards against buying the superficiality that feeds insecurity. What if we stopped thinking about it and started doing it? If you have no idea where to begin, search out some volunteer opportunities in your area. Look into hospice. Go sit beside a person with AIDS, dying to be loved. Go read to the elderly. People out there need help. And you have something inside you that *needs* to help them. So do I. It's the way our souls were built.

Unless we choose to drop out of public life entirely, we're still going to pass alluring storefronts, billboards, magazine covers, and Internet ads that shout all sorts of promises they can't keep. Unless we want to let them completely consume and corrode us, we're going to have to know beyond a doubt that life is about something greater. I am not nearly as affected by plunking a new pair of jeans on the counter at Gap if I know in my heart that it's the furthest thing on earth from what really matters.

When Keith and I get home from doing food relief work in Angola or AIDS work in South Africa, our fleshly appetites are always dramatically dulled and our insecurities are veritable nonissues. We have much more important things to think about. We've both become convinced that the less we are willing to get outside our own lives, the more self-absorbed and miserable we become. I'll never forget Keith walking through the front door a year or so ago, slamming it behind him, and stomping to the bedroom, where he grabbed his checkbook.

"Honey, what on earth is the matter?" I could tell he was as mad as a hornet.

"I just caught myself counting our money in my head while I was driving around town. Apparently I haven't given enough away lately."

And he wrote a check to a charity. Now don't go thinking that he's Mr. Hyper-Spiritual, because he's not. He's just a man who has lived long enough to know that the more selfish he is, the more miserable he becomes. The greedier he is, the less secure he feels. If he feels like hoarding, he knows he needs to give something away.

With awe and gratefulness to a merciful God, we have watched our children also pour their passions into the needs of people. Yes, both my daughters will shop their feet to nubs, spending the day with me at an area mall where we might end up with more than lunch. But they will also board a plane en route to the remotest parts of the world and stare poverty in its ugly face.

Our youngest daughter, Melissa, wrote these words after her recent return from mission work overseas. Her experience suggests to all of us that a person doesn't have to wait until she has lived fifty-plus years to figure out that life is not all about her.

Oh, what a deep imprint [the children] have made on this hard heart of mine. And not just them, but all the people, so deeply loved by God, in Calcutta and India at large who must fight for their survival each and every day. I could never have prepared myself for all that I saw last week. For example, during one of my visits to a devastating slum, a half-clothed, poverty-stricken crippled man with his back hunched over at a ninety-degree angle limped slowly over to me. He had purchased a coconut for me with whatever small amount of money he did have and then proceeded to slice the top open for me to drink so that I could be protected from the heat. And mind you, I was the one going back to the air-conditioned hotel. Not him. What was I supposed to do with that? And that is just one of about several hundred stories I could tell.

Because we each had experiences like

this and because I am sure our eyes were about to glaze over, the leaders of our group called for a debriefing in lieu of a corporate lobotomy. During this debriefing they gave us a safe place to talk about what some of us were feeling and thinking. It was great, but we really needed another entire week to hash it all out. I'll never forget the [question one leader posed] before we left the debriefing.

"Now that you know, what will you do?"

He continued by saying, "You've spent your words lavishly on sharing your stories; now it's time to spend your lives." Talk about messing me up. And so it was to this tune that our reentry began.

I will confess something about myself. You know that I'm going through an emotionally or spiritually trying time when I bust out one of the movies from The Lord of the Rings trilogy. Other girls may want *Sleepless in Seattle* or even *Pride and Prejudice,* but for me, it's Tolkien. There was one awful season in my life when, along with reading the books, I actually watched at least one of the films every night for two months. I wish I were exaggerating. You can ask my dad, because he was so ready for me to get a grip. I was totally hogging the television, and he had deer-show watching needs that definitely were not being met. And, yeah, I know . . . spending three hours a night watching movies wasn't exactly good stewardship of my time. But it's the truth. I nearly have the entire trilogy memorized. And that is saying a lot since most of the proper names sound exactly the same.

Well, yesterday it happened again. This time my victim was [the third in the trilogy] *The Return of the King.* Have you ever seen it? Do you remember the last scene when Frodo unexpectedly boards the ship to sail to the Grey Havens? Throughout their life-threatening journey to Mordor, Frodo and Sam kept dreaming about such things like the taste of the strawberries on the Shire, but when Frodo actually does get back to the Shire, for some reason, it is like he can't fully enjoy the normal comforts that the Shire has to offer. I've always speculated about why exactly Frodo has to sail to the Grey Havens. I think that Frodo has just been through too much. His scars run too deep. After years of being back at the Shire they still haven't healed. In the movie he asks the rhetorical questions: "How do you pick up the threads of an old life? How do you go on when in your heart you begin to understand there is no going back?" And then he explains, "There are some things time cannot mend. Some hurts that go too deep . . . that have taken hold."

But I'm not a hobbit.

And this is real life.

I don't get to sail off and escape from the white shores into a far green country under a swift sunrise with Gandalf.

Ironically, my life just happens to be deep in the heart of excessive American culture. And I'd be lying to you if I said I don't enjoy it. The honest truth is that I know myself. I know that normal life will quickly pick back up and the temptation will be to forget all I have seen. To move forward without any change. While others around me may wish for me to hurry up and acclimate to normal life again, my fear is that I will too quickly move ahead. That I will forget all I have seen, heard, touched, smelled, and felt.

I know myself.

I'm just an all-American twenty-six-year-old girl, consumed with comfort, security, vanity, wealth, and materialism like the "best" of them. In light of who I know I am, I feel compelled to ask that the Lord would perform a miracle on my behalf — that He would keep the emotional wounds that were carved during the past few weeks from healing. Now I know you may think I'm a bit morbid, eccentric, or even just plain weird. But that's okay, because I've been called far worse, I'm sure of it. So this is my prayer today: that time won't have its typical way with me. That the sharp edge of the sting I feel deep in my soul won't ever be dulled or alleviated.

You see, Melissa didn't just want to care. She knew that deep within her soul, she *needed* to care. She realized that, just like the rest of us, she'd never be healed of her self-centeredness until she was wounded irreparably with love for an aching world. To help others would become life to her own lungs. As it turns out, the prophet Isaiah told us something similar centuries ago. Absorb it into the marrow of your bones, dear one, and then, before the dust can settle on the cover of this book, let's start acting on it. So long, superficiality. You've fueled our insecurity way too long.

Is not this the kind of fasting I have chosen: to loose the chains of injustice and untie the cords of the yoke, to set the oppressed free and break every yoke?

Is it not to share your food with the hungry and to provide the poor wanderer with shelter — when you see the naked, to clothe him, and not to turn away from your own flesh and blood?

Then your light will break forth like the dawn, and your healing will quickly appear; then your righteousness will go before you, and the glory of the LORD will be your rear guard.

Then you will call, and the LORD will answer; you will cry for help, and he will say: Here am I. If you do away with the yoke of oppression, with the pointing finger and malicious talk, and if you spend yourselves in behalf of the hungry and satisfy the needs of the oppressed, then your light will rise in the darkness, and your night will become like the noonday.

The LORD will guide you always; he will satisfy your needs in a sun-scorched land and will strengthen your frame. You will be like a well-watered garden, like a spring whose waters never fail.

ISAIAH 58:6–11

CHAPTER 17
WHAT ARE YOU AFRAID OF?

Any communicator worth her salt knows that the last points a decent listener hears in a message will probably be what she remembers best. That's why I've waited until now to discuss the subject matter in this chapter. If you forget one hundred other references in this book, I am hoping and praying you will not forget this one. Think of it like a Quick Start button on an exercise bike. If you take the time to customize your program by entering your age, weight, and interval preference before the pedals start spinning, you'll undoubtedly get a better workout. But sometimes you just don't have the time or patience to enter the information. If you hit Quick Start, you may not get the optimum, personalized effects, but you can count on a workout.

Your road to a prevailing sense of security will be most effective and life energizing if you take the customized route that we've spent multiple chapters discussing. Sometimes, however, you just need to know how to hit Quick Start. For each of those moments, there's a powerful pair of words:

Trust God.

Plain and simple. Not easy, mind you, but basic and uncomplicated. You don't always have to hash it all out. Sometimes you can make a single swift decision. As Christ said to a wavering disciple, you just have to make up your splintered mind to "stop doubting and believe" (John 20:27). Believe that He loves you and has you covered and takes every one of your hits as if they were aimed at His own skin. Get down to the bottom of what frightens you, and then pitch it to Him like a hot potato. Let's freeze on those three words tucked into the middle of the previous sentence for a minute:

What frightens you?

Whenever you get hit by a wave of insecurity, the wind driving it is always fear. This is true whether the flare-up is monumental or comparatively mild. The moment you're cognizant of an outbreak of insecurity, learn to check your heart for what you're afraid of. If you're honest with yourself, you'll rarely come away from that diagnostic test empty-handed. No need to make this complicated. Imagine two simple scenarios.

1. You're standing at a coworker's desk. A simple conversation ensues. "Did you hear about . . . ?" No, you hadn't heard. Suddenly, a wave of insecurity wells up inside of you. A fear of some kind is driving it. Learn to instantly identify it. Trade it in for trust.
2. You're at a crowded restaurant with your man. While waiting for an available table, he and a woman you've never met greet each other enthusiastically. She turns out to be a coworker you've heard him mention here and there. You had no idea she looked like that. Suddenly, a wave of insecurity wells up inside of you. A fear of some kind is driving it. Learn to instantly identify it. Trade it in for trust.

If you and I were at a sidewalk café having this conversation over cappuccinos, you might be in a position to respond to the second scenario like this: "But Beth, I don't know if I can trust my man or not. What if I've seen red flags and something really is up?"

412

I'm not talking about trusting your man in the middle of that wave of insecurity, although I deeply hope you can and do. I'm talking about something much less reliant on frail flesh and blood: trusting God. Trusting God *with yourself. With your husband. With your job. With your health. With your family. With your friends. With your threat.* I'm talking about entering into a transforming, two-sentence dialogue with a very real, very active God who sees all things and is intimately acquainted with everything concerning you:

You: "Lord, I don't know if I can trust _____ or not."

God: "But can you trust *Me?*"

Any time insecurity hits, you can be sure that you are afraid of something. The question is, *what?* The answer could be one of many possibilities depending on our present vulnerabilities, but it can get subtly ignored behind the upheaval of insecurity. You have to look beyond the obvious to see the wind driving the wave. Maybe you could use a jump start so you'll know the kinds of things you're looking for. Beneath that sudden outbreak of insecurity:

You may fear proving stupid.
You may fear rejection.

You may fear anonymity.
You may fear being alone.
You may fear being unimportant.
You may fear betrayal.
You may fear being replaced.
You may fear disrespect.
You may fear being hurt.
You may fear pain of any sort.

Nothing has come more naturally to me than fear. I understand the insanity of some of it and the sheer normalcy of most of it. I'm often afraid because the world proves over and over to be a scary place. Like yours, the majority of my fears have been unfounded, but some of them have been almost prophetic — as if my rehearsals did anything at all to make the reality easier. Listen carefully: either way, whether founded or fictional, our fears will never do us a single favor. If fright would somehow insulate us from specific outcomes, I'd say let's jump out from behind a door and scare ourselves half to death every morning for good measure. If imagining it would keep us from living it, let's all quit our jobs and spend our days transfixed on the couch in a mental horror flick of our own making. The fact is, fearing something doesn't jinx it — even though we wish it would. Neither does it prepare us for it. Fear consumes massive amounts of energy and focus and can chew a hole through our intestines, our relationships, and countless great opportunities. At the risk of oversimplifying, the kind of fear we're talking about is a colossal waste of time.

I used to think that the essence of trusting God was trusting that He wouldn't allow my fears to become realities. Without realizing it, I mostly trusted God to do what I told Him. If He didn't, I was thrown for a total loop. Over more time than should have been necessary, a couple of realizations finally dawned on me about this thing I was calling trust: (1) It wasn't the real thing. (2) It constantly failed to treat the core issue. Trusting God to never let our fears come to fruition doesn't get to the bottom of where insecurity lurks. It's too conditional. It suggests that if any of our terrors come to pass, God is not trustworthy after all. If, like me, you tend to think that the essence of trust is counting on God to obey you, go ahead and wave bye-bye from a country mile to any semblance of lasting stability. If we can't count on God, for crying out loud, who can we count on? In the words of Isaiah 33:6, "He is your constant source of stability" (NET).

Travel the earth and sail the seven seas. Delve into the world's great philosophies and tinker with its religions if you can risk the time. If you're candid with yourself, you'll still discover that there is no other constant than God. Nothing else will hold.

Anyway, when we set certain conditions for trust, we offer the enemy of our souls the perfect playground for toying with our minds. No, he can't read our thoughts, but he can certainly study our behaviors. Once he pinpoints our emotional Achilles' heel, he draws back the bow and aims the poisonous dart straight at it. He figures out what we're most afraid of, and then he taunts us unmercifully with expert marksmanship.

See if this sounds familiar: your teenager is late coming in from a date, and you can't reach her on her cell phone. You've called six times and texted ten. You have her dead and buried in your mind by 1:00 a.m. By the time she tiptoes through the front door, you've eaten everything in the refrigerator and overdosed on antacids. Most of the enemy's power is in his bluff, but he has been around long enough to know that the constant fear of disaster can be as disabling as the disaster itself. Your daughter begs your forgiveness, drops into bed, and sleeps like a baby. You're up half the night trying to quiet unrequited anguish.

You know somewhere deep down that there's got to be a better way. And thankfully, there is. In order to plant our feet on solid ground, we can drop the conditions off of our trust and determine that God will take care of us *no matter what.* Let me say that again.

No matter what.

I'm not saying it's easy. I'm stating that if we want to be secure people, this mind-set is a necessity. Sometimes trusting God means taking no further action. That's when a verse like Psalm 46:10 speaks loudest: "Be still, and know that I am God." Other times trusting God means regrouping with Him until the fog clears so we know how to take the next step. Nothing can mislead us or make us jump the gun faster than fear. For times like these when action is necessary but not obvious, Proverbs 3:5–6 hits the nail on the head: "Trust in the LORD with all your heart; do not depend on your own understanding. Seek his will in all you do, and he will show you which path to take" (NLT). I love the succinct way Psalm 37:3 says something similar: "Trust in the LORD and do good" (NLT).

A couple of years ago God put me through a peculiar exercise that caused a total

417

earthquake in my long-held perception of trust. With your permission, I'd like to replay it to you in the form of a dialogue because when it occurred, it was as if God spoke every word concretely and audibly to me. In reality, what I'll describe was expressed in my spirit rather than in my physical hearing. After spending years in relationship with God, seeking what He's like and how He operates in Scripture, I, like many people, can get a sense of something He's strongly impressing upon me without "hearing" precise words. When thoughts come to me out of the blue that I'm convinced did not originate in my own mind, if they're consistent with God's character and sound like something He would say in Scripture, I usually assume it's Him. Ultimately, time proves whether or not I discerned the voice correctly. If it produces substantial fruit, I know it was God and I was on target. If nothing comes of it, I probably misunderstood or accidentally ascribed it to Him. None of us are beyond confusing our own thoughts with God's, no matter how many times we've been around the bend with Him.

That said, here's what happened. God saw me in inner turmoil *again* about a relentless relational challenge, and while I was wrestling before Him in prayer, my stomach twisted like a wrung-out wet rag, He interrupted.

Child, tell Me your worst fears.

I was a little taken aback. After all, I was in the throes of a particularly descriptive lament. Still, in my human estimation, He had no doubt spoken, so who was I to ask Him to wait His turn? I did what He requested. I told Him my worst fears. Then He "said" something I never could have anticipated, and this, beloved, is precisely what I mean by "out of the blue."

Let's say those things happened.

Trust me when I tell you, that is *not* what I wanted to hear from God. I wanted reassurances like, "I will never let any of those things happen to you." I sensed Him continue the interaction despite my bewilderment and dread.

Beth, picture yourself going through the whole process of one of your worst fears becoming a reality. Get all the way to the other side of it. What do you see there?

So I did. I saw myself getting the news I feared most, bawling my eyes out, grieving a loss, or going through all the emotions of betrayal. The tears stung in my eyes. Butterflies flew to my stomach. My insides turned out. But something odd happened

419

on the other side. I'll use a specific example to illustrate the process:

One of the fears I confessed to God was that, in my older years, Keith would stop loving me and fall for somebody else. Somebody younger. After all, a few of his good friends had done exactly that. It wasn't unreasonable. It's not like it doesn't happen. I pictured my worst-case scenario: not only would Keith find someone new, my daughters would also love and embrace her. Now *that* would be a nightmare.

Okay, Beth, you did a good job thinking up something terrible. What then?

That's when I figured out what God was after. He and I both knew what I would do. I would be devastated at first. I would probably sin in my anger and say all sorts of things and act all sorts of ways I would live to regret. I would feel inexpressibly lonely and rejected and probably old and ugly. But I knew that finally I'd go facedown before God just as I have a hundred other hard times, accept His grace and mercy, believe Him to take up my cause and work it together for good, and then I would get up and choose to live.

The excruciating emotional exercise was the best thing God ever could have asked from me. He knew I had pictured the

420

devastation and defeat over and over, but I had never gotten any further than that in my imagination. It was as if He said, "As long as you're going to borrow trouble on the future, why don't you just go ahead and borrow the grace to go with it and see yourself back up on your feet defying your enemy's odds . . . just as you and I have done a dozen other times."

Even now I could clap my hands over it. The devil took a harsh blow that day because I've never fallen back into that old pattern of thinking. And further, the victory over such a long-term mental stronghold caused me to entertain the thought that I could be equally free from my lifelong battle with insecurity. After all, the two are inseparable. These days I far less often pray, "Lord, I trust You to . . ." I simply try to say over and over again, "Lord, I trust You. Period."

I've always been afraid of losing my most cherished loved ones. When giving way to particularly advanced forms of self-torment, I have even pictured myself at their caskets (morbid, I know, but don't try to tell me you haven't done it). But I never once pictured myself several years later, back on my feet to the glory of God, heart sore and scarred but pouring my life into hurting people. Helping other people get through what I've gone through is redemption to me. It's the only way on earth to plunder the pain.

Of course, I realize God would prefer for me to refrain from rehearsing those kinds of fears altogether, but He also knows my weaknesses and how deeply and subconsciously I associate love with risk. As long as I insist on torturing myself with these terrifying possibilities, He seems to suggest that I think them all the way through to the other side. The prospect of losing a loved one is horrifying. I cannot imagine enduring it, but because I know God is faithful, I must trust that somehow I would. Can you bring yourself to believe that you would as well?

God has promised that His grace will be given according to our need and that not only will we survive by the skin of our teeth, if we trust Him and hang on to Him for dear life — grieving, yes, but as those who have hope — we will also thrive again. We can give ourselves to something greater than painlessness. We can give ourselves to *purpose.* If we cooperate, good will indeed come to us and others around us, and glory will most assuredly come to God. Otherwise, He would have forbidden the tragedy.

Those of us who are in Christ will also spend eternity with the loved ones who have shared our faith, and this life will seem like a vapor in comparison.

Romans 8:18 promises that the future we have coming is so glorious that nothing we've suffered will compare to the magnitude and splendor of it. We must not let the enemy of our souls get away with convincing us that anything can utterly destroy us. If we do, we will hand him an engraved invitation to attend our constant torment. Over and over Jesus implores His followers, "Take courage!" as if His hand is outstretched and His palm opened with offered treasure. It's time we took Him up on it. Do we really want to spend our time rehearsing deaths of all kinds rather than engaging in the effervescence of life? In the words of Shakespeare, "Cowards die many times before their deaths; the valiant never taste of death but once."

When I got sick and tired of my lifelong battle within security and began this bumpy journey, I found a segment of Scripture that has since become my mantra. The portion echoes in rich tenor everything we've talked about in this chapter. It describes a human with an honest-to-goodness secure heart, and I was bound and determined to become one. I have no idea how many times I've recited this passage over the last twelve months. I voiced it as recently as yesterday and often enough in recent weeks to taste the lingering sweetness on my tongue from sipping through that straw of truth. For our present purposes, I don't think God will mind one bit if we change the "he" to "she" for impact.

> [She] will have no fear of bad news; [her] heart is steadfast, trusting in the LORD. [Her] heart is secure, [she] will have no fear; in the end [she] will look in triumph on [her] foes.
>
> PSALM 112:7–8

Absorb the statement again: *Her heart is secure.* As our journey narrows toward its end, imagine those words being used to describe you and me. Let's make a pact this moment and this close to our conclusion to not let up until our hearts are consistently secure. Those words are vastly truer of me today than they were nine months ago. Fix your eyes upon the bookends propping up those four glorious words:

She will have no fear of bad news. . . . Her heart is secure. . . . She will have no fear.

You and I know by now that a chronically insecure person is invariably eaten alive with fear. Some of us have lived with it so long it feels like part of the fabric of our souls, but the time has come to treat the unhealthy variety as an enemy alien. The most repetitive command God gives His people in the entire stretch of Scripture is "Do not fear!" When we began this chapter, we talked about trading our present fear for trust in order to take the wind out of insecurity's sails. It will have no choice but to hit the ground like a kite with no air. Take note of the very specific fear the person in Psalm 112 traded for trust.

[She] will have no fear of *bad news.* (emphasis mine)

I don't think the psalmist meant that the person described had a lifetime guarantee from God that he would never get any bad news. Hard things happen to all of us, and they often come in the form of "news." It's part of pumping blood on this fretful planet. The psalmist meant just what he said. She doesn't live in fear of bad news. Why is she free from such self-torment? Stay with me here, because this connection is crucial: she is free because she knows that "in the end [she] will look in triumph on [her] foes."

Translation? God will work all things — no matter how difficult or devastating — out to her advantage. Her enemy will not triumph over her. It may hurt in the beginning, but it's going to be beautiful "in the end."

The teacher in me loves nothing better than tying two dangling concepts into one big, fat, beautiful bow. Let's do that right this minute. Remember our key verse in Proverbs 31 that we learned to recite to ourselves every time we feel insecure? I'll refresh your memory. Proverbs 31:25 says of an extraordinary woman of valor, "She is clothed with strength and dignity." That's only half the verse, however. It's time we looked at the rest.

She is clothed with strength and dignity;
she can laugh at the days to come.

Both Psalm 112:7–8 and Proverbs 31:25 describe secure people. Not coincidentally, they have one profound characteristic in common. Neither gives the future the right to intimidate them. Their hearts are "steadfast, trusting in the LORD." Insecurity feeds like a starving wolf off fear of the future — and not just the distant future of aging, infirmity, or death. Insecurity fears what might happen later today. Tonight. Tomorrow. Next week. Next year. Next decade. Its constant mantra is, "What will I do if . . . ?" Fear of the future makes people settle for things in the present that completely defy abundant life. It also insults the grace of God that will be piled in heaps for us when hardship comes. We agonize over how we'll possibly make it, yet all the while we can glance over our shoulders and see where God has carried us. And often through worse than what we're afraid of now.

When you feel that familiar panic begin to rise in your heart like a river coursing its banks and your soul begins to roll with another round of "What will I do if . . . ?" what would happen if you were willing to hear the voice of God whisper these inaudible words?

Child, you are asking the wrong question. Here's the one that would assuage your fears: What will God do if . . . ?

Here's a smattering of answers to that mighty good question. *I, the Maker of heaven and earth, will:*

perfect everything that concerns you (Psalm 138:8, KJV).

work all things together for your good (Romans 8:28).

contend with those who contend with you

(Isaiah 49:25).

fight this battle for you (2 Chronicles 20:15).

equip you with divine power (2 Corinthians 10:4).

delight to show you mercy (Micah 7:18).

meet all your needs according to My glorious riches in Christ Jesus (Philippians 4:19).

give you grace that is perfectly sufficient (2 Corinthians 12:9).

be your power in weakness (2 Corinthians 12:9).

do immeasurably more than all you could ask or imagine, according to the power that is at work within you (Ephesians 3:20).

There is so much I don't know. So much I'm uncertain of. So much that makes me wonder. But sister, I'm certain of this. I promise you, based on the authority of God Himself and centuries of witnesses to His faithfulness, if you will place your trust in Him, He will always — I said always — make sure that in the end you will look upon your foes in triumph. No illness, loss, rejection, or betrayal will ever get the last word. You will stand to your feet stronger than ever. And oh, may your unseen enemy regret the day he set the crosshairs of his weapon upon your forehead.

CHAPTER 18
A CLEAN ESCAPE

This has been a messy book. In case you're wondering if I'm aware of it, I am. Passion isn't always the best ink. It tends to get splattered and spit instead of scripted thoughtfully and melodiously like notes on a composer's score. The writer of Proverbs talked of words "fitly spoken," but I'm afraid what you've gotten here were words spoken in a fit. Things are better said in retrospect, but had I waited until I worked through my pathetic insecurity, the pressure would have waned and a written message would never have materialized. The next phase in my life would have come with all its demands, and stopping to look back would have been an unaffordable luxury. If this book is as messy as I fear it is, at least it's messy in a cleansing sort of way. That can happen, you know.

My sister-in-law was in Houston recently for a long-overdue visit. She has lived abroad with her family for several years and adjusted to taking trains most places instead of cars. Apparently it's left her a little rusty on how things are done in the wide-open spaces of Texas, where trains are still best suited for cattle drives and the metro rail system is primarily for people who refuse to drive a pickup truck. While running a few errands, my sister-in-law decided to do her parents a favor and fill up the miniature gas tank of their silver four-door Toyota Corolla. She paid at the pump and fed the tank every ounce it could stomach, and as she stuck the nozzle back in place, she was met with the familiar question on the screen: "Do you want a car wash?" Judging from the layer of dirt coating the back of her pants from where she had leaned on the fender, my sister-in-law decided a double favor was in order.

She coughed up seven bucks for the Super-Wash, drove around to the back side of the convenience store, found the "Enter here" sign, and punched in her six-digit code. The automated voice instructed her to put the car in neutral, and imagining how pleased her parents would soon be, she cheerfully complied. That was the last clear thought she had for the four longest minutes of her life. Some of the details are sketchy, but based on my well-honed investigative skills of peculiar human behavior, this is what I've deduced:

The conveyor belt began pulling her neutralized car into the drive-through as promised, but the automatic voice was still chattering instructions. As my sister-in-law recounts it, she poked her head out the driver's side window and yelled back at it, "What? What did you say?" If you're not from our part of the country, where manners trump authenticity and sometimes plain sense, you may not comprehend our reluctance to drive off while someone is still talking. Yes, even if it's an automated voice of indiscernible gender trapped in a metal box with bad speakers. Around here, it's just plain rude.

Exasperated, she turned around just in time for the first squirt. She couldn't describe the color of it because it hit her square in the eye but as someone experienced in drive-through car washes, I was sharp enough to already know. It was the color of a well-aged woman's cotton-white hair when it has a tinge of blue rinse from the beauty shop in it. No doubt in my mind. I've seen the shade a thousand times at church. In her momentary blindness and considerable surprise, my sister-in-law began slapping frantically at the inside of her car door in search of the electric window switch. Mind you, she had only driven her parents' car a few times, so it's perfectly understandable that she hit the button that rolled down the backseat window instead of rolling up the front. What ensued was quite simply the SuperWash of my sister-in-law's life. By the time she exited the car wash, she'd been primed, shampooed, slapped senseless with long gray rags, and then rinsed and waxed with impressive effectiveness. Only the power dryer at the exit failed to perform comprehensively. Of course, this was no small deficiency in terms of her hair. I have purposely omitted her name to protect her last semblance of dignity, but she knows who she is and by now has sizable reservations about having told me. Good sport that she is, she'll willingly take one for the team.

Anyway, I'm not making fun of her. I'm relating. That's precisely what I've endured for the last nine months of toiling over this book. I feel like a person who's walked barefoot through a car wash and paid good money to do it. The firm slapping with the long gray rags particularly resonates. Lo these many months later, I am considerably cleaner but in serious need of a spa day.

Speaking of salons, in case we happen to run into one another someday, perhaps you're better off knowing in advance what you can expect out of your buddy in the wake of this book. After all, I hate in the worst way to fail to measure up to someone's expectations, but unfortunately, it's one of the most predictable job hazards in the briary field of writing. I would rather tell you up front that, should we meet, you could bet your girlfriend a friendly cup of coffee that I'll still have highlights, still have a manicure or need one, and still be in search of the ultimate smoky gray eyeliner or, better yet, a great pair of jeans.

I don't do any of those things out of insecurity. I do them because I like them, not because I don't like myself or need you to like me. I'm also hard-pressed to find those kinds of things unbiblical unless they're becoming idols or heaping debts. First Peter 3:3–4 does a brilliant job of reminding women not to get confused about where true beauty emanates from and removes all doubt about the priority of the internal over the external. Taken in context with the whole counsel of Scripture from start to finish, however, you would have a pretty tough time substantiating the idea that it's wrong for a woman to look her

434

reasonable best as long as it doesn't teeter the precedence of her character. In actuality, the Bible doesn't saint plainness *or* adornment. God simply "doesn't see things the way [we] see them. People judge by outward appearance, but the Lord looks at the heart" (1 Samuel 16:7, NLT).

My goal in the wake of this journey of heart is to cease being motivated to thought or action in any way by insecurity. From an observer's perspective, the line may seem fine at times, but to the person herself, the difference in the internal struggle can be as clear as day if she's willing to pay attention. Insecurity has a certain sick feel to it. A niggling of urgency and desperation. If the feeling gets masked behind a half dozen others, we only have to ask ourselves why we're thinking what we're thinking or doing what we're doing. Insecurity is, above all, an anxious motivator. We can cut straight to the core of our drivenness with these kinds of inquiries:

Am I doing this . . . or buying this . . . or saying this . . . or selling this out of any semblance of insecurity?

If the honest answer is yes, then it's time to be brave and say no. I'm not sure what this plumb line will look like next to your unique life, but I can tell you that next to mine, it means that while the shopping mall is still in, a few other practices and possibilities are probably out because I know good and well they're motivated by nothing but insecurity. We who are in Christ possess the supernatural insight to know the difference and the divine power to act on it.

Not long ago we got a blog comment that brought Amanda, Melissa, and me untold joy. Between our two generations and three diverse personalities, we have the privilege of serving all sorts of women of every age and walk of life. We have college students and Web-savvy retirees in our online community, and in between you'll find occupations running the gamut from anesthesiologists to missionaries. Like most blog communities, ours has its regulars who post comments often enough to become welcome friends. One of them is Sister Lynn. In this case "Sister" isn't just a figure of speech for a fellow Christian. Lynn is a real, live sister in the ecumenical sense of the word. She and her merry group of social networkers are nuns who log in from the simple world of their convent's wireless connection.

Not long ago I wrote a blog post about a song I had been singing repeatedly in the middle of work havoc and a small heartbreak; the words and tender melody reminded me how very much I love Jesus. It's the kind of song you don't just sing *about* Him. You sing it straight to Him. I shared the lyrics on the post and then asked our bloggers to name a song they often sing to Jesus when they either feel the love or want to. Comments poured in like a glad torrent. Bloggers offered hundreds of titles lifted off the charts of Christian contemporary music and peeled from the slick silver pages of ageless hymnbooks. Sister Lynn? She came through with a soulful late-sixties classic by Aretha Franklin. Those of us fortunate enough to be young or sober when R & B was the reigning king of AM radio probably know the chorus by heart. Slow down for a moment before you read her last two lines. You can't rush a lyric like this. Each syllable was meant to hang like a summer dress on a country clothesline until a woman who'd almost forgotten who she was could feel the breeze blow life back in her lungs:

"You make me feel like a nat-u-ral wo-man. [Even slower here:] A nat-u-ral wo-o-o-man."

I threw back my head and laughed out loud at Sister Lynn's bold selection, but I also knew exactly what she was talking about. Jesus has been the purest, most consistent romance of my life, and despite the inevitable aches and shocks of living for five decades, somehow with Him my youth is inexplicably renewed. In the light of His presence I am so glad to be a woman and feel oddly adept at it even in a world gone mad. Away from the active awareness of Him, I am at the bitter mercy of my next bad mood. That's where Sister Lynn would happily consent to being one-upped a tad. Actually, with Jesus, we are so much more than natural women. Remember? We have this *Treasure* — this all-surpassing power in these imperfect jars of clay. Every time we glance in a mirror, we come face-to-face with a supernatural work of God. So what if our hair color is not exactly natural? Admit it. Sometimes natural is overrated.

As we wrap things up around here, wouldn't it be wonderful if the two of us could grab a table at a restaurant and sit right across from each other for a little while? I would ask if God had accomplished anything discernible in your life through the pages of this book, and then I would tell you that the God part of this process has been monumental for me. If, truth be told, it has been substantially less for you, I would also tell you how sorry I am for dropping the ball. Nothing brings me more relief than the absolute certainty that human handprints can't smudge the face of God when He's bound and determined to reveal a glimpse of Himself.

One of the things I love about Him is His strong penchant for authenticity. Neither the hypocritical nor the ill-equipped can use Him as an excuse. If any message, whether in print or in person, was truly His idea and doused in His anointing, He has tested it meticulously on the messenger. In order to prove me genuine as a writer on this subject, God has spent this last year systematically exposing every ugly insecurity I had and testing these methods in circumstances too uncanny to be coincidence.

For starters, He allowed Keith and me to endure a challenging season that, based on my history, should have turned me inside out with self-doubt. Before we came out on the other side, I got countless opportunities to say to myself, *I am clothed with strength and dignity* and say silently to anyone or anything that came to rob me of my security, *God gave it to me. It is mine. You cannot have it.*

And then one of my dearest loved ones has battled an untimely health crisis in her young adult years, and it is as of yet unresolved. After remaining stalwart on her behalf through months of medical tests, I finally gave way to panic over the growing concern of specialists and was cut to the quick with conviction over the concepts I taught late in this book. One night while driving home from spending the day with her, I spoke these words aloud to God between honest-to-goodness wails:

"Lord, I am asking You to heal her completely. You know that is the desire of my heart. I love her so much. More than my own life. But neither she nor I will find lasting security in trusting You only to do what we want You to do. My conditional faith is leaving the door wide open for the enemy to torment me. Therefore, with every bit of determination in me, I choose to trust You. Period."

There with my face soaked and my throat contorted, I felt my strength return. Amid these two overriding tests of security came the everyday variety that may wear on a person slower but over time are often surer. Like you, I'm too plugged in to real life not to have work issues, personal problems, and relational difficulties. I've felt attacked, misunderstood, and criticized at times, probably a lot like you. I've also seen somebody another day older in the mirror, and regardless of your age, so have you. I've felt afraid of the dark and twice as afraid of the light. I've second-guessed my motivation for everything I do.

And meanwhile, the concepts we've discussed in this book have stood the test. Come what may, whether well received or not, God wanted me to be able to hold my head up when this message hits the shelves and know beyond a doubt that I am not the same woman who penned the first page. Storms came, and the methods worked . . . at least on one chronically insecure woman. God and I are a long way from where we started. I'm no longer seriously ticked. Concerned, yes, but I'm now a block or two past ticked. I've stumbled through a car wash and had my anger rinsed into passion — a passion that longs to see girls from elementary school to assisted living thrive in their God-given right to security in a culture that is brutal on our gender.

As we go our separate directions, I want you to know how much I care and how deeply I thank you for taking this journey with me. It began out of my own severe need, but it never would have gone this far without you. Let's each refuse to give up a single inch of the ground we've gained. I do not want to relapse.

To help instigate an ongoing victory, I've written a prayer involving our concepts and supported by Scripture that I plan to use as long as it takes for these thought processes to become second nature to me. You'll find it at the end of this chapter if you want to join me. Use it any day. Use it every day. Think of it as your <u>maintenance prayer</u>. If life knocks the wind out of you and you lose your grip on a strong sense of personal security, return to the longer prayer journey in chapter 9. That's your <u>repair prayer</u>. Between the two of them, you should rarely be at a loss for words when you need a fresh gain of security.

I'm about to shut my mouth, but rest assured, God's is wide open. He is calling you, beloved. He is summoning you to freedom. He is wooing you to joy. He's inviting you to live on purpose and spin around with childlike faith in the acute awareness of His love for you. His hand is outstretched. Take your dignity back no matter where you've been or what has happened to you. Hold on to your security for all you're worth. It is yours. Nothing and no one can take it from you.

The LORD is your security. He will keep your foot from being caught in a trap.
PROVERBS 3:26, NLT

Now get out there and show some wide-eyed little girls what a secure woman looks like.

My Father in heaven,
I thank You for breath this day
    to give You praise.
I thank You for a life where nothing
    is wasted,
a life where pain turns into purpose and
    Your providence assigns a personal
    destiny.
You will never allow anything in my path
that cannot bring You glory or me and
    those around me good.
No matter what this day holds,
I am clothed with strength and dignity.
I have divine strength to overcome every
    obstacle and all oppression
because I belong to Jesus Christ, and His
    Spirit lives within me.
You, Lord, are my security.
No one and nothing can take You
    from me.
You will keep my foot from being caught
    in a trap.
I choose to turn my back on fear because
    You are right here with me.
I can smile over the days to come
    because Your plan for me
    is good and right.
My heart is steadfast, trusting in You,
    Lord.

In the end, I will look in triumph on my
    foes.
Because of You,
I, _____, am secure.
In Jesus' triumphant name,
Amen.

SO, YOU'RE CONSIDERING CHRIST

I could have no greater privilege in all of life than introducing you to a saving relationship with Jesus Christ through a simple prayer you fill with your faith. You will realize as time goes on that no human being could draw you here. This invitation is from Christ alone. He has been pursuing you for years, and now if you are willing and so desire, the time has come to start living the life you were created for. The simplicity of the gospel is often a stumbling block for people. We reason that eternal life in heaven and internal power on earth should take longer to acquire than five minutes, but that's where we misunderstand who is doing the work.

Jesus already spent the time, energy, and unimaginable turmoil when He went to the cross. All you're asked to do is receive the gift He has placed with unbridled affection before you. Once you've accepted His gift of grace, you don't need to ever doubt your salvation again. Your eternal condition is not based on how you feel from day to day. Stand steadfastly on what you know. The very moment you accept Christ as your Savior, you receive His Spirit. Once He resides within you, He will never leave or forsake you. When you die, you will awaken immediately to brand-new life in a glorious Kingdom, where you will be more alive than you ever dreamed of being on earth. Let this matter be settled once and for all. Know that nothing and no one, including you, can sabotage your salvation.

Romans 10:8–13 gives every seeker the uncomplicated steps to becoming a Christian.

> "The word is near you; it is in your mouth and in your heart," that is, the word of faith we are proclaiming: That if you confess with your mouth, "Jesus is Lord," and believe in your heart that God raised him from the dead, you will be saved. For it is with your heart that you believe and are justified, and it is with your mouth that you confess and are saved. As the Scripture says, "Anyone who trusts in him will never be put to shame." For there is no difference between Jew and Gentile — the same Lord is Lord of

all and richly blesses all who call on him, for, "Everyone who calls on the name of the Lord will be saved."

With confidence in what the Scripture has just said to you and with a willing heart, say these words to God. If you're in a position to do so, consider saying them from your knees to help sanctify this moment so you'll remember it forever.

Father of heaven and earth,
Thank You for sending Your Son
to die for all my sins —
past, present, and future.
Today on _____
I receive Your gift of grace,
turn from my own destructive ways,
and accept Your Son as
    my personal Savior.
I believe with my heart
and confess with my mouth
that Jesus Christ is Lord.
Lead me daily to fulfill my destiny.
Flood me with Your Spirit.
Empower me to do the impossible.
Today the matter is settled.
I am Yours, and You are mine.
In Jesus' delivering name,
Amen.

Beloved, if you prayed that prayer with a willing, sincere heart, you have just become a child of God. Your eternity is secured, and your salvation is complete and absolute. Every time you're tempted to doubt it, thank God for it instead. You will honor Him by believing Him to have accomplished exactly what He promised. Welcome to the family of God! Words fail me to express how happy I am to point you to the Savior, who has been my joy, my strength, and my entire life purpose. May He show Himself mighty and merciful to you.

Please don't do anything that makes you feel awkward, but if you're willing, I would dearly love to know that you made this decision. I will not broadcast or post your name or embarrass you in any way. I'd just love to celebrate your salvation with you. Here's how you could let me know: visit www.so longinsecurity.com.

NOTES

1. Interviews of 953 respondents done by Adrienne Hudson, statistician, November 2008, Living Proof blog site.
2. Joseph Nowinski, *The Tender Heart: Conquering Your Insecurity* (New York: Fireside Publishers, 2001), 23.
3. Ibid., 23–24.
4. Taken from "Mostly Late at Night" by Kate Crash; quoted in "Poet Turned Songwriter: An Interview with Kate Crash," *Carpe Articulum Literary Review* (March–April 2009).
5. Nowinski, *The Tender Heart,* 57.
6. Michael Levine and Hara Estroff Marano, "Why I Hate Beauty," *Psychology Today* (July/August 2001): 41.
7. Sermon at Houston First Baptist Church, April 26, 2009.
8. *Merriam Webster's Collegiate Dictionary,* 11th edition (Springfield, MA: Merriam-Webster, Inc., 2003).

9. Richard Winter, *Perfecting Ourselves to Death* (Downers Grove, IL: InterVarsity Press, 2005), 125–126.

10. Original source: Terry D. Cooper, *Sin, Pride and Self-Acceptance* (Downers Grove, IL: InterVarsity Press, 2003), 166.

11. *Word Biblical Commentary,* volume 22 (Nashville: Thomas Nelson Publishers, 1998), 243.

12. Lexical *hadar* (pronounced *huh-DAR*), *Key Word Study Bible* (Chattanooga, TN: AMG Publishers, 1996), OT Lexical Aids, #2077, 1511.

13. Joseph Nowinski, *The Tender Heart,* 138.

14. Ibid., 139.

15. Rob Jackson, "Confronting Your Spouse's Secret Sin," http://www.pure intimacy.org/piArticles/A000000483.cfm (last accessed September 4, 2009).

16. This Scripture quotation is taken from *God's Word.® GOD'S* WORD® is a copyrighted work of God's Word to the Nations. Quotations are used by permission. Copyright 1995 by God's Word to the Nations. All rights reserved.

17. Jennifer Rothschild, *Me, Myself, and Lies* (Nashville: LifeWay Press, 2008), 119.

18. Cooper Lawrence, *The Cult of Celebrity* (Guilford, CT: Skirt Publishers, 2009), 233.

ABOUT THE AUTHOR

Beth Moore is a bestselling writer, Bible teacher, and speaker whom God has used to touch the lives of millions of women around the world. A love for Jesus was planted in her heart at a young age and budded when she sensed God calling her to work for him at the age of eighteen.

Beth graduated from Southwest Texas State University with a degree in political science, married Keith Moore in 1978, and gave birth to two children, Amanda and Melissa. As a young wife and mother, Beth served the Lord by speaking at luncheons and retreats, working at Mother's Day Out, and teaching Christian aerobics.

From a growing passion to know God's Word, Beth eagerly learned how to study it. She then founded Living Proof Ministries in 1994 with the purpose of teaching women how to love and live on God's Word. Since then she has authored numerous Bible studies and books, including *Get Out of That Pit, Believing God,* and *Breaking Free,* which have been read by women of all ages, races, and backgrounds. In 2004 she began a radio ministry called *Living Proof with Beth Moore.*

Beth attends Houston's First Baptist Church, where she hosts an interdenominational Tuesday-night Bible study for women in her city. Because of her burden for unity in the body of Christ, Beth counts serving women of all denominations as one of her greatest privileges in life.

Beth and Keith reside in Houston, Texas, where they enjoy traveling, hiking, drinking coffee on the back porch, eating Mexican food, making each other laugh, walking their dogs, and being grandparents to Jackson and Annabeth.

The employees of Thorndike Press hope you have enjoyed this Large Print book. All our Thorndike, Wheeler, and Kennebec Large Print titles are designed for easy reading, and all our books are made to last. Other Thorndike Press Large Print books are available at your library, through selected bookstores, or directly from us.

For information about titles, please call:
   (800) 223-1244

or visit our Web site at:
   http://gale.cengage.com/thorndike

To share your comments, please write:
   Publisher
   Thorndike Press
   295 Kennedy Memorial Drive
   Waterville, ME 04901